Clinical Medical Ethics

VOLUME 2

The titles published in this series are listed at the end of this volume.

MAKING SENSE OF ADVANCE DIRECTIVES

Making Sense
of Advance Directives

NANCY M.P. KING, JD

*Department of Social Medicine, School of Medicine,
University of North Carolina at Chapel Hill, U.S.A.*

Kluwer Academic Publishers
Dordrecht / Boston / London

Library of Congress Cataloging-in-Publication Data

King, Nancy, 1953–
    Making sense of advance directives / Nancy King.
        p.   cm. -- (Clinical medical ethics ; v. 2)
    ISBN 0-7923-1163-9 (HB : alk. paper)
    1. Right to die. 2. Right to die--Law and legislation.
I. Title. II. Series.
R726.K5 1991
362.1'75--dc20   91-6695

ISBN 0-7923-1163-9

Published by Kluwer Academic Publishers,
P.O. Box 17, 3300 AA Dordrecht, The Netherlands.

Kluwer Academic Publishers incorporates the publishing programmes of
D. Reidel, Martinus Nijhoff, Dr W. Junk and MTP Press.

Sold and distributed in the U.S.A. and Canada
by Kluwer Academic Publishers,
101 Philip Drive, Norwell, MA 02061, U.S.A.

In all other countries, sold and distributed
by Kluwer Academic Publishers Group,
P.O. Box 322, 3300 AH Dordrecht, The Netherlands.

Printed on acid-free paper

To my family

Table of Contents

Acknowledgments

I am grateful for the thoughtful critical commentary of Richard Robeson, Carol Leininger, and Larry Churchill, and for the patient secretarial expertise of Angie Boudwin, Jackie Jones, Deborah Eakins, and Carolyn Winn.

Notice

Except in the instance of cases that have been reported in the public media or have become public through court hearings, all identifiable information used in case examples has been changed, and the structure of the case example altered, so as not to identify the individuals and institutions involved. Instead, case examples have been constructed out of numerous clinical experiences so as to illustrate a general problem in bioethics, health care delivery, or health care policy. Any similarity to actual individuals living or dead is purely coincidental.

Also, though legal cases and principles are examined in this volume, there is no intention to provide legal advice. For legal advice there is no substitute for directly subvening the legal profession.

Chapter One

Introduction

> The first time I read the medical consent and
> authorization, it had registered in my mind simply as
> a legal document. Now I began to understand what it
> meant. It was a letter of ultimate love and trust.
> (Schucking, 1985, p. 268)

Ever since Karen Ann Quinlan slipped into permanent unconsciousness in
1975 and her father agonized publicly over whether she should remain
indefinitely on a respirator (*In re Quinlan*, 1976), the desires of patients, their
families, and their friends to limit the application of apparently limitless
medical technology have been a pressing concern for ethics, law, and public
policy. Ms. Quinlan's case contained nearly all the elements of the problems
we still face: vague, general, but sincere prior oral statements suggesting that
she would not want continued treatment; a family attempting to do what they
saw as best for her; and physicians uncertain whether to use medical
judgment alone (and if so, what the "right" medical decision was), to
preserve her life at all costs, or to honor the family's interpretation of their
daughter's choice. Most ironically, once she was removed from her
respirator, she did not die.

Karen Quinlan – like dozens of other names made famous by court
decisions, newspaper stories, and television evening news – has come to
symbolize a tangled knot of issues surrounding the end of life and who
controls it. Of all the contenders for that control – patients, their families,
their doctors, ethics committees, legislatures, and courts – patients themselves
have an overwhelmingly strong claim to make end-of-life health care
decisions about their own bodies, lives, and futures. Much of the time,
however, the health care choices patients make will not be effectuated until
they have lost their decisional capacity, their ability to ratify prior choices,
and their ability to consider their current condition. To rely on patients'
choices under these circumstances means to give effect to their *advance
directives* about medical treatment.

This book is for clinicians and others who wish to understand and make use of advance directives as a primary vehicle for end-of-life decisions that concern the health care of patients. It addresses why patients' advance directives are a better means of making such decisions than reliance on other possible decisionmakers, and it examines how advance directives should be written, interpreted, and implemented. Though directed primarily to clinicians, this book will also help persons wishing to write their own advance directives to make sense of the issues that make these health care choices so highly charged.

An advance directive is a written statement[1] that is intended to govern health care decisionmaking for its author, should he or she lose decisional capacity in the future. Though by this definition advance directives can apply to any health care decision, they are almost always addressed to end of life issues, and it is in this context that they are best known. As "living wills" (directives giving lists of instructions), durable powers of attorney (directives naming proxy decisionmakers), or both, advance directives are becoming commonplace. Attorneys and advocacy groups often counsel the elderly and the chronically ill to write advance directives in order to ensure that physicians will honor their wishes for "death with dignity." And courts deciding the ever-increasing number of "right to die" cases often express the wish that the patient had written an advance directive instead of just telling family and friends "I hope I never become another Karen Ann Quinlan" or "I would not want to live as a vegetable" – as did Paul Brophy (*Brophy v. New England Sinai Hospital*, 1986) and perhaps now the most famous name of all, Nancy Beth Cruzan (*Cruzan v. Director*, 1990). The implication is that advance directives provide needed – and wanted – guidance, certainty, and legal and moral protection for certain kinds of important, value-laden health care decisions.

But what are advance directives really? How should physicians view them and what should they accomplish? Should everyone have one? And above all, when should an advance directive be honored? Many patients believe strongly that advance directives give them the only possibility of dignity and control at the end of life. At the same time, however, many caregivers, sometimes from an excess of caution but often through bitter experience, see advance directives as barriers to doing what is best for patients, engendering a false sense of certainty and promoting misunderstandings between health care providers and the patient's friends and family.

For the clinician, making sense of advance directives means (1) understanding how to help a patient prepare a directive and how to discuss a patient's directive, with the patient and the patient's family or friends, so that it contains what the patient wants and can be understood by caregivers, and (2) knowing how to respond to an advance directive: how to read it, apply it, and decide whether and how it should be honored. Ideally, the doctor and the patient will write the patient's advance directive together – a directive that the doctor will later honor. But many clinicians will also help patients write directives that *others* will have to honor, and will also face the question of honoring existing advance directives that they have not helped prepare. Thus, all clinicians must have a sound understanding of what advance directives are, and what it means to write them, so that all directives may be read and judged practically and fairly.

Making Sense of Advance Directives

The basis for the moral (and legal) validity of advance directives is the patient's right of autonomy or self-determination. To understand why advance directives are desirable and should be implemented, it is necessary to understand the patient's right of autonomy or self-determination as it applies to health care decisions that are intended to be acted upon both contemporaneously and in the future. Establishing the validity of advance directives does not end the matter, however – or responsible caregivers would not have the concerns they do about implementing directives. Yes, the patient's right of autonomy implies a duty of others – physicians and other caregivers in particular – not to interfere with its exercise. Yet this duty of noninterference by itself does not help guide physicians in interpreting and implementing directives or in helping patients to formulate and articulate their wishes by means of directives.

The enforceability of directives depends on more than just their basis in autonomy; it also depends, in an important way, upon *community*: upon the willingness of patients and doctors to talk together about health care choices, to share values and goals, confront differences, and make true efforts at understanding. The values of community – trust and respect for others – give content and workability to the requirement that patients' directives be honored, by providing a basis for (1) requiring patients to make good-faith efforts to write directives that others can interpret and apply without undue difficulty and confusion, and (2) requiring caregivers and others to make good-faith efforts to understand patients' directives so that they may be implemented as they were intended, regardless of personal disagreement with the patient's values and choices. Patients' most significant choices about treatment are, at the same time, in one sense truly private and in another sense necessarily social, shared, the products of a community. Recognizing the duality and tension in these difficult choices is essential. In order to understand and use directives well, therefore, this book must address three distinct but related issues: the patient's right of choice; the meaning of that right for choices that will be applied in the future; and concerns of fairness and practicality in the interpretation and application of directives.

The First Issue: The Extent of Consent

First, we must look at patients' legal right of consent. What health care choices may patients with decisional capacity make? Are there any limits to their power to decide? (For example, are their legal rights greater when they are dying; or perhaps less because death is an irrevocable and socially disfavored choice?) Do they have less right to refuse treatments when death could be readily avoided with treatment (for example, refusal of blood transfusions or antibiotics), or when the refusal seems like suicide? In addition to their legal right to refuse, may patients *request* any treatments? And may physicians morally or legally refuse to comply with patients' decisions?

This book argues that patients have a strong and clear moral interest and legal right to act as the ultimate decisionmakers about their own medical care. The interest extends to any and all decisions, including decisions viewed by others as wrong, that are made by persons who have the ability to make autonomous choices.

When a patient refuses medical interventions intended to preserve or prolong his or her life, health professionals and others may often quite reasonably question the *authenticity* of the patient's choice. We are at pains to assure ourselves that such patients are not speaking solely out of fear, pressure from family, financial worries, delirium, or despair. We want to know that the choice represents the will of the patient, as free, knowledgeable, and unimpaired as possible. In serious illness, with its attendant impairments and constraints, decisions may be less authentic, more pressured; they will certainly be suspected of being so. Nonetheless, patients may still make valid choices at difficult times – including decisions to refuse treatment. Indeed, the more consequential the decision, the more expressive of important personal values and human ends it may be, so that honoring patients' wishes may become more necessary than ever. This issue is examined in Chapter 2.

The Second Issue: Past Choices, Future Consequences

Second, we must consider the "future factor." Having gained some understanding of the choices decisionally capable patients may make, what basis is there for applying these choices when the patients have irretrievably lost their decisional capacity? Why do patients want their wishes honored at a time when they often cannot perceive their circumstances, and have certainly lost their ability to understand their own past preferences and reasoning? Why should caregivers not simply be empowered to act in the patient's best interests once the patient can no longer make decisions? And if the patient has in a directive named someone else to decide on his or her behalf, why should we not limit such a proxy's power to decide, since the patient cannot dissent from the proxy's decision?

This book argues that the patient's right to choose extends also to choices that are meant to affect medical care in the future, in anticipation of future decisional incapacity. There are several reasons for extending the patient's right of choice to include prospective choices. In practical terms, to recognize only contemporaneous choices would permit caregivers to alter an agreed-upon plan of care as soon as a patient became unable to reaffirm previously made care choices. This could result in decisions, by persons other than the patient, to administer recently refused treatments on the patient's deathbed. To avoid this obvious unfairness, a decision-making standard labeled "substituted judgment" has been identified as a primary means of determining how decisions should be made for a patient no longer capable of making them. Substituted judgment requires a reconstruction of the prior competent self in an effort to determine what this patient would have wanted. Evidence of the patient's prior wishes and views is assembled, and only if the evidence available is insufficient to enable such a reconstruction should outside decisionmakers, acting on behalf of the incompetent patient, turn instead to a more objective "best interests" standard, which may, if necessary, rest heavily on medical judgment.

Some have argued, however, that prospective decisions can never be sufficiently informed to be valid; that persons who have not yet experienced the circumstances about which they are deciding cannot sufficiently appreciate them; and that the existence of genuine unknowns about consciousness and the end of life makes it impossible, even theoretically, to dismiss the possibility of disagreement between the present, deciding self and the future, decided-about self. The issue is not whether unconscious, demented, dying patients have value, or whether they experience their existence as valuable, but whether the possibility or even the certainty that the future self might have such value precludes anyone in the present from choosing death instead of a diminished future existence.

The argument in support of the validity of prospective choices rests upon an understanding of the continuity of the self and of the individual's right to make choices that reflect a valuation of the self. An individual's own self-definition depends upon embracing and developing a certain set of attributes while refusing or discouraging the adoption of others. Recognizing prospective choices requires not only that individuals be permitted to prefer some attributes over others, but also that individuals be permitted to reject some attributes that are partially unknown and even unknowable.

Making decisions that include unknowns of all kinds, as well as considerations about the future, is nothing new in medical decisionmaking or in decisionmaking about anything else. Thus, the "future factor" does not represent a barrier to acceptance of advance directives. This issue is examined in Chapter 3.

The Third Issue: Practicalities and Particulars

Third, we must read and use particular directives well. Having established a basis for honoring a patient's previously expressed wishes, we face the very central and practical questions of certainty in advance directives:

Does/did the author have decisional capacity? How do we test for that, and what is our standard? How thoughtful and reasonable and persuasive must patients be for their directives to be honored?

Is/was the person informed? What does it mean to be informed about potential situations that do not yet exist? How much uncertainty can patients be permitted to deal with? Is there a point at which it becomes unreasonable to ask caregivers to apply a directive to a given decision, either because we cannot be sure what the patient meant or perhaps even because we can not be sure that the patient has not changed his/her mind?

And lastly, what is the difference between answering these essentially practical concerns in the *writing* of a directive, with patient and physician talking together, and addressing them in the directive's *application*, when the patient can no longer be consulted? If every clinician who cares for a patient is tempted anew to second-guess the patient's advance directive, no certainty at all can exist for patients. Yet if we do not scrutinize advance directives, and require patients to take some care to make them clear and unambiguous, the adverse consequences could be significant for the patient.

If advance directives are valid in theory, should individuals who wish their choices to be known and honored think carefully and deeply about them? Of course they should. Everyone who decides to write an advance directive must take into account that each of us can only imperfectly understand the future; and everyone who must decide whether to honor a directive must understand that it represents a free choice in the face of an uncertain future, a choice between what we know ourselves to want and the chance that with new information what we want could diverge from what is morally best for us. Writing, assessing, and implementing directives, then, is a matter of weighing their goals against their effects, their benefits against their risks, and making choices about them that are both personal and principled. If the directive is valid, it is also, in at least some sense, binding on others. Thus, individuals executing directives have some duty *to others* to provide circumstantial guarantees of a directive's validity – simply in order to be able to expect that the directive will be implemented. A crucial concern of this book, then, is an inquiry into what gives a directive sufficient apparent validity that it *ought to be honored.*

Advance directives should not be primarily intended to protect physicians who implement them from legal liability. Such a goal would be futile no matter what; *there is no "suit-proof" living will.* Directives should seek to memorialize patients' prospective decisions, for reasons of evidence, certainty, and clarity. If caregivers are willing to implement only directives executed in accordance with narrowly drawn state "living will" statutes – or if they believe that only such statutory directives are legally valid – the patient's interest in decisionmaking is jeopardized. In contrast, a directive that is intended to facilitate the mutual decisional progress of the physician-patient relationship is far more likely to provide physicians with the opportunity to satisfy themselves as to the patient's mental state, decisionmaking character, level of appreciation of the facts and issues at hand, and relevant personal values. The physician-patient relationship provides the physician with the opportunity to encourage a high degree of reflection in the patient and to assist the patient in writing an advance directive that demonstrates the patient's seriousness of consideration.

How far does the physician's duty to trust the patient's expression of choice extend? And how far may patients' trust in others' obedience to their choices extend? These questions may not be possible to answer with any precision in general terms. Physicians must be willing to consider each situation closely and carefully, and patients may have to accept the practical necessity of persuading others of the validity of their directives. But once the patient's interest in prospective decisionmaking is recognized as valid, the guiding principles underlying that recognition will order and ease the practical difficulties that remain. Chapters 4, 5, and 6 further address these concerns.

Easy Cases, Hard Cases, and Advance Directives in Perspective

Advance directives are not usually treated as an isolated matter, but instead are often considered as one of the many available means of caring for "hopelessly ill patients" (Wanzer *et al.*, 1984, 1989) or of addressing the problem of "life-sustaining treatment" (Wolff *et al.*, 1987). Living wills and durable powers of attorney; do-not-resuscitate orders and hospital ethics committees; and reasoning based on the patient's autonomy, the patient's best interests, the needs of the family, and the interests of society are often considered all together in analyzing decisionmaking at the end of life. As a result, there is at least some societal agreement about "easy" cases involving terminally ill patients and refusal of invasive life-sustaining treatments like artificial ventilation, resuscitation, and chemotherapy. And there is a redundancy of reasoning about these cases as well: there are many good reasons to support the decision to stop treatment. Both patients' rights and patients' best interests can justify treatment withholding and withdrawal in these cases. Treatment cessation can be supported by an advance directive, a verbal declaration, a family request, a statute, a hospital policy, or a medical decision.

So many reasons come together in these easy cases that we can get fuzzy and fail to distinguish among them. The result is that when we go beyond the easy cases and consider the hard ones – namely, refusals of treatments that are clearly life-saving or life-preserving and refusals of treatment when patients are not terminally ill – we are less than certain about which of these reasons, if any, can still apply.

This book is primarily concerned with *written documents*. This helps to distinguish the discussion of advance directives from the potentially more difficult practical problems of determining what a patient with no written document would have wanted, as well as from the theoretical question of whether trying to make such a determination for patients is a better approach than trying to determine their best interests. The written expression of wishes (in the form of instructions, the naming of a proxy decisionmaker, or both) establishes the patient's seriousness of purpose and at least begins to show *that* the patient wanted his/her wishes honored and *what* those wishes were at the time of writing (Cohen, 1991). Problems of the meaning and application of written directives may still exist, but these problems will usually not be as severe as the problems that arise when nothing is in writing and when caregivers must make decisions with little or no information about the patient's prior views.

Moreover, discussion here will not be limited to the class of written advance directives that appear in *state legislation*. It is true that the form, content, and application of such statutory directives are sufficiently narrow and particular to provide solutions to some of the potential problems raised by directives. Statutory directives are written to describe and define the "easy" cases. They also offer a small amount of legal insulation for physicians who honor them, and sometimes even the hint of a remedy for patients whose physicians fail to do so. This book is also concerned with advance directives that are not statutorily prescribed, and seeks to promote the use of directives that are more detailed and extensive than those prescribed by statute. This distinguishes the discussion here from that of many legally oriented articles and advocacy group publications, whose focus is on the documents approved by the various states. Though these statutes serve as useful starting points for writing directives, and may be sufficient for many people, concentrating on statutes obscures both the general issue of the basis of the patient's authority to write directives – which is not merely statutory in *any* state – and the particular question of how to deal with directives that do not fit the template provided by the relevant statute.

Many patients seek to make choices that statutory directives do not address. More and more patients are attempting to refuse treatments when they are not "terminally ill"; most definitions of terminal illness do not include patients in persistent vegetative state, who may live for many years. More and more patients are attempting to refuse food and water when they are supplied by artificial means, ranging from nasogastric tube feeding to total parenteral nutrition. In more than a few states this currently cannot be done by statutory directive.[2]

There are potentially many other decisions patients might choose that are not contemplated by narrowly drawn "living will" statutes. The importance of these most difficult decisions by patients highlights the problem of how to think about advance directives. Are they legal documents? Or are they fundamentally something else? Are directives "letters of trust"? Binding contracts? Non-binding documents? Legal protection for caregivers? Moral statements? Or just a way to begin a conversation about health care choices and expectations? Which of these effects are intended by an advance directive's author, which are looked for by those responding to a directive, and which of them all should be decisive? By examining the legal foundations of treatment refusal as well as statutory forms of advance directives, Chapters 2 and 4 consider the legal status of advance directives, conclude that they are not primarily legal documents, and suggest ways they can secondarily fulfill that role while remaining faithful to their primary purpose of *effectuating patients' previously expressed wishes within the patient's decisional community of caregivers, family, and friends.*

The following case examples are meant to illustrate the ways in which advance directives appear in medical practice and the ways in which the issues they address are interwoven with many other issues for patients and for doctors. Discussion of these cases is far from exhaustive and is intended to stimulate the reader's reflection.

Example 1: Thinking about Directives

The Carpenters have been your patients for three years, since retirement brought them South from New Jersey, where Betty, a school librarian, and Herman, a middle manager in light industry, raised three children. Herman's arthritis is mildly disabling; Betty is recovering from cataract surgery. Today they have come for a routine visit, a check on their medications, and prescription renewals. They also have some questions.

"We went to see a lawyer recently", Herman explains. "One of our daughters was divorced last year, and we've also become grandparents again, so we decided to update our wills for the first time in about 20 years. The lawyer told us we should also make out 'living wills', to make certain that we will be able to control the care we receive in case of some serious illness."

"This lawyer was recommended to us by a friend we met at a Weekend Retirement College seminar", Betty explained. "He was quite helpful and professional, but he wasn't really able to answer our questions about this 'living will'. He left the impression that if we didn't have one of these documents we would have difficulty in dealing with doctors and hospitals; but he wasn't clear on how we should use it to avoid those problems. So we decided to ask you", Betty concludes, handing you a one-page photocopied form. You recognize it as the Standard Living Will that is contained in the Natural Death Act for your state; unsuccessfully, you try to recall what the continuing education lecturer said about it in the Practice Update keynote speech last year.

The lawyer who proposed to the Carpenters that they needed "living wills" meant well, but his advice did not help the Carpenters much. The brief standard directives contained in state statutes tend to be both vague and narrowly applicable; therefore they are potentially quite difficult for caregivers to interpret and apply. In order to know what it is they are signing, patients must know what the terms of such documents mean: what is included in "lifesaving treatment"? When is a person "terminally ill"? etc. Legal definitions can help make this clearer, certainly; but because directives will be interpreted and applied by caregivers, it seems necessary to know how they, too, would define such terms. Moreover, a directive that has been left in a lawyer's hands along with family wills, or placed in a safe-deposit box, or even filed with important personal papers at home is unlikely to be available when it is needed. Anyone who writes a directive must think about ways of bringing it to caregivers' attention. The best way for patients to address both of these concerns is to discuss them with their physicians.

The answers to the Carpenters' questions may, under the circumstances, be easy to give. As their physician of several years, you may assure them that you intend to act in their best interests in any instance of serious illness. You might explain that if one of them were unable to express choices you would consult the other to help decide what is best; you might emphasize your commitment to keeping them well-informed and honoring their wishes. Because they currently have no serious health problems that could trigger the need for an advance directive, you might advise the Carpenters that a living will is probably not necessary so long as you can be contacted when needed. If they are concerned about relying on other caregivers to contact you in an emergency, an advance directive might be only one of several appropriate mechanisms to deal with that situation.

Example 2: Discussing Directives

A year later, the Carpenters are back in your office. Six months ago, Herman was diagnosed as having amyotrophic lateral sclerosis (ALS, or Lou Gehrig's Disease); his disease has progressed during that time but he is still able to care for himself, with substantial assistance from Betty. His principal complaints are increasing difficulty in getting up out of chairs and into and out of the car, and shortness of breath, which he confesses he finds frightening. Herman and Betty have been seeing you regularly, to keep up with Herman's illness, to plan for changes in his care, and to discuss what can be expected in the future. On this visit, it is Betty who brings up the subject of advance directives – she has written one for herself, and it is several pages long.

"I've joined one of those groups that help people to control their own health care", she announces. "I brought you my living will, so that we can discuss it; I've thought a lot about this lately and I just don't want to be dependent. I want to die with dignity. I don't want, ever, to be resuscitated, to be on a ventilator, to have radiation therapy or chemotherapy, or to be fed intravenously or by a tube. If I am not able to make my own rational choices and my mental capacity can't be restored, I don't want *any* treatment except to keep me comfortable. I've prepared a durable power of attorney, too, and I'm naming my sister Clara to make these decisions for me. Herman says he could never do that – could never tell a doctor *not* to do something that would help keep me living a little longer. Well I think that's barbaric; I guess I see why he feels that way but I know Clara will stand up for me and do what I want. What do you think, Doctor, will this living will make certain that I die the way I choose?"

While devoutly wishing Betty had not asked you such a loaded question, you scan her document, which fairly bristles with instructions, explanations, and philosophical statements. Gently you suggest that Betty's concerns are more likely to be well addressed if you and she talk about what she wants and why than if she attempts to present an ironclad contract to every potential caregiver. You steer Herman and Betty into a discussion of their difference of opinion over the durable power of attorney, explaining that many caregivers would be troubled by such a disagreement unless they could be assured that Herman understood his wife's position and would not object to Clara's role. You debate with yourself whether you should ask Herman whether he would also like to write an advance directive, and decide to do three things instead:

1. You strongly suggest that Herman and Betty begin talking separately, with a counselor you recommend, about how they are coping with Herman's diagnosis. Because you suspect that some of the stress of Herman's illness has influenced Betty's thinking, you would like to be more sure that the influence is productive.
2. You make an appointment to discuss with Herman and Betty how you intend to cope with Herman's increasing respiratory problems; you will instruct them about what to do in a crisis, and explain the likelihood that Herman could require temporary ventilatory assistance in the near future.
3. A month from now, after they have had some counseling sessions, you will return to the topic of advance directives. You intend to emphasize the importance of discussing the future, sharing decisions, and respecting others' wishes and needs. You want both Herman and Betty to be able to express their choices, and to count on your support and each other's, even though their choices may differ.

Example 3: Reading Directives

Brenda Harmon has just arrived by ambulance to the critical care nephrology unit where you are the chief resident.[3] Her private physician is a division chief in the hospital; you do not know him personally. He is not in the hospital now; he has called and left word that Mrs. Harmon appears to be infected. You know that she is an insulin-dependent diabetic who has been on home dialysis for eight years, and that she has been treated at your hospital in the past. Now she is somnolent and is not responding to questions. Her husband, who has arrived with her, has given you what information he can about her condition over the past 36 hours. He appears upset and agitated, and you have asked him to wait outside the unit; he stands in the doorway as you begin to examine Brenda and draw blood for tests.

Before you have gotten very far, she suffers an arrest and you begin resuscitation. Suddenly her husband rushes into the room brandishing a sheaf of papers: Brenda Harmon's "living will" and a durable power of attorney naming him as her decisionmaker. Professor Harmon demands that the resuscitation cease, claiming that the documents show that Brenda has specifically expressed a wish not to be resuscitated in circumstances like this.

You leave the bedside, ordering the team to continue the resuscitation, and examine Professor Harmon's papers. They seem perfectly authentic, combining a statutory living will form, handwritten notarized instruction statements, and the durable power of attorney. But what are you to do with them now? Should you stop the resuscitation, or continue?

Although you do not know Brenda Harmon or her husband, perhaps you can verify the authenticity of these documents and begin to determine how they should be applied by contacting her physician immediately to see whether he knows of their existence. (It is also possible that copies of the documents could have been made part of her medical record already, since she has been treated here before. Unfortunately, that is not often done; moreover, it could be done and still go unnoticed during emergencies.) In this case, Mrs. Harmon's doctor knows about the documents and informs you that Brenda has strong opinions and is indeed deeply opposed to any resuscitative efforts. He points out, however, that because an infection is potentially curable, he would not have discouraged or opposed resuscitation if consulted before it was begun. You are puzzled and a bit annoyed at this: Who would think of consulting about an emergency resuscitation before beginning it, unless previously alerted to a patient's potential objections? If her physician knew of her objections and did not convey them when Mrs. Harmon was admitted, is it not true that he has refused to honor her wishes – in a way that leaves *you* with the responsibility?

Professor Harmon certainly thinks so. He is furious when you convey to him the substance of your conversation with the division chief and explain that you are obligated to continue the resuscitation until it either is effective in restoring function or shows itself to be futile. He claims that his wife does not care whether her infection is treatable; she wants no resuscitation *no matter what*. You wish that Professor Harmon had showed you these documents half an hour ago, when you were asking him about his wife's medical history; to be fair, however, if *you* did not know they would be relevant, how could he? And even then, you do not know how you could avoid an emergency resuscitation anyway; maybe he should not have come to the hospital at all. Mrs. Harmon's reasoning sounds like a suicide wish to you, but if she had stayed home, at least you would not be involved.

Returning to the bedside, you find that heartbeat has been restored and that the patient has been placed on ventilatory support. But Professor Harmon wants the ventilator withdrawn; he wants no further resuscitation, cardiac drugs, or intervention of any sort. In response, you call the hospital administrator, the chaplain, and the unit social worker to an emergency care conference. Professor Harmon will have to live with the fact that until he can explain his wife's views to these people and to you, her care will go forward. You cannot see that you have any other choice right now.

These case examples were crafted to describe some of the implications that advance directives have in the different settings in which they may be discussed or employed. Our discussion of them has not been exhaustive; it should be clear that advance directives can apply to situations ranging from home care to nursing home care to hospitals; to critical or to chronic care; and to choices ranging from "do not resuscitate" and "do not hospitalize" to "do not tube-feed" and "do not give antibiotics." Every situation is further modified by the involvement, and the perspectives, of the patient's family or intimate friends, all of the patient's caregivers, institutions in which the patient is residing or to which the patient wishes to go, and even the patient's insurer. We are just at the beginning.

Four Models of Advance Directives

"Advance directive" is often popularly seen as synonymous with "living will" – a short, official document, in a form either legally prescribed or prepared and distributed by some prominent organization, that refuses treatments which impede "death with dignity." This popular portrait is beginning to change, however; it is being amplified to include the naming of a proxy decisionmaker authorized to refuse treatments on the patient's behalf, and it is even beginning to be viewed as a flexible documentation of patients' preferences. Four models of advance directives demonstrate both a core understanding of what advance directives are and some of the bewildering array of points and variations that gives rise to confusion about the legal, practical, and moral significance of their different forms. The first and third directives are distributed by Concern for Dying/Society for the Right to Die,[4] the second is model legislation drafted by a law school project, and the fourth was developed by physicians in response to problems they saw in existing models.

In addition to these models, persons interested in promoting the effective use of advance directives may consult many other sources of exemplary documents, such as Cantor's excellent "annotated living will" (1990) and the model legislation drafted by the Concern for Dying Legal Advisors Committee (1983). These and other models are discussed further in Chapter 4.

....

To My Family, My Physician, My Lawyer and
All Others Whom It May Concern
(Concern for Dying, 1990):

Death is as much a reality as birth, growth and aging – it is the one certainty of life. In anticipation of decisions that may have to be made about my own dying and as an expression of my right to refuse treatment, I, _____, being of sound mind, make this statement of my wishes and instructions concerning treatment.

By means of this document, which I intend to be legally binding, I direct my physician and other care providers, my family, and any surrogate designated by me or appointed by a court, to carry out my wishes. If I become unable, by reason of physical or mental incapacity, to make decisions about my medical care, let this document provide the guidance and authority needed to make any and all such decisions.

If I am permanently unconscious or there is no reasonable expectation of my recovery from a seriously incapacitating or lethal illness or condition, I do not wish to be kept alive by artificial means. I request that I be given all care necessary to keep me comfortable and free of pain, even if pain-relieving medications may hasten my death, and I direct that no life-sustaining treatment be provided except as I or my surrogate specifically authorize.

This request may appear to place a heavy responsibility upon you, but by making this decision according to my strong convictions, I intend to ease that burden. I am acting after careful consideration and with understanding of the consequences of your carrying out my wishes. *List optional specific provisions in the space below.*

....

Durable Power of Attorney for Health Care Decisions

To effect my wishes, I designate _____ ,
residing at _____ , (phone#) _____ ,
(or if he or she shall for any reason fail to act, _____ ,
residing at _____ , (phone #) _____)
as my health care surrogate – that is, my attorney-in-fact regarding any and all health care decisions to be made for me, including the decision to refuse life-sustaining treatment – if I am unable to make such decisions myself. This power shall remain effective during and not be affected by my subsequent illness, disability or incapacity. My surrogate shall have authority to interpret my Living Will, and shall make decisions about my health care as specified in my instructions or, when my wishes are not clear, as the surrogate believes to be in my best interests. I release and agree to hold harmless my health care surrogate from any and all claims whatsoever arising from decisions made in good faith in the excercise of this power.

I sign this document knowingly, voluntarily, and after careful deliberation,
this _____ day of _____ . 19 _____ .
Signature_____
Address_____

I do hereby certify that the within document was executed and acknowl-edged before me by the principal this _____ day of _____ , 19_____ .
Notary Public _____
Witness _____ Printed Name _____
Address_____

Witness _____ Printed Name _____
Address _____

Copies of this document have been given to: _____

This Living Will expresses my personal treatment preferences. The fact that I may have also executed a declaration in the form recommended by state law should not be construed to limit or contradict this Living Will, which is an expression of my common-law and constitutional rights.

....

DECLARATION (President's Commission, 1983, p. 314)

Declaration made this _____ day of _____ (month, year).
I, _____, being of sound mind, willfully and voluntarily make known my desire that my dying shall not be artificially prolonged under the circumstances set forth below, do hereby declare:

If at any time I should have an incurable injury, disease, or illness certified to be a terminal condition by two physicians who have personally examined me, one of whom shall be my attending physician, and the physicians have determined that my death will occur whether or not life-sustaining procedures are utilized and where the application of life-sustaining procedures would serve only to artificially prolong the dying process, I direct that such procedures by withheld or withdrawn, and that I be permitted to die naturally with only the administration of medication or the performance of any medical procedure deemed necessary to provide me with comfort care.

In the absence of my ability to give directions regarding the use of such life-sustaining procedures, it is my intention that this declaration shall be honored by my family and physician(s) as the final expression of my legal right to refuse medical or surgical treatment and accept the consequences from such refusal.

I understand the full import of this declaration and I am emotionally and mentally competent to make this declaration.

Signed _____

City, County and State of Residence _____

The declarant has been personally known to me and I believe him or her to be of sound mind.

Witness _____

Witness _____

....

Living Will Declaration (Society for the Right to Die, 1990)

To My Family, Doctors, and All Those Concerned with My Care

I, _____ , being of sound mind, make this statement as a directive to be followed if I become unable to participate in decisions regarding my medical care.

If I should be in an incurable or irreversible mental or physical condition with no reasonable expectation of recovery, I direct my attending physician to withhold or withdraw treatment that merely prolongs my dying. I further direct that treatment be limited to measures to keep me comfortable and to relieve pain.

These directions express my legal right to refuse treatment. Therefore I expect my family, doctors, and everyone concerned with my care to regard themselves as legally and morally bound to act in accord with my wishes, and in so doing to be free of any legal liability for having followed my directions.

I especially do not want: (You may list specific treatment you do not want. For example: Cardiac Resuscitation; Mechanical Respiration; Artifical feeding/fluids by tube. Otherwise, your general statement will stand for your wishes.)

Other instructions/comments: (you may want to add instructions or care you do want – for example, pain medication; or that you prefer to die at home if possible).

Proxy Designation Clause: Should I become unable to communicate my instructions as stated above, I designate the following person to act in my behalf:

Name _____

Address _____

If the person I have named above is unable to act on my behalf, I authorize the following person to do so:

Name_____

Address_____

This Living Will Declaration expresses my personal treatment preferences. The fact that I may have also executed a document in the form recommended by state law should not be construed to limit or contradict this Living Will Declaration, which is an expression of my common-law and constitutional rights.

Signed: _____ Date: _____

Witness: _____ Witness: _____

Address: _____ Address: _____

Keep the signed original with your personal papers at home. Give signed copies to doctors, family, and proxy. Review your Declaration from time to time; initial and date it to show it still expresses your intent.

....

Lastly, the *Medical Directive* (Emanuel and Emanuel, 1989) is a comprehensive and quite helpful one-page document. It includes conventional textual statements, like those of other model directives, but its centerpiece is a chart allowing patients to clearly mark whether they want, do not want, are undecided about, or want a trial of an extensive list of treatments ("if considered medically reasonable"), including: cardiopulmonary resuscitation (defined as "if on the point of dying the use of drugs and electric shock to start the heart beating and artificial breathing"); mechanical breathing; artificial nutrition and hydration (defined as "nutrition and fluid given through a tube in the veins, nose, or stomach"); surgery (major or minor); kidney dialysis; chemotherapy; diagnostic tests, either "simple" or "invasive";

blood or blood products; antibiotics; and "pain medications, even if they dull consciousness and indirectly shorten my life."

Patients make those choices for the following four situations:

SITUATION (A): If I am in a coma or in a persistent vegetative state, and in the opinion of my physician and several consultants have no known hope of regaining awareness and higher mental functions no matter what is done.

SITUATION (B): If I am in a coma, and I have a small likelihood of recovering fully, a slightly larger likelihood of surviving with permanent brain damage, and a much larger likelihood of dying.

SITUATION (C): If I have brain damage or some brain disease which cannot be reversed and which makes me unable to recognize people, or to speak understandably, *and I also have a terminal illness,* such as incurable cancer which will likely be the cause of my death.

SITUATION (D): If I have brain damage or some brain disease which cannot be reversed and which makes me unable to recognize people, or to speak understandably, *but I have no terminal illness,* and I can live in this condition for a long time.

Additional text in the Medical Directive amplifies the chart with a clear explanatory statement of how the Directive should be used and an invitation to consider the underlying philosophical reasons for particular treatment decisions:

The Medical Directive states a person's wishes for or against types of medical interventions in several key situations, so that the person's wishes can be respected even when he or she cannot communicate.

A Medical Directive only comes into effect if a person becomes incompetent, or unable to make decisions or to express his or her wishes. It can be changed at any time up until then. Decisions not involving incompetence should be discussed directly with the physician ....

A copy of the completed Medical Directive should be given to a person's regular physician and to his or her family or friend to ensure that it is available when necessary.

Medical Directives should be seen not only as legal protection for personal rights but also as a guide to a person's physician. Discussion of Medical Directives with the physician can help in making plans for health care that suit a person's values.

Especially helpful is the following discussion, which precedes the chart listing of Situations on the Medical Directive form:

A person's wishes usually reflect personal, philosophical, and religious views, so people may wish to discuss the issues with his or her family, friends, and religious mentor as well.

Before recording a personal statement in the Medical Directive it may be helpful to consider the following question. What kind of medical condition, if any, would make life hard enough that attempts to prolong life would be undesirable? Some may say none. For others the answer may be intractable pain. For other people the limit may be permanent dependence on others, or irreversible mental damage, or inability to exchange affection.

Under such circumstances as these the goal of medical treatment may be to secure comfort only, or it may be to use ordinary treatments while avoiding heroic ones, or to use treatments that offer improved function (palliation), or to use all appropriate interventions to prolong life independent of quality. These points may help to clarify a person's thoughts and wishes.

The Directive also contains a Durable Power of Attorney, with a statement giving priority among documents and decisionmakers:

I understand that my wishes expressed in these four cases may not cover all possible aspects of my care if I become incompetent. I also may be undecided about whether I want a particular treatment or not. Consequently there may be a need for someone to accept or refuse medical interventions for me in consultation with my physicians.

Should there be any disagreement between the wishes I have indicated in this document and the decisions favored by my above named proxy(s), I wish my proxy(s) to have authority over my medical directive/I wish my medical directive to have authority over my proxy(s). (Please delete as necessary.)

Should there be any disagreement between the wishes of my proxies, _____ shall have final authority.

Finally, the Medical Directive contains an organ donation authorization and includes space for a Personal Statement, encouraging patients to include as extensive a statement as they wish. Space is provided for the signatures of three witnesses.

* * *

All these directives are intended to be formal documents, supplementing their formality of tone with witness statements and even notary seals, after the fashion of a last will and testament. All assert the writer's soundness of mind at the time of writing, in the same way a last will and testament does. All of the directives state that they expect physicians, family, and others to honor them, and assert that they are based upon legal rights. Three also appeal to their *moral* authority, and one points out that directives serve as guides to physicians and should be discussed with them. Three claim to be based upon the patient's understanding or to be the result of the patient's consideration; two of these go further by asserting a basis in the patient's settled values.

Significantly, only one of these directives limits its applicability to terminal illness; the others apply whenever the patient is unlikely to recover from extreme disability, which could include non-terminal conditions like coma, persistent vegetative state, or even severe dementia from Alzheimer's disease. This is an important difference from most statutory directives, as will be seen in Chapter 4. All four of these model directives explicitly or implicitly refuse life-sustaining procedures, but only one, the 'terminal condition' directive, tries to define that term. The physician-drafted model directive tries to avoid all difficult-to-define terms in favor of particular circumstances and treatments, and is one of two directives specifically to list artificially administered nutrition and hydration among the things that may be withheld.

Finally, three of these directives include a proxy designation. Linked as they are to the patient's expressed wishes, which these directives encourage to be specific, these proxy designations by implication require the proxy to make decisions based on those wishes, rather than on what the proxy thinks is best for the patient. However, one of these directives allows the patient to select whether the document or the proxy should have final authority; one mentions no decisional standard; and one permits the proxy to use a best interests standard where the patient's wishes, as detailed in the document, are not clear.

There is another difference among these directives that is not apparent in the documents themselves. Only one, #2 (the 'terminal condition' directive), is part of model *legislation*, so only it is accompanied by interpretive materials outside of the directive itself. However, all directives that appear in state statutes are similarly part of a whole scheme, and are meant to be read in light of the scheme's other provisions, which generally include a statement of legislative purpose, definitions of key terms, a revocation provision, a declaration about the enforceability of the directive, penalties for noncompliance, if any, and some assurance of protection from liability for caregivers who comply with a proper directive. The presence of these additional provisions in statutory directives amplifies caregivers' concerns about interpreting and applying directives '*legally*'. Yet these concerns derive much (though not all) of their force from the belief that advance directives are properly to be viewed as legal documents rather than as guides for difficult choices.

Advance Directives in Context

Advance directives, as substitutes for patients' own contemporaneous decisions, could potentially authorize *any* decisions that decisionally incapable patients might make if they still had decision-making capacity. Thus, advance directives could go well beyond their popular association with drastically diminished existence and dying, to apply to any treatment choice about which a patient feels strongly enough. Advance directives can specify decisions or categories of decisions to be made, or name values and preferences that should influence decisionmaking on the patient's behalf, or appoint a substitute decisionmaker, or all of the above. Directives potentially may either refuse or request treatment, or specific treatments or temporary trials of treatments; the same power of personal decision underlies both types of directive.[5] And directives can apply in the absence of terminal illness, as we have begun to see in the many cases of permanently unconscious patients. This is because advance directives are meant to perpetuate patients' preferences and values whenever patients cannot speak for themselves. They presume that individuals have the right, while capable of making choices, to decide about their own futures.

This potentially broad reach of advance directives, combined with the softness and generality of the language employed, as in our examples, to convey the patient's sense of self and value and reasons for refusing treatments, may result in a paradox. The more clearly and poignantly detailed are the patient's values, the harder it may be for the patient's caregivers to apply those values to the particular decisions faced. This is one of the reasons why advance directives work best when addressed to common and commonly understood disabilities and treatments at the end of life, and why proxy directives appointing contemporaneous decisionmakers, which shift the responsibility of applying a directive away from caregivers, are gaining favor. However, these two solutions, sticking to certain kinds of easy cases and requiring the appointment of a proxy decisionmaker, do not answer the paradox nor address the wishes of patients in different circumstances or patients who do not have available to them a suitable candidate for proxy decisionmaker. Therefore, the task of making sense of advance directives belongs to the caregiver – both by default and by the nature of the caregiver's role. Because the legal, moral, and practical meaning of each directive is different, it is the clinician's task to attempt to understand what the patient expects from the directive. Yet the patient's wishes are not the only factor. Because every person and institution affected by a directive has expectations, needs, interests, and duties with regard to the directive, all of these concerns must also be placed in perspective.

Making sense of advance directives for the clinician is not the same as determining when nontreatment should be considered or recommended. It is not the same as understanding hospital policy on "do not resuscitate" orders or trying to decide what to do for nursing home patients or patients in the intensive care unit. Those are questions of overwhelming importance, that must be addressed; but they are also questions that may be unnecessary, in many instances, if discussion of advance directives is initiated, and taken seriously, with decisionally capable adult patients, including those apparently not at risk of decisional incompetence or serious illness. Much literature is available on terminating treatment for incompetent dying patients, including extensive guidelines for clinicians and institutions (Cohen, 1991; President's Commission, 1983; Wanzer *et al.*, 1984, 1989; Wolff *et al.*, 1987; *see also* Meisel, 1989). Law and policy alike address the question of appropriate care for persons whose wishes are unknown. Here we should principally be concerned with patients who seek to make their wishes known through some form of directive, and with the clinicians who seek to assist them and who are charged with honoring their wishes.

Every institution should have a treatment termination policy in place and as part of that policy should make provision for honoring advance directives. All clinicians should have some familiarity with the applicable law in their states: case law and statutes on advance directives and termination of treatment. It is vital, however, for clinicians in all jurisdictions to recognize that implementing an advance directive that does not perfectly mirror institutional policy or state law is not wrong, nor is it unduly risky, either legally or morally. Advance directives, besides responding to patients' most important rights and interests in making their own decisions, provide clinicians with the best available means of avoiding the postponement of crucial choices. They assist caregivers both by substituting for and by supplementing patients' decisions when their decisional capacity is uncertain. When we wait until the patient is in intensive care, or until somebody brings up the question of a do not resuscitate order, or until the patient is incapable and the family in disagreement, time is short and clear evidence of the patient's wishes is often unavailable. The results of such postponement are often disastrous – physically, psychologically, and financially – for the patient, the family, all of the caregivers, and the institution. Lawsuits start here, *not* when foresight is encouraged and reflection facilitated by timely discussion of the patient's choices.

Clinicians should prepare to understand and use advance directives by taking the following general steps:

1. Identify the most pressing questions addressed by the model directives given in this chapter and the statutory directive provided by the law of your state;

2. Determine the kind of information necessary to answer these questions, so as to be prepared to obtain this information from patients, if possible, from their named proxies, or from their families and friends;

3. Be ready to suggest to patients that they consider the difficult choices they may face, and be ready to discuss directives and difficult choices fully and frankly with them, or with their friends and family; and

4. Acknowledge that when patients have tried, in a directive, to make known wishes about the future direction of their lives and deaths, it is necessary to try in good faith to understand and implement those wishes.

Similarly, persons wishing to write their own directives should talk with their clinicians about their wishes, in order to identify and address the kinds of questions that health care providers may have about interpreting and implementing directives. Whatever the form or content of an advance directive, it will work best when its potential problems are anticipated, so that others who read it are assured that its writer was thoughtful and serious in considering its implications.

Family, friends, policy, and the values of others have a place and a meaning when there is a directive, though it is a lesser place than that held by the patient's wishes and a different meaning than if there were no directive. Advance directives depend for their validity first on the value of the individual, which entails recognition of individuals' rights to shape their own goals, values, and lives. But they further depend for their enforcement upon the values of community – mutual trust, and respect for the choices of others. Advance directives are, unavoidably, social documents. To understand and use them well is to make explicit the assumptions and obligations entailed in acknowledging ourselves members of a society that recognizes advance directives as valid expressions of these important values. Such an understanding will enable clinicians to assist their patients by discussing, preparing, and implementing advance directives.

Notes

[1] By convention and for reasons of proof, advance directives are generally understood as *written statements*. Like informed consents, advance directives need not be in writing to be effective, but should be in writing to ensure that they are effective. Oral statements may be forgotten or misremembered; may not be disseminated to all the people who need to hear them; and are sometimes difficult to prove at all. Patients should be encouraged to put their wishes into written form – not necessarily into a '*legal*' document, but into any form that is understandable and usable, such as a personal statement, a note in the medical record, or a letter to a chosen proxy decisionmaker. Thus, it should become easier to write a valid advance directive. In addition, however, when a written directive is not available, patients' oral directives should become better accepted, though still subject to proof problems.

[2] As of 1989, the Society for the Right to Die listed Oklahoma, Maine, Missouri, and Wisconsin as having statutes that clearly prohibit withdrawal of tube feeding. Statutes in fourteen other states do not address it; ten specifically authorize it; and another ten permit it under some circumstances, potentially requiring judicial interpretation (Society for the Right to Die, 1989).

[3] This example is taken from Schucking (1985), with modifications.

[4] As this book went to press, Concern for Dying and the Society for the Right to Die were in the process of merging. Persons interested in requesting documents published by either organization will be able to reach both at their address, which is listed in the Bibliography.

[5] Popular knowledge of 'living wills' centers on the refusal of treatment, but there is nothing to preclude the execution of a directive that requests treatment, whether 'routine' or 'heroic'. However, whether such a 'request directive' should carry exactly the same practical, moral, and legal authority as a refusal directive is a separate question (Brett and McCullough, 1986). Request directives are further discussed in Chapter 6.

Chapter Two

Treatment Refusal and the Patient's Choice: Foundations in History, Law, and Ethics

This chapter addresses the first of the three central issues for advance directives: the nature and extent of the patient's right of choice. What kinds of health care decisions should patients be permitted to make? The chapter provides a general foundation in the moral and legal basis for informed consent and refusal of treatment, a brief look at the impact of technology upon how patients' choices are regarded, and an examination of what it means to say that a patient has, or lacks, the capacity to make his or her own health care decisions, especially decisions that will or may result in death.

Refusing Treatment and Dying Well

Even though advance directives embody such a broad range of possible forms, most advance directives are written to refuse treatment in the case of terminal illness or permanent unconsciousness. Their popular identification with the refusal of treatment has associated advance directives with newly emerging concerns for the acceptance, and compassionate management, of dying.

For as long as we humans have concerned ourselves with the good life and how to lead it, we have also hoped for a good death. Dying well may in the past have meant dying in battle, or after a long life of service to family, or with one's soul free of blemish. It might entail purification through suffering, or time enough to settle accounts, or just a swift and painless end. Whatever the good death may be, we have wished for it, prayed for it, reasoned about it, and sung about it throughout history. In this respect a good death is an integral component of a good life.

Before the healing arts developed to a degree genuinely able to affect the course of illness, disease and death were simply things to be borne. Living and dying well meant accepting disease and facing death in ways that accorded with cultural and religious views of nobility and virtue. Essentially these views instructed us to shoulder whatever was our lot, because there was no choice.

Things are different now, in some ways; in others, not different at all. Medicine now has more power, both to heal and to harm. Choices abound – choices of ends (e.g., restoration vs. enhancement of performance or of appearance) as well as choices of means (e.g., surgery, drugs, diet, exercise, radical therapies, conservative therapies). And choosers and advisers often disagree – among themselves as well as between them – about a choice to be made and its basis. It is this availability of choice that unmasks the fundamental possibility of disagreement between patients and caregivers about health care treatment.

Disagreement about the management of illness can be an unwelcome surprise. We are often not prepared to expect disagreement in medicine, either disagreement among healers, who are after all people of science, or disagreement between healers and their patients, who presumably wish nothing but to be healed. Even if we realize that medicine not only is an imperfect science but also contains value choices, we may be surprised at the range of values held by patients and the number of courses of action they might therefore select. Each offer of health care entails, at the very least, acceptance or refusal of that offer; often there are further choices, and a process of negotiation unfolds between healer and patient.

Refusing an offer of care is a particularly sensitive situation. By approaching a physician, a patient enters into a setting and a relationship designed for healing, in which refusal may scarcely seem credible. Many times patients, rather than stating their decision to refuse, simply remove themselves from the relationship entirely. At other times, anticipating the need to negotiate extensively or to refuse, they may never seek care at all, or delay until they feel they have no choices.

Some refusals of care carry a double burden. These are the refusals that form part of the process of "dying well." These refusals of care are the least amenable to the bureaucracies of healing that exist in modern society, because they decline services that may offer at least some benefit to their recipients. They are also not amenable to management through withdrawal from relationship with those bureaucracies, because they concern patients who cannot refuse care without the cooperation of their caregivers.

Technology and Treatment Refusal

Lewis Thomas (1975, pp. 35-42) has divided medical technology into three categories: nontechnologies, halfway technologies, and decisive technologies. Nontechnology, or supportive care, has always been a mainstay of healers. Provision of supportive care was the aim of almshouses and early hospitals, and it underlay the founding of the nursing profession. Supportive care is comparatively painless, nonintrusive, and inexpensive. Nobody seems to have made much of an issue out of refusal of supportive care, and current institutional policies for the withholding or withdrawal of other levels of care from patients generally provide that such "comfort care" will always be given. This is not to say that refusals of supportive care are invalid or likely to be viewed as invalid; they are simply uncommon.[1]

Decisive, or effective, technology is a phenomenon both recent and rare. Thomas cites immunizations and antibiotics as prime examples. The essential characteristic of decisive technology is a genuine understanding of the mechanisms of disease; Thomas claims that with such an understanding this technology is relatively inexpensive and easy to deliver. Refusal of effective technology is not rare. It is often based on religious or idiosyncratic reasons (*Application of President and Directors of Georgetown College*, 1964).

Halfway technology – a term now well-entrenched in the vocabulary of medicine – is a label most often applied to innovative procedures, techniques, and treatments that have entered the medical armamentarium only recently. Prime examples, for Thomas, of halfway technologies are organ transplants, artificial organs, and most of the treatment of heart disease and cancer. Renal dialysis, treatment of AIDS and diabetes, and psychotropic medication for mental illness are other examples. The essential characteristic shared by these technologies is a lack of understanding about the underlying disease mechanisms sufficient to prevent or cure the disease itself.

This characteristic ineffectiveness is shared by nontechnology, or supportive care, as well. What makes halfway technologies different is that, in addition, they are generally expensive and intrusive, and are very often risky, unpleasant, or harmful in themselves. Sometimes it is said – as has been said of dialysis and organ transplantation – that a halfway technology merely replaces one chronic disease with another.

Although the term has had an almost exclusively modern application, 'halfway technology' is an appellation that is surprisingly apropos for most early medical treatment that was not mere supportive care. Amputations, many tuberculosis treatments, bleeding, purging, medications containing heavy metals and other extremely dangerous ingredients, hysterectomies as treatment for nervous conditions – all these treatments commonly employed at different times up through the 19th century fit the definition of halfway technology extremely well. By recognizing that halfway technologies have been employed for most of the history of medicine, we can identify and understand the refusal of treatment throughout most of the history of medicine as well.

It has been said that not until the 20th century did patients have a better than even chance of benefiting from an encounter with a physician (Stevens, 1971, p. 135). If care is likely to be ineffective, costly, risky, and painful, refusal of care should not be surprising; and certain treatments historically enjoyed a very high rate of refusal. Amputations and other major surgical procedures were often refused, both because of the pain in the era before anesthesia and because of the high risk of fatal infection in the era before asepsis and antisepsis. Resistance to the assault on body image represented by amputation, as well as fear of being rendered handicapped and unemployable at a time when limb prostheses were very primitive, also figured into many refusals of amputation (Pernick, 1982).

In the 19th century, when medical cultism was at its height in the United States, the existence of medical movements advocating treatments that challenged the theories of prevailing allopathic medicine gave evidence of public rejection of harsh and harmful treatments. The best example of such movements is homeopathy, whose gentle, almost infinitely diluted herbal remedies certainly must have seemed a pleasant alternative to the bleeding, purging, mercury-containing compounds, and other drastic measures favored by allopaths of the day. Popular accusations of deception by physicians in connection with surgery and drug dispensation also support that period's concern about refusal of surgery and of some drug treatments (Pernick, 1982).

Further evidence of treatment refusal for reasons of pain, risk, and expense comes from an unusual and much earlier source: religious writings from Europe, dating from as early as the 16th century, in which theological scholars explain the nature of the individual's duty to preserve his or her own life in the case of illness. These writings agree that, especially where cure is not entirely certain, patients need not undertake surgical, drug, or dietary treatment if so doing would cause excessive and overbearing pain, disgust, or even financial hardship. Cardinal De Lugo, an influential 17th century Catholic theologian, seems to capture aptly the problem of halfway technology by supposing a situation in which a person is condemned to death by fire. While surrounded by the flames, he notices that he has sufficient water to extinguish some of the fire but not all of it. Must he use this water? De Lugo says no, and gives his reason:

> ... if a man condemned to fire, while he is surrounded by the flames, were to have at hand water with which he could extinguish the fire and prolong his life, while at the same time other wood is being carried forward and burned, he would not be held to the obligation to conserve his life for such a brief time because the obligation of conserving life by ordinary means is not an obligation of using means for such a brief conservation – which is morally considered nothing at all... (De Lugo, 1868).

This reasoning would seem to apply generally to decisions refusing treatment that is likely to be futile or that merely prolongs dying in the case of terminal illness. However, theologians of this era also held that patients could be permitted to refuse certain treatments even where cure is possible, stating that "no one can be forced to bear the tremendous pain in the amputation of a member or in an incision into the body: because no one is held to preserve his life with such torture" (Soto, 1582).

Theological discussions of the individual's duty to preserve life even included consideration of the propriety of forgoing changes in diet and place of habitation. These discussions are especially interesting because the most healthful foods and climates recognized at the time were also the most costly, without being in themselves risky or unpleasant. Religious authority held that it was not sinful to choose not to spend one's entire income on a drug, a diet, or a move to a new place, despite the fact that one's life would be shortened as a result. Similarly, health policymakers in the 20th century have recognized that patients are often forced for financial reasons to choose between food and medication, supporting their families and consulting a specialist, caring for their own health and for the health of their spouse or children (Stevens, 1971, pp. 135-137).

It seems abundantly clear, therefore, that in the days before medicine was so effective, refusals of harsh, costly, dangerous, or ineffective treatment were far from unknown. By the end of the 19th century in the United States, however, the circumstances that had created the climate of skepticism and vigilance which supported such refusals had changed. Medicine was being transformed in the popular view into a noble science; physicians were being trusted as scholarly professionals rather than scrutinized as tradesmen and quacks; hospitals were growing in numbers, becoming oriented toward acute care, technologically sophisticated, and safer (Starr, 1982; Stevens, 1971, p. 145).

On the one hand, these developments seemed to undo many of the early reasons for refusal of treatment. Surgery was less painful and less risky; better chances of cure were available for many ailments. On the other hand, technology greatly increased the expense of care and the shift to the hospital eliminated many lower-cost, low-technology alternatives, like midwifery and home birth (Stevens, 1971, p. 179), leaving other reasons for treatment refusal intact. At the same time, the growth of institutional medicine, with its employment of new technologies, its greater numbers of providers and support staff, and its large facilities, made treatment refusal more difficult to initiate and to sustain.[2]

The full flowering of the high-technology acute-care hospital did not come until the 1950s and 1960s. It was in the 1950s that the first intensive care units were established, premature nurseries began to use intensive care, open heart surgery was begun, and mechanical ventilation was first used extensively for polio patients and others. In the 1960s, kidney dialysis and kidney transplants became generally available, cardiopulmonary resuscitation became a hospital routine, coronary care options grew by leaps and bounds to include coronary artery bypass surgery, heart transplantations, and cardiac care units, and radiotherapy and chemotherapy for cancer were introduced (United States Congress, Office of Technology Assessment, 1987, p. 40).

By no coincidence, it was precisely during this period of burgeoning technical capability that the legal doctrine of informed consent was named and became notorious – most notably in the 1957 *Salgo* case (*Salgo v. Leland Stanford*, 1957) and the 1960 *Natanson* case (*Natanson v. Kline*, 1960), which dealt with complications arising from new technology: in *Salgo* a new diagnostic procedure, lumbar aortography, and in *Natanson* cobalt therapy as an adjunct to mastectomy for breast cancer.

The legal doctrine of informed consent does not merely require that doctors provide information to patients. Patients in informed consent cases make the claim that although they agreed to the physician's treatment, "If I had the right information, I would have refused treatment." Thus, beginning in the 1950s, law and society implicity approved of treatment refusals through the developing doctrine of informed consent, even though patients in informed consent cases have not refused treatment.

At the same time, the unique circumstances of high-technology catastrophic medicine made it unlikely that the informed consent doctrine could be successfully applied to many patients' circumstances. Many of the traditional exceptions to the informed consent doctrine (*Canterbury v. Spence*, 1972; Meisel, 1979) were present in cases where patients might have sought to refuse treatment. The patient was often considered incapable of making decisions because of unconsciousness, dementing conditions, depression, or stress. In addition, many situations calling for high-technology intervention developed as emergencies: by the time consent was needed, there was no time to obtain it. Resuscitation efforts, artificial ventilatory support, and the like were usually instituted on an emergency basis. Thus, the issue of informed consent was often sidestepped when life-prolonging treatment was at issue.

This brief history shows us two things. First, it is apparent that treatment refusal is a familiar occurrence historically. Patients have always refused treatments, sought forms of treatment of their own choosing, and generally acted independently of the advice of recognized caregivers of all eras; for it is the patient who ultimately controls health care choices about his or her body. Second, in all eras philosophers, theologians, and jurists have attempted to probe for moral guidance about treatment refusals.

Such guidance is most likely to be found by placing the issue of the patient's treatment decisions within a larger context of discussion: the principles which properly underlie morally and legally justifiable decision-making in health care. In the remainder of this chapter, we will examine the development of informed consent and the philosophical foundations of the patient's choice.

The Nature and History of Informed Consent

Informed consent is the name for a doctrine of 20th century American common law that upholds a patient's moral and legal right to make choices about recommended medical therapies (Faden *et al.*, 1986). As a byword of the recent patients' rights movement, informed consent holds a central place in justifying respect for every patient's autonomy in health care decisionmaking. A brief examination of the doctrine is useful in understanding the scope of patients' power to control their treatment.

First, it should be recognized that truth telling in medicine, though a necessary prerequisite to informed consent, is not the same issue as informed consent. The question of what patients should or should not be told about their health has historically been viewed as distinguishable from questions about patients' decisions whether to seek care and whether to accept or reject their physicians' recommendations about care (Faden *et al.*, 1986). Before the 19th century, truth telling generally was viewed by physicians as counter-productive, largely because, in what was often a highly competitive atmosphere, patients were accustomed to doctor-shopping according to whether they liked what they heard. Because therapeutic alternatives were few, diagnosis and prognosis were all-important, and accuracy warred with optimism as the approach most likely to help patients.

The lack of effective therapy similarly severed any potential connection between information and choices. Truth telling might be seen as beneficent, because it enabled the dying patient to put his affairs in order and compose himself to face death well, or as harmful because it destroyed hope and thus might hasten the patient's decline (Pernick, 1982); but it was not considered relevant to the patient's choice among therapies, for usually there was no such choice.

Nonetheless, the choice between therapy and no therapy has always existed, even when no other choices did. The Hippocratic physician was enjoined to refuse to treat those who were "overmastered" by their diseases (Hippocrates, *The Art,* in Reiser *et al.,* 1977), thus indicating early recognition by physicians that there was a time to stop. Moreover, to refrain from treating the hopelessly ill was a professional choice, designed to improve medical practice (Amundsen, 1987). It was not until centuries later, when heroic measures like bleeding, purging, and amputation became commonplace, that significant attention began to be paid to patients' decisions, since many chose not to pursue these extreme but potentially "lifesaving" treatment alternatives (Pernick, 1982). And it was not until the recent advent of scientific medicine that it became professionally acceptable to intervene in hopeless cases (Loewy, 1987). Thus, there has always been one choice available – acceptance or refusal of whatever might be offered. Sometimes in the past there have been other alternatives as well. Until recently, however, the giving of information was not generally viewed as related to patients' choices.

What we now know as informed consent is essentially a 20th century idea (Appelbaum *et al.,* 1987; Faden *et al.,* 1986; Katz, 1984; Pernick, 1982). It developed along two separate paths, both of which had important histories and significant implications. One of the two paths of development of informed consent was the human rights concerns that arose during the mid-20th century, particularly in connection with abuses of human subjects during medical and scientific research (Faden *et al.,* 1986). The 1947 Nuremberg trial of *United States v. Karl Brandt* (Katz, 1972, pp. 292-306) brought to light the work of the Nazi 'experimenters' in World War II, and the Nuremberg Code, which emerged in 1948 from that trial, became the first widely known statement of research principles to require the informed and voluntary consent of all human subjects. The Code's first principle provides in part:

> The voluntary consent of the human subject is absolutely essential....[T]he person involved...should be so situated as to be able to exercise free power of choice, without the intervention of any element of force, fraud, deceit, duress, over-reaching, or other

> ulterior form of constraint or coercion; and should have sufficient knowledge and comprehension of the elements of the subject matter involved as to enable him to make an understanding and enlightened decision. This...requires that...there should be made known to him the nature, duration, and purpose of the experiment; the method and means by which it is to be conducted; all inconveniences and hazards reasonably to be expected; and the effects upon his health or person which may possibly come from his participation in the experimentation (Katz, 1972, p. 305).

In 1964, the World Medical Association's Declaration of Helsinki also required physicians engaged in nontherapeutic research to obtain the subject's "freely given informed consent" (World Medical Assembly, 1964). These influential pronouncements began to focus attention on the rights of human subjects of research – that is, upon the nature of their humanity and the obligations of researchers to respect that humanity.

Deception in research received great attention in the mid-20th century, further reinforcing public and professional consciousness of what is owed by researchers to subjects. In the Tuskeegee Syphilis Study, subjects were led to believe that they were receiving treatment, when in fact effective treatment was withheld (Faden *et al.*, 1986 pp. 165-167). In the Jewish Chronic Disease Hospital case, subjects were given injections of cancer cells without their consent (Faden *et al.*, 1986); the injections were considered by the investigators to be harmless, but the word 'cancer' was not. And in Stanley Milgram's obedience experiments, subjects were allowed to believe they were seriously injuring another who was posing as a subject (Faden *et al.*, 1986 pp. 174-177).

All of these notorious cases helped set the stage for federal regulation of federally funded research. Regulations issued by the FDA and DHEW (now DHHS) imposed relatively stringent informed consent requirements that contained "laundry lists" of the material to be disclosed, including a statement that the study constitutes research, a description of the research itself, its risks, discomforts, possible benefits, and alternatives, confidentiality protection if any, injury compensation if any, names of persons to contact with questions, and the subject's right to refuse or withdraw from participation.[3]

In all of these concerns for informed consent in research, the connection between information and choice was clear: for a subject's consent to have meaning, he or she must know that the consent is for research rather than for therapy. The nature of the research and its potential risks must be known. This information is necessary for choice – the choice to participate or not.

However, the role of informed consent in therapy is not necessarily the same as its role in research. Research and therapy are not the same. Indeed, in much of the notoriously deceptive research mentioned above, the deception lay in permitting research to be taken by the subjects for therapy. The promise of benefit is a strong inducement to consent to therapy, so that if research not expected to benefit the subject is presented as therapy, potential subjects might be more likely to consent. It is surprising to no one that this form of deception should be thought wrong. By the same token, it should not be surprising that it is still occasionally questioned whether informed consent is necessary or desirable in the ordinary, therapeutically oriented doctor-patient relationship,[4] where benefit to the patient is the physician's goal.

The second path of development for the informed consent doctrine focuses on the patient's role in the therapeutic relationship. Entering into the physician-patient relationship is a matter of mutual quasi-contractual consent for physician and patient, even when both seek the patient's benefit. There is a sort of presumption that the goals of physicians and patients tend in the same direction; after all, the relationship is a therapeutic alliance, and physicians generally treat only patients who have voluntarily sought their services. The patient's decision to seek care is usually not an issue discussed between them, and patient and physician begin their relationship with at least some expectation of agreement. It seems reasonable to assume that a patient who knowledgeably chooses a physician because of that physician's superior skill and knowledge should be prepared to trust the physician's judgment and embark upon the proffered treatment in reliance upon that judgment. Surely we generally expect people to consider favorably what is offered for their therapeutic benefit; that is exactly why patients go to doctors, and also exactly why we are concerned that research not masquerade as treatment.

Yet there are limits to the scope of any consent to become a physician's patient. Physicians are required, under the threat of malpractice, to treat patients according to the custom of the profession, delivering care that meets at least minimal standards of effectiveness and safety. Patients are understood to consent only to treatment that is according to custom. They may not consent to treatment so inferior as to be negligent or to unheard-of or outlandish procedures, even those claimed to be beneficial.[5] Whatever the precise limits of the physician-patient relationship may be, it is clearly wrong to assume that the patient, in entering into one, implicitly consents to everything offered by the physician for ever after (*Mohr v. Williams*, 1905; *Pratt v. Davis*, 1906).

Furthermore, it has always been acknowledged that patients may sever their relationships with physicians at will (*Carpenter v. Blake*, 1871). A patient who knows what the physician proposes to do, and wishes to avoid it, may do so by dismissing the physician entirely – an effective but unwieldy protection against unwanted treatment. The fact that the patient can terminate the physician-patient relationship at will, without "good reason" or even "against medical advice", illuminates the central moral tenet of that relationship: its purpose is not simply the best interest of the patient, but the patient's own determination of his or her best interest – even to the point where the patient refuses to accept continued care.

If then the physician conceals his or her treatment intentions from the patient in order to preclude the patient from severing the relationship, the physician is practicing deception. Such deception may be rectified by recognizing the patient's right to select a new physician when he or she wishes to refuse a proffered treatment, or by acknowledging the patient's interest in making choices directly about the proffered treatments themselves. The dilemma that remains for physicians is how to maintain relationships with patients who make treatment choices that do not accord with their physicians' recommendations. This is a dilemma that is often at the heart of the clinician's ambivalence and confusion about advance directives.

Informed consent in the therapeutic relationship has its conceptual origins in the bare right to be left alone – a fundamental principle of the common law, or judge-made law, of England and the United States (*Satz v. Perlmutter*, 1978). According to the law of *battery*, to make any intentional physical contact with someone without that person's consent is offensive, and the offended party may be entitled to collect damages in court.

The root premise of "bodily integrity", dignity, autonomy, independence, or self-direction upon which the offense of battery is based is simply treated as a given by law. If consent is obtained, then there is no battery. (As a matter of social policy, consent is implied in many circumstances, from social handshaking and kissing to emergency medical treatment for unconscious persons.) According to the law of battery, it is the patient who initiates the physician-patient relationship; regardless of how the encounter has proceeded, the relationship can begin only when the patient consents to the physician's touch.

Battery also makes clear that because it is the *touch* that is consented to, the patient's consent to the relationship does not automatically encompass all treatments. Each recommendation must be examined on its own terms; that first consent cannot reasonably be construed as a consent to anything the physician recommends unless the patient understands it in precisely that way (*Mohr v. Williams*, 1905; *Pratt v. Davis*, 1906). Sometimes patients do so understand their consents: "I know you will do what is best for me, Doctor, so whatever you recommend is fine with me." When patients consent on these terms, the operative factor for them is the doctor's judgment of their best interest. Even under these circumstances they understand their consent as being for a particular purpose, their best medical interest, even though that purpose may encompass a very broad range of recommended procedures.

All consents are therefore born of some understanding of what is consented to. Patients may consent to particular "touchings" by their physicians, or they may consent to any touchings necessary to accomplish a particular purpose, their well-being. The law of battery holds that a consent given without any such understanding of what is consented to is not valid. A touching that follows upon a consent obtained by deception or by withholding of crucial information is still a battery. Early cases where patients consented to a particular treatment and received a different one, or more than they asked for, thus paralleled cases in the 1950's where patients claimed they were given an incomplete understanding of their treatments.

The importance of the patient's self-determination in informed consent (*Canterbury v. Spence,* 1972) is a reminder that in the physician-patient relationship, the purpose of the touching is the crucial determinant of what makes a consent informed. Patients consent to medical treatment not for the sake of the touching itself, as we consent to being touched while dancing or playing basketball, but for its benefits. Informed consent is an issue because *benefits* are offered and because a *choice* is available.

Self-determination is also a reminder that it is the *patient's* view of benefits that matters. It is the patient's autonomy, dignity, and independence that are protected by informed consent, and it is the patient's own judgment and understanding of the situation that turn what would otherwise be a battery into a permitted intrusion. Informed consent gives to patients the right to receive information relevant to decisions about therapy, and to physicians the opportunity to educate and advise patients in order to bring the patient's and physician's views of benefit into closer alignment. Ultimately, though, the patient's decision controls.

Informed consent acknowledges patients' control of their own bodies and their control of caregivers' access to their bodies for treatment purposes. This control furthers patients' interests in making life choices, including medical choices, that serve their own views of their best interests. The information in informed consent comes from physicians, in the form of recommendation and advice. In addition, patients often decide with the help and consultation of family and friends. The patient's process of decision is a process of reasoning, just as other decisions in life – small and large, common and uncommon – reflect a reasoning process. The variety of decision-making processes engaged in by ordinary people in ordinary life is staggering. Still, patients and physicians alike lead ordinary lives that have at least some things in common – enough to engage in discussion of a decision and gain some degree of understanding of each other's views.

The first reported cases requiring the physician to obtain consent to medical treatment appeared around the turn of this century. These were cases based on battery. They simply required the physician to obtain consent before performing a procedure and to remain within the bounds of the consent given unless there was some emergency which made delaying for consent unsafe (*Mohr v. Williams,* 1905; *Pratt v. Davis,* 1906).

Later cases, still using the reasoning of battery, began to enumerate the information that patients need to have (and that therefore physicians are required to give them) in order to give a valid consent with some understanding of what they are consenting to. The issue of information disclosure is the focus of modern legal action based on informed consent, and there has come to be a legal laundry list for it: Physicians must disclose to patients the nature of the procedure, its expected consequences, the significant risks associated with it, the expected benefits, and the available alternatives to it – always including the alternative of no treatment at all. To know what you are consenting to, say the courts, you need to know what it is and what it is for, which includes what the chances are that it will work, what might go wrong, and what other choices there are (*Berkey v. Anderson,* 1969; *Cooper v. Roberts,* 1971; *Gray v. Grunnagle,* 1966).

Once the cases began to be concerned with disclosure of so much information to patients, the legal theory of informed consent began to undergo a subtle shift away from its simple vision of the patient's right of choice. This happened for a very simple reason: the disclosure physicians were required to make had to be measured largely according to medical standards. Even though the patient's judgment of benefit ultimately guided the treatment decision, only the medical profession could say what the proffered procedure entailed, what risks and benefits were likely to arise from it, and what alternatives were medically feasible.

The modern disclosure "laundry list" was to be given to patients regardless of whether the medical profession thought that was a good idea, but the standards of the medical profession had to be applied to determine the precise content of this required disclosure. Many courts soon decided to treat informed consent as a form of professional negligence – as medical malpractice, an injury of carelessness in disclosure rather than an intentional contact without valid consent. This shift was probably more than anything else a matter of judicial convenience, but it served misleadingly to overemphasize the physician's judgment about the patient's benefit

(Comment, 1967; McCoid, 1957; *Natanson v. Kline*, 1960; Note, 1970; Plant, 1968; Waltz & Scheuneman, 1970).

Despite this shift in emphasis, informed consent has preserved its focus on the patient's autonomy in a number of ways. Most significant is its recognition of the patient's right to refuse treatment regardless of whether nontreatment is a medically acceptable option. The physician's obligation to disclose alternative treatments need not include a complete discussion of treatment refusal, but any patient's refusal will always trigger an obligation to disclose the risks and consequences of refusal (*Truman v. Thomas*, 1980). The doctrine of informed consent thus acknowledges that nontreatment is always an option the patient may consider – that the patient's judgment of his or her own best interests might be best served by nontreatment even though such a choice runs counter to good medical judgment.

In this way, informed consent raises the possibility that the patient may make a choice that runs counter to the physician's medical judgment. Informed consent raises the question of the physician's freedom (or obligation) to respond to the patient's choice – but it alone cannot answer it. The question of whether physicians may be required to support patients in the making of decisions against medical advice goes beyond informed consent and into the related but still distinct issue of the patient's right to refuse treatment.

Contemporaneous Choice: Autonomy versus Beneficence

Many health professionals who think about health care decisionmaking tend to view informed consent as no more than a means of arriving at more accurate determinations of the patient's best interests (Pernick, 1982). The basis for informed consent, the patient's interest in autonomy or self-determination, is by this reasoning protected and honored because patients know themselves better than doctors do. These caregivers consider the patient's autonomy interest only as a means to the right decision, and when they are reluctant to honor patients' choices, they may explain their reluctance as a disagreement about whose judgment is better – theirs or their patient's.

This weak view of autonomy is in reality a version of the this-is-for-your-own-good reasoning characteristic of the principle of beneficence. Though willing to allow patients to make many disapproved choices, some courts and caregivers wrongly believe that the patient's right of autonomy has substantive limits – that patients do not have the right to make choices that will result, or are highly likely to result, in death. They reason that death cannot, by definition, be in anyone's best interest.

Although many moral and religious traditions hold that continued existence is in the individual's best interests, the assertion that the principle of beneficence outweighs the principle of autonomy *whenever* the patient's autonomous choice would result in death cannot be sustained. The duty to preserve one's life always has limits.

A patient who makes a choice to refuse treatment, even if it will result in death, may have many reasons for doing so. All of these reasons in some sense reflect that patient's own view of his or her best interests, but some of them may stray far afield from what health care providers are accustomed to consider in their determination of what is best for the patient. Patients may wish to avoid pain or disfigurement or loss of dignity, or to spare spouse and family from emotional pain or financial hardship; or patients may make particular choices just because health is not the same issue for them as it is for their doctors.

The patient's decision-making autonomy is important not because patients may be best at determining what is best for them, but because they are the only ones who can say who they are and what matters to them (Dworkin, 1986). The uneasiness that some caregivers feel in the face of patients' decisions to refuse treatment provides a basis for discussion with the patient and perhaps even for moral persuasion; it alone does not provide a basis for interference with autonomous choice (Annas & Glantz, 1986; Buchanan & Brock, 1986; Faden *et al.*, 1986).

The principle of autonomy is a powerful one – so powerful that modern philosophers are properly alert to the risk that an autonomy-based theory of health care decisionmaking could become atomistic and compassionless (Veatch & Callahan, 1984). Yet this risk is minimized greatly with a proper and responsible recognition of the true meaning of autonomy for patients, including the proper and responsible exercise of that autonomy (Childress, 1990).

Autonomy has been defined by Beauchamp and Childress as "a form of personal liberty of action where the individual determines his or her own course of action in accordance with a plan chosen by himself or herself" (Beauchamp & Childress, 1979, p. 56). They explain that autonomous persons are able to deliberate, choose, and act on their choices, and that persons of diminished autonomy are dependent and less able to think and act freely. Two figures in the history of philosophy, Immanuel Kant and John Stuart Mill, have shaped our understanding of autonomy as, respectively, freedom of the will and freedom of action. For Kant, autonomy is governing oneself, including making one's own choices, in accord with moral principles that are one's own but that can be willed to be universally valid for everyone.

Mill's concern was about autonomy of *action*. In his *On Liberty*, Mill argues that social and political control over individual actions is legitimate only if necessary to prevent harm to other individuals affected by those actions. All citizens should be free to develop their potential according to their own convictions, as long as they do not interfere with a like expression of freedom by others (Beauchamp & Childress, 1979 p. 57).

Respect for autonomy is a societal obligation imposed on each of us to recognize the autonomy of others and to respect their judgments even when we believe them mistaken. In Kant's view, respect for autonomy is a part of perceiving persons as "ends in themselves", able to determine their own destiny, rather than treating them merely as means to the ends of others. Moral relationships, for Kant, are essentially characterized by mutual respect for autonomy. Mill's view further requires that society refrain from interfering with autonomous actions, however foolish, so long as they do not harm others (Beauchamp & Childress, 1979, pp.58-59).

No reasonable argument can be made to support the position that either the autonomy of the patient, or the authority of health care providers or of society, is absolute, that is, capable of outweighing *all* other principles, rights, interests, and reasons in all cases. Legitimate moral authorities provide reasons to explain and justify their commands; legitimate exercises of autonomy are similarly reflective, and therefore explainable. The expectation of communication about moral choices is critical: Moral beliefs arise from shared experiences and perceptions, and moral conflicts between autonomous patients and beneficent medical authorities properly take place within a community able to share traditions and examine commonly held values (Beauchamp & Childress, 1979, p. 61-62). For advance directives, questions must be asked about what sort of communication about patients' decisions is necessary, and what is sufficient, for those decisions to be recognized and honored as autonomous.

Arguments Against Refusal

It cannot be said that there are no grounds at all for questioning a patient's autonomous decision. In law, autonomous choices may be curtailed for significant public policy reasons or to prevent harm to others. Moral reasoning about whether treatment may or may not be refused is closely related to legal reasoning in this area, though some of the argument structure is dissimilar. Legal reasoning provides a relatively clear and handy model for moral reasoning about treatment choices, and will be so used here.

We have already discussed the law's battery-based concept of autonomy or self-determination in the context of informed consent. This legal concept is a matter of common (judge-made) law; it has evolved from court decisions in the various states over the years, and rests upon basic principles inherited from early Anglo-Saxon legal traditions. In the law of treatment refusal, the right of autonomy also has an additional basis: a federal constitutional right, which many courts have labeled the right of privacy (*Gray v. Romeo*, 1988), but which the United States Supreme Court has recently identified as a Fourteenth Amendment liberty interest (*Cruzan v. Director*, 1990).

The right of privacy has a controversial constitutional history and origin (Tribe, 1978, pp. 886-990). Beginning in the 1960s, privacy was viewed as an expansive right of personal decision and control, carrying implications of dignity and intellectual sophistication not yet shared by the common-law self-determination basis of informed consent. Informed consent cases as a rule arise after the claimed injury has occurred; the only remedy is money damages. constitutional privacy paved the way for preventing injury by controlling actions prospectively instead. Currently, the two rights are viewed as fundamentally similar in nature, though not in origin (Faden *et al.*, 1986, pp. 39-42). The United States Supreme Court's reliance on "liberty" rather than "privacy" appears to focus the constitutional analysis on the physical intrusion of unwanted treatments; nonetheless, there is at last no doubt that both Constitution and common law support the right of treatment refusal.

The advantage of thinking in constitutional terms is that constitutional rights are ranked according to how powerful they are, and the right of privacy is in the most powerful category: it is a *fundamental* right.[6] Thinking about self-determination in constitutional terms has reinforced society's understanding of its importance by labeling it fundamental, without going so far as to consider it absolute.[7]

Once the right to refuse treatment is established as fundamental, legal reasoning examines the nature and strength of the countervailing interests that may be present. The rights and interests on both sides are balanced in a sort of cost-benefit calculation in order to reach a conclusion about whose should prevail. If the patient's right to refuse treatment – the right to make one's own medical decisions – is a powerful, "fundamental" right, then in order to overcome its power, the countervailing interests asserted by the state on behalf of its citizens must also be very powerful, or, in constitutional analysis, "compelling" (Tribe, 1978, pp. 886-896).

The power of these state interests depends on the particular facts of each case, but the interests themselves are constants, and there are four of them that are regularly discussed in the cases. They are:
- the preservation of life;
- the prevention of suicide;
- the protection of innocent third parties; and
- safeguarding the integrity of the medical profession (President's Commission, 1983, pp. 31-32; *Satz v. Perlmutter,* 1980; *Superintendent of Belchertown State School v. Saikewicz,* 1977).

The *protection of innocent third parties* is in some ways the easiest of these four interests to analyze. The analysis should be a straightforward weighing of the harms anticipated from alternative courses of action. It is a staple of moral reasoning that if one person's actions harm others, and if those others can be protected best by controlling that individual's actions, then control may be appropriate. A classic example of this reasoning is the state's exercise of its public health power to isolate or treat persons suffering from contagious diseases. Another example is the state's power of compulsory vaccination, which was justified by the U.S. Supreme Court in the early part of this century on the grounds that persons who refuse to be vaccinated present a risk to others who are not yet, or cannot be, vaccinated (*Jacobson v. Massachusetts,* 1905). Modern legal analysis requires that the risk to others be comparatively great and not reasonably avoidable except by curbing the actor's rights, and that those rights be curtailed to the minimum extent possible that effectively removes the risk to others (Tribe, 1978, pp. 886-896).

In refusal of treatment cases, the innocent third parties whose interests are at issue are the born and unborn children of the refusing patient (who in the cases is usually, but not always, female). An early decision, once influential but now recognized as having been hastily decided and poorly reasoned, was the *Georgetown College* case (*Application of President and Directors of Georgetown College,* 1964), in which the court ordered a blood transfusion for the mother of an infant because of the infant's interest in the mother's continued support. The mother was a Jehovah's Witness, who according to the beliefs of that religious sect faced the possibility of eternal damnation from receiving blood.

There are now many decisions upholding refusal of transfusions by Jehovah's Witnesses (*Fosmire v. Nicoleau,* 1990; *In re Jamaica Hospital,* 1985; *In re Melideo,* 1976; *In re Osborne,* 1972). Such decisions reject the reasoning of the *Georgetown College* case as it applies to already born children. Though parents may have a moral duty to their children not to risk their own lives unnecessarily, judgment about the acceptability of the risk should be left to the parents and the state should not seek to interfere except in extreme circumstances.

Already born children can be supported emotionally and financially by others if a parent's treatment decision results in death. Unborn children, however, are dependent upon their mothers and usually cannot be safely separated from that dependence, even if they are viable, without contravention of the mother's right to refuse treatment. A number of cases deal with pregnant women who, for religious or otherwise personal reasons, refuse blood transfusions needed for their own care or for their fetuses, or refuse Cesarean sections when their fetuses are thought to be at risk of injury or death from vaginal delivery.

Probably the majority of courts asked to order treatment in cases like this have issued such orders (Rhoden, 1987). The orders are usually contingent – for example, blood is made available to be used only if necessary; surgery will be ordered only if the placenta continues to block the cervix at the beginning of labor. In several of the reported cases (a surprisingly high percentage) the dangerous condition that served as the basis for the court's order later resolved itself without need for implementation of the order. Thus, serious questions exist as to the factual reliability of medical judgments of emergency and necessity in these cases. As a result, courts have become somewhat more cautious about ordering treatment. It is probable that in many cases such orders are not sought, or not issued, and that the matter is resolved by sensitive discussion and sharing of information between patient and physician.

In these unborn child cases the mother's self-determination interests are exactly the same as before, but the harm to the child cannot be minimized without affecting the mother's interests. Yet it is not settled that the balance therefore favors infringing upon the mother's choice. In the analogous situation where a patient in need of a bone marrow transplant locates an unwilling potential donor, the courts have declined to order the transplant, even when the potential donor is related to the patient (*McFall v. Shimp*, 1978). Donating bone marrow is less risky (though perhaps no less painful) than a Cesarean section, the patient's death without the donation is always certain, and the potential donor is usually the best or only tissue match available. This apparent inconsistency between two types of cases that should be treated similarly is focusing new attention on the reasoning behind enforced treatment for pregnant women (Annas, 1986; Rhoden, 1987).

End-of-life treatment refusals such as those addressed by advance directives are not very likely to raise problems like these cases involving pregnant women. The sole exception might be where a pregnant woman could possibly be kept alive until her fetus is viable. It is possible, but by no means certain, that under some circumstances a dependent fetus' interests could override a mother's decision to refuse treatment. In making such an assessment, however, physicians need to resist the temptation to count the mother's wishes as less important than they would be if her family circumstances were different.

The case of Angela Carder, though factually sharply different from our hypothetical case of a pregnant woman who refuses treatment that could prolong her life, has raised concern about the balancing of maternal and fetal interests in treatment refusal cases. Angela Carder, near death from cancer, refused a treatment – a Cesarean section to deliver her infant prematurely – because it would probably end her own life *sooner*. It was clear that she could not survive until her pregnancy came to term. She hoped to stay alive till her unborn child reached 28 weeks' gestation, and had agreed to a Cesarean at that time; instead her condition deteriorated and the surgery was performed against her will at 26 weeks. The child died within hours; Angela died the following day.

In a much criticized opinion that was soon vacated (that is, rendered ineffective) and was later reversed after a rehearing, the court reasoned that Angela's interests were outweighed by those of the fetus because she would die very soon no matter what happened (*In re A.C.*, 1987). The new decision (*In re A.C.*, 1990) states clearly that pregnant women have no greater legal duty to their fetuses than potential bone marrow donors have to dying patients for whom they are the only tissue match, and holds that only in very rare cicircumstances will a mother's refusal of care harmful to herself (whether she is decisionally capable or through substituted judgment) be overridden on behalf of her unborn child. This decision too will no doubt prove controversial, as indicated by one judge's vociferous dissent. Moreover, it remains to be seen, in some future case, whether a woman's refusal of potentially life-prolonging treatment will be subject to the same or similar analysis.

The other interests potentially running counter to the patient's right to refuse treatment do not directly weigh the patient's right against the interests of other identifiable individuals. Instead they raise broader societal concerns about the appropriateness of treatment refusals.

Two of these remaining interests, the *prevention of suicide* and the *preservation of life*, at first may seem to amount to the same thing, but they are distinguishable. Social, moral, and legal prohibitions against suicide historically stemmed at least in part from the principle of beneficence; that is, the individual's suicide is prevented for his or her own good. Suicide is no longer a crime in the United States. Disapproval of suicide persists, however, and concerns about the psychological well-being of would-be suicides are genuine. Therefore, many states retain laws making it a crime to assist a suicide. Prevention of suicide is a legitimate beneficent concern where the would-be suicide is too mentally disabled to make an autonomous choice for death; criminal penalties against such persons are considered pointless. Whether there can ever be "rational suicide" is a different issue. Still another issue is whether preventing suicide is a legitimate societal concern in refusal of treatment cases. The courts have uniformly held that it is not.

Courts addressing this question have often disposed of it simply by reasoning that refusal of treatment is not suicide. There are two ways to make this argument. First, the courts reason that the patient does not wish to die, but rather does not wish to live under the conditions of treatment – and therefore accepts death, but only as the outcome of his or her refusal of burdensome treatment. Jehovah's Witnesses do not refuse blood in order to die, but in order to avoid damnation. Patients who refuse to stay on their respirators do not want to die, but want to end the discomfort of enforced artificial ventilation, and know that they may not survive without it.

Second, courts argue that the cause of death is not an act by the patient, the physician, or anyone else, but rather the underlying disease. This argument is easiest to make when the refusing patient is terminally ill and the issue is thus merely postponement of death; but it also is applied to cases in which life support is withdrawn and death results from an underlying chronic disease, as when, for example, a patient withdraws from dialysis.

Although in many cases of terminal illness and severe impairment these arguments about intent and cause may seem appropriate, and therefore may help us to support most patients' refusal of treatment, it is easy to find more troubling cases in which this reasoning is less persuasive. The cases of Dax Cowart and Elizabeth Bouvia are excellent examples.

At the age of 26, Dax suffered extremely serious full-thickness burns over 67% of his body as a result of an accidental explosion. He was left blinded, badly deformed, and seriously impaired, but survived. His continual refusals of burn treatment were not honored (Areen *et al.*, 1984, pp. 1112-1117).

The treatment of severe burns to promote healing and prevent infection is agonizingly and unavoidably painful, and lasts for many months. The pain of graft surgery and rehabilitation is also severe and long lasting. Dax asserts that he refused treatment in order to avoid that pain, with the expectation that he would then die from infection. He preferred death to pain, and perhaps it could be said that he did not wish or intend to die, but the line is very hard to draw.[7] If he had left the hospital, as he wished, and developed an infection, he would have died of an eminently treatable condition.

Elizabeth Bouvia's case is even more destructive of the fine lines courts have tried to draw. She is a young woman afflicted with severe cerebral palsy since birth, which has resulted in almost total paralysis, severe limb deformities, and increasingly extensive and painful arthritis. She needs constant care and has had difficulty obtaining support from either friends or the state. In 1983, she entered a California state hospital facility with the announced intention of starving to death and receiving palliative care in the process. A court determined that the hospital could discharge her rather than comply (Annas, 1984; *Bouvia v. County of Riverside*, 1983). But in 1985, when she entered another hospital in order to obtain care and pain relief for her arthritis, she was no longer able, because of her increasing pain and disability, to swallow enough food to sustain her. The hospital then, over her refusal, inserted a nasogastric tube in order to ensure the sufficiency of her nutritional intake.

This time, when she sued for the tube's removal, the appellate court agreed with her that she could refuse the treatment (*Bouvia v. Superior Court,* 1986). The court's majority pointed out that she did not intend to starve; she was simply incapable of eating enough, did not wish to undergo the discomfort of the nasogastric tube, and accepted that her capacity to swallow would gradually decrease and that she would ultimately weaken and die. It was her underlying muscular incapacity that would cause her death, not the act of will represented by a hunger strike. However, one justice, in a separate opinion concurring with the majority's conclusion, failed to see these distinctions as real differences from the first case involving Ms. Bouvia, in which she simply did not make her own argument for death carefully enough to assuage the conscience of the court. This justice was prepared to assert that suicide is a right of all individuals, and that it stems from autonomy as clearly as does refusal of treatment.

On the basis of cases like those of Dax Cowart and Elizabeth Bouvia, it seems evasive to attempt to argue that it is still appropriate to prevent suicide (for the individual's own good) but that suicide is never, or almost never, involved in treatment refusal. A more plausible posture might be to assert a moral interest in discouraging suicide but not a legal power to prohibit it, thus maintaining respect for the autonomy of individuals while still addressing their wishes and needs.

The cases of Dax Cowart and Elizabeth Bouvia received enormous attention, and many accounts and discussions of them can be found in professional and popular literature. Our fascination with them, and with others like them, stems from our uneasiness about such cases; we search for a 'true' description of their circumstances that will explain which decision is the 'right' one. For example, a prominent scholar, Robert Burt, has examined Dax's case and concluded that his refusal of treatment was not really autonomous and not really a refusal – that it stemmed from unmet needs for support from his mother and caregivers, and from other unresolved issues (Burt, 1979). Burt's sensitive and probing psychological analysis quite naturally strikes a chord with those concerned lest "autonomy" become a catchword for oversimplifying a profoundly complex human situation; yet it is also easy to grasp at psychological explanations as a means of distrusting patients' choices.

Similar speculations proliferated about Elizabeth Bouvia's 'true' reasons for her decision to stop eating; moreover, she became a focus for advocacy groups for the handicapped, who argued that judicial support of her refusal to be artificially fed would send the public message that life is not worth living for handicapped persons, and that therefore, those who choose to live with handicaps deserve no public assistance in so doing (Kane, 1985). This argument would have placed her symbolic value, as a means of fostering certain views, above her own autonomous choice – which brings us to an examination of whether society has an interest in the preservation of life that can curtail autonomous treatment refusal.

Preservation of life is the term used in court decisions to describe a societal interest in the sanctity of life. It is not an interest that is set up directly to challenge individual autonomy, like the prevention of suicide. Instead, the argument goes, we need to promote social values that help to ensure respect for others and the well-working of society as a whole. Preservation of life accomplishes these goals by preventing patients from making medical choices that ultimately would devalue others' lives in our eyes and weaken the social fabric overall. This asserted interest is the counterpart of a general moral proposition that discouraging treatment refusal is part of promoting the proper valuation of human lives. Individuals' choices are not contravened for their own good but because of the negative message that would be sent to society if their choices were honored: the "slippery slope" of progressive contempt for weak, imperfect, or disfavored human beings (*Bouvia v. County of Riverside*, 1983).

Here also the courts have argued, in many refusal cases, that although the state's interest in preservation of life is real, it does not apply to the facts at hand. The first widely known expression of this position came in the celebrated *Quinlan* case, where Karen Quinlan's parents sought to remove her respiratory support in the full expectation that she would die very soon thereafter: "We think that the State's interest *contra* weakens and the individual's right to privacy grows as the degree of bodily invasion increases and the prognosis dims" (*In re Quinlan*, 1976, p. 644).

During the 1960s and 1970s, many of the celebrated treatment refusal cases were cases like Karen Quinlan's was thought to be; if the patient was not "terminal", death was nonetheless not very far away. Perhaps the archetypal situation might be something like the Joseph Saikewicz case (*Superintendent of Belcherton State School v. Saikewicz*, 1977). Mr. Saikewicz was a profoundly retarded institutionalized adult, 67 years old and diagnosed as having acute leukemia, which in his age group has a very dim prognosis. With vigorous chemotherapy, there was a 30-40% chance that he might experience a 2- to 13-month period of remission; cure was not possible. If Mr. Saikewicz had not been retarded, his choice to refuse chemotherapy would almost certainly have been honored by a court using the *Quinlan* balancing test. The prognosis is dim – certain death, albeit a small chance of a short postponement – and the invasiveness of chemotherapy is devastating. The prospect of a remission period might be enough to encourage many patients to try chemotherapy, but a contrary decision is certainly understandable, and many rational arguments might be offered in its support.

But what would the court that permitted the withdrawal of Karen Quinlan's respirator have decided had it known then that she would breathe on her own for many years (finally dying, in 1985, from pneumonia that her family decided should not be treated)? Is ten years of significantly demented existence the kind of dim prognosis originally envisioned by the court? And is artificial nutrition and hydration "invasive"?

The preservation of life interest is important but not specific. It does not belong to identifiable individuals but is really a societal posture that seeks to forestall certain choices but not others. Courts have not had much difficulty with medical decisions that "merely hasten death", as the decisions in the *Quinlan* and *Saikewicz* cases were viewed as doing. In cases like those of Dax Cowart and Elizabeth Bouvia, many courts and caregivers have more difficulty with upholding decisions that cannot be said to "merely hasten death" and thus appear to be based on disvaluing the patient's life. Yet there are some lives that are genuinely unbearable in the eyes of those living them, and often courts and caregivers can identify with patients' decisions to end them. The risk to society is that we will come to prefer the choice of death to giving support and help to persons who choose to live with their discomfort and pain. The risk seems remote, however, when we are face to face with patients' own choices. As the concurring justice in the second *Bouvia* decision (*Bouvia v. Superior Court*, 1986) pointed out, refusing to permit a patient to refuse treatment because of the message that choice would send to others is – no matter how honorable that concern – to force the patient to endure a continued existence that the patient believes unendurable. Understood in this way, the preservation of life interest, important though it may be as a cautionary influence, appears cruel.

In cases like Elizabeth Bouvia's, where the patient's autonomous choice is clearly expressed, many courts have articulately shown themselves willing to support termination of treatment. The case of William Bartling (*Bartling v. Superior Court*, 1984) is an example.

Mr. Bartling was hospitalized for multiple severe chronic problems including depression and emphysema. Routine diagnostic procedures were complicated by his poor health, and he was placed on a mechanical ventilator when a poorly healing biopsy incision resulted in a collapsed lung. He found the pain, discomfort, and degradation of the respirator and its attendant restrictions unbearable; but none of his afflictions were "terminal" and he was considered likely to live another year.

After a lower court refused to permit removal of the ventilator, the appellate court phrased the central question as "whether the right of Mr. Bartling, as a competent adult, to refuse unwanted medical treatment is outweighed by . . . the preservation of life . . . ." And its answer was straightforward: "[I]f the right of the patient to self-determination as to his own medical treatment is to have any meaning at all, it must be paramount...."

However, in many cases the patient is not "terminally ill", continued treatment is somewhat painful or burdensome, and in addition the patient cannot make a contemporaneous choice and has not written an advance directive memorializing a strong autonomous statement refusing treatment under such circumstances. Such cases are therefore complicated by several additional factors: (1) by questions about the reliability of any evidence of the patient's preferences, (2) by the possibility that treatment termination decisions in these cases may reflect a devaluing of the lives of the helpless handicapped and demented rather than a genuine attempt to honor their wishes, and (3) by uncertainties about the meaning and role of the patient's "best interests" when the patient appears to have no real experience of his or her circumstances.

Nonetheless, patients' choices have been upheld under these circumstances as well. The case of Paul Brophy (*In re Brophy*, 1986) is a good example. Mr. Brophy, a fire fighter, suffered a ruptured aortic aneurysm. After brain surgery he lapsed into a persistent vegetative state, able to breathe on his own but with no higher brain functions and virtually no chance of recovering any consciousness. He required extensive personal care, and had to be fed liquid nutrition through a gastrostomy tube directly into his stomach. Although he apparently was conscious and communicative at times between the onset of his illness and surgery, he never specifically gave directions expressing his treatment wishes during that time. However, as the Supreme Judicial Court of Massachusetts stated:

> About ten years ago, discussing Karen Ann Quinlan, Brophy stated to his wife, "I don't ever want to be on a life-support system. No way do I want to live like that; that is not living." He had a favorite saying: "When your ticket is punched, it is punched." Approximately five to six years ago, he helped to rescue from a burning truck a man who received extensive burns and who died a few months later. He tossed the commendation he received for bravery in the trash and said, "I should have been five minutes later. It would have been all over for him." He also said to his brother regarding that incident, "If I'm ever like that, just shoot me, pull the plug." About one week prior to his illness, in discussing a local teenager who had been put on a life support system he said, "No way, don't ever let that happen to me, no way." Within twelve hours after being transported to Goddard Hospital following the rupture of the aneurysm, he stated to one of his daughters, "If I can't sit up to kiss one of my beautiful daughters, I may as well be six feet under." (*In re Brophy*, 1986, n. 22).

The court viewed these statements as sufficient to conclude that Brophy would refuse continued gastrostomy tube feeding, even though he could potentially live for many years. Other courts might disagree, or require more specific declarations; these are matters of interpretation and fairness, to be discussed in a later chapter. For our present purposes, it is most significant that the Court applied the *Quinlan* balancing formula here, weighing the interest in preserving life against the burden to the patient, even though Mr. Brophy was not likely to die soon and could not be said to be in pain or currently experiencing the burdens of his treatment:

> [W]e must recognize that the State's interest in life encompasses a broader interest than mere corporeal existence. In certain, thankfully rare, circumstances the burden of maintaining the corporeal existence degrades the very humanity it was meant to serve.
>
> * * *
>
> The duty of the State to preserve life must encompass a recognition of an individual's right to avoid circumstances in which the individual himself would feel that efforts to sustain life demean or degrade his humanity....While...continued use of the G-tube is not a highly invasive or intrusive procedure and may not subject him to pain or suffering, he is left helpless and in a condition which Brophy has indicated he would consider to be degrading and without human dignity....Additionally, in our view, the

maintenance of Brophy ["bathing, shaving, mouth care, grooming, caring for his bowels
and bladder, changing his bed linens and clothing, turning him in bed to prevent bed
sores and providing him with food and hydration through the G-tube"], for a period of
several years, is intrusive treatment as a matter of law (*In re Brophy*, 1986).

Thus, the societal interest in preservation of life is unable to override
meaningful refusals of treatment. Indeed, the United States Supreme Court
so recognized in its recent *Cruzan* decision (*Cruzan v. Director*, 1990),
though the question of what constitutes a meaningful *prospective* refusal of
treatment is still unsettled. That is the subject of the next chapter and will not
be addressed here. However, there remains the state's fourth interest to
consider. Should caregivers like Mr. Brophy's physician, who believe that
clamping Mr. Brophy's G-tube is professionally unethical, be able to prevent
it for this reason?

The last of the state's four interests, preserving the integrity of the medical
profession, is one that is often sidestepped. The issue is raised when
physicians, other caregivers, and hospitals object to a patient's refusing
treatment and continuing to receive other care from them; or when
withdrawal of support is authorized by the court and someone has to actually
pull the plug. It is a distillation of the problem that physicians face with all
patients who fail or refuse to follow advice. What do you do with the rest of
the patient's care? How do you as a caregiver understand your role, your
freedom to give the best possible care? Facing a patient's treatment refusal
is harder than the dilemma of how to treat the patient who will not quit
smoking, however, because not only is the physician's effectiveness at stake,
but the patient's whole life and freedom are at stake as well.

The courts get around this, essentially, by questioning whether good
medical practice is always consistent with the prolongation of life. The
Quinlan court first raised this issue with a historical discussion demonstrating
that "physicians have always distinguished between curing the ill and
comforting the dying" (*In re Quinlan*, 1976). In addition to citing the
Hippocratic Oath's reference to avoiding futile treatments, the court in
Quinlan examined Roman Catholic theology to find additional support for the
distinction between "ordinary" and "extraordinary" efforts to preserve life.
The court viewed it as a proper medical judgment to determine the point at
which preservation of life was futile; therefore there could be no categorical
determination that refusal of treatment contravened a professional
commitment to the best care. It then remained to determine, in each instance,
whether the care refused was under the circumstances "ordinary" or
"extraordinary" – whether the refusal was something no physician could
condone or something the profession in general could support.

This analysis is easy in some factual settings – namely, where the patient is clearly terminal and the proposed treatment invasive and plainly futile, or where the caregivers in question agree with the patient's decision and are simply seeking protection for their actions, or where transfer to a willing physician is possible. It is unsatisfactory in other settings, however. When physicians oppose the patient's choice and no other caregivers stand ready to support it, when transfer is not possible, or when the patient's choice does not merely hasten death but chooses death over disability, this view of the physician's interest does not necessarily protect the patient. On this view, the medical profession as a whole could decide to continue the treatment of a patient who has nowhere else to go and no effective way to refuse. But why should medicine have the definitive say in these matters?

Perhaps there are medical values that identify preservation of life and health as a good, and condemn futile care, which is predicted to accomplish neither (Schneiderman *et al.*, 1990). But suppose the care being considered is usually but not always futile. It cannot be solely *medicine's* place both to assess the risk of futility and to decide when it is too great or too small. The values of the patient must also be considered, and may be in some cases decisive. These are not simply medical questions, no matter how entangled with medicine they may be.[9]

If the integrity of the medical profession is a legitimate interest, it surely should ensure that physicians who choose not to participate in the care of persons refusing treatment should not be compelled to participate. Other health care professionals and institutional providers should similarly be empowered to withdraw from the care of such patients. Nonetheless, there are limits to the physician's power to disengage from a patient's care. All caregivers and institutions are obligated never to abandon a patient in need. In this context, the prohibition against abandonment effectively means that the patient should not be forced to endure treatment because no caregivers are willing to support nontreatment. New Jersey courts have held that an institution that failed to give a patient timely notice of its policy against cessation of treatment cannot force the patient to leave the institution (*In re Jobes*, 1987; *In re Requena*, 1986); presumably, then, the institution must permit the patient access to caregivers (from other institutions) who are willing to withdraw treatment. So long as there are some caregivers who will support a patient's choice to refuse treatment and some who will not, the question of whether there is a genuine issue of professional integrity involved in these cases will be obscured, just as the *Quinlan* court obscured it.

The patient's right to make contemporaneous treatment decisions that are likely to result in death is thus stronger than the four interests commonly arrayed against it. A last ground exists, however, upon which to oppose the decisions of patients. It does not interpose a new countervailing interest but instead challenges the validity of the patient's decision directly, by challenging the patient's ability to make it.

Decisional Capacity, or the "Competence Conundrum"

"Competence" is the term generally employed in health care to describe a patient's ability to make autonomous decisions about his or her treatment. A competent patient is one whose treatment decisions are considered valid and to be honored by caregivers. "Incompetence" describes the condition of patients who cannot make decisions about their care, or cannot make decisions that carry sufficient validity to be honored. About this much there is general agreement. In fact, however, incompetence is properly a term applied only to persons *legally* determined to be incapable of autonomous decisionmaking. It has therefore been suggested that the term be limited to this use and that "capacity for autonomous decisionmaking" be used instead of "competence" where a more general term is wanted (Wolff *et al.*, 1987, pp. 131-132). "Decisional capacity" is rapidly gaining ground over the common but imprecise "competence."

There is little or no agreement about how decisional capacity and its absence are recognized and determined, what kinds of decision-making skills are necessary for decisional capacity, and what skill levels are sufficient. To delve fully into this large, rich, and freewheeling debate is beyond the scope of this volume, but some acquaintance with the problem is clearly necessary (Annas and Glantz, 1986; Appelbaum *et al.*, 1987; Buchanan and Brock, 1986; Culver and Gert, 1982; Dworkin, 1986; Faden *et al.*, 1986; Lo, 1990; President's Commission, 1983).

In common language, "competence" is a term with two possible meanings. According to one of these, competence is the ability to do anything adequately: "He is a competent accountant"; "She is an incompetent orthopedic surgeon"; "Jane is competent at golf"; "Bill is incompetent behind the wheel." Thus, competence is by itself contentious, but when an answer is supplied to the question "Competent at what?" we know in a general way how to decide what skills are necessary for a particular competence – that is, competence at a particular activity – and what level of skill is required.

The second common meaning of "competence" is more specific. It refers to our common understanding of incompetence as a mental state resulting in the inability to look after one's own life: "We had to commit Cousin Herbert because he'd become completely incompetent"; "The family is contesting Grandfather's will on the ground of incompetence." Although only one particular activity is referred to by this usage, it is usually left unspecified. And because this meaning refers to a mental state, it is often conflated with the even more specific issue of decisional capacity. It is easy to forget that the capacity for medical decisionmaking is more than just a generalized psychological status, and that it must be associated with particular decision-making activity. How that activity is defined and measured when a patient's medical decision making capacity is at issue is crucial.

"Making health care decisions" is the most general statement of the relevant activity; for advance directives, making *prospective* health care decisions is a better definition. Whether it is necessary to go further and distinguish between different decisions or at least different categories of decisions (e.g., life and death choices versus decisions with less serious consequences) is still debated, even though most agree that because competence is task-specific, decisional capacity should be measured in terms of the particular decision(s) faced by the patient. Patients with limited mental capacity, who might be viewed as "generally incompetent", may still be capable of making certain decisions – just as a "generally competent" person may be incapable of making some choices.

Assessing decisional capacity in the health care setting is a problem principally because there is no common understanding of what is "normal" under the circumstances of health care decisionmaking. When decision-making capacity in other areas is assessed, the inquiry is a little bit easier: we have at least some idea what it means to be able to manage one's business affairs, provide food, clothing, and shelter for oneself and one's family, dispose of one's property by will. When it comes to health care decisions, however, it may be difficult to assess the appropriateness of a decisionmaking process in such an unfamiliar setting. Once we recognize that decisional capacity does not necessarily mean following the doctor's advice, we have to have some way to evaluate "normal" decisionmaking under conditions of stress, pain, discomfort, invasion of privacy, pressures of various kinds, depression, separation from family and routine, helplessness, reduction of dignity, poor communication, and the assimilation of new information very much outside of the patient's previous experience.

With such a catalogue of adverse conditions, it is not surprising that there should be a widespread temptation to underestimate the decision-making capacity of the ill and the institutionalized. It is easy to overlook the fact that a similar catalogue might be made for other kinds of decisions: what if a person writing a will did so while very near death, or after an emotional dispute with an expected beneficiary? What if the young mother who just bought a new station wagon was distracted by her misbehaving children; pressured by her isolation and by her husband's complaints about her inefficiency; manipulated by the salesman's charming sleight-of-hand; handicapped by her poor grasp of mathematics, budgeting, and automotive engineering?

Thinking clearly about the capacity to make health care decisions requires the recognition that health care decisions do not need to be 'better' decisions than other kinds of decisions about other matters. They need to be only as good as the decisions we will accept that are of comparable magnitude. Buying a car; buying a house; investing in the stock market; choosing a college major, a career, a spouse; having children; engaging in a potentially dangerous sport or recreation; all of these major life decisions may be of comparable magnitude to many of the health care decisions about which people are most concerned, while many other health care decisions are nearly trivial by comparison. Recognizing that health care decisions in general are like other decisions causes us to realize that there is in fact little agreement about how to measure the capacity of ordinary day-to-day life decision-makers. We know that as a general principle, decision-making capacity is presumed, and decision makers are given a lot of leeway; but beyond that, what? Are there reasons for making some decisions, like buying a car, or getting married, that are so bad we should not allow some decisions to be made?

In general, society does three kinds of things to regulate decisionmaking. We institute some type of regulation of the transaction (e.g., truth in advertising; marriage blood tests) to reduce – usually minimally – some of the harmfulness of bad decisionmaking; we use information, education, and persuasion to improve decisionmaking; and we rely on psychiatric determinations of mental incapacity if we believe that the decision in question demonstrates a deeper problem. We do not usually intervene in particular decisions that are not about health care simply because we believe that they are not sufficiently well reasoned, have failed to appreciate certain information, are not mature enough, or have been affected by any of the adverse circumstances recited earlier. Yet we are tempted to intervene in health care decisions for all these reasons.

Many people wish to argue that health care decisionmaking is different from all other decisionmaking because of its 'life and death' character. Not all health care decisions are life-and-death matters, however, and when stress and illness are present they affect all decisions, not just health care choices.

Decisions to refuse treatment and decisions at the end of life are (usually but not always) more important, with more serious and irrevocable consequences, than many (but not all) other life choices. It has been argued that therefore they must be required to be 'better' decisions than others before they are honored by others. This argument ignores the fact that in the case of advance directives the most important decisions are also the decisions most important for the decisionmakers – decisions that implicate deeply held wishes and values, decisions about which people feel most strongly. To require a higher decisional standard because of the importance of the decision runs the risk of disenfranchising people from the choices most important to them, unless the strength of the wishes, values, and convictions underlying these choices is taken into account in evaluating the choices.

Medical choices seem different because many of them entail risks and/or certainties of very bad outcomes. It must be acknowldeged that many ordinary life choices also contain significant risks, and also that, though many people would describe themselves as risk-averse, many others are forced by circumstances to choose between the proverbial "devil and the deep blue sea." Though hard decisions may be unprecedented in the life of a given patient, and therefore more difficult to make well, the very difficulty of end-of-life choices between certain death and the risks and burdens of continued treatment suggests that the decisional standard for such choices ought perhaps to be lower than the standard chosen for other decisions, where the better choice is clearer. This would more readily permit patients to make their own choices when there is no obviously 'good' option available. At least, standards of capacity based solely on rational decisionmaking should not necessarily be dispositive in the hardest cases.

The argument that medical decisions are different really amounts to a declaration that some choices should not be permitted, for the patient's own good. When the patient is able directly to contest others' views of his or her own good, it is hard to maintain this position except by claiming that the patient lacks decisional capacity; but where the only evidence of that lack of capacity lies in this disagreement with caregivers and others, no valid grounds exist to support the claim.

Certainly we would like to be able to ensure that medical care decisions, and all decisions, are mature, well-reasoned, adequately justified, sufficiently informed, and sufficiently appreciative of all relevant issues. Yet agreement is lacking about what constitutes sufficient maturity, appreciation, and reasoning and how they should be measured. It seems only sensible to do what we do outside the health care context inside the health care context as well: set a minimal standard that is enforced by regulation of the setting or the provider (e.g., informed consent law); use psychiatric evaluation to uncover disorders that preclude 'normal' life decisionmaking; and attempt, by means of information, discussion, and persuasion, to encourage the best possible decisionmaking process.

Advance directives clearly present a special problem in this regard. Like wills, they are put into effect only when their writers do not have the capacity to write them, and are not even 'available' to be examined, questioned, informed, or persuaded. The retrospective evaluation of decisional capacity at the time the document was written is very different from a contemporaneous analysis, because the evidence available for consideration is likely to be quite limited.

As a result, in the case of wills, property law has developed a very commonsensical (and frequently litigated-about) definition of testamentary capacity: Did the testator know "the natural objects of his bounty", and did he understand the consequences of the distribution he chose? The capacity of the testator is examined by establishing the formal validity of the will document itself; by examining its terms; by interviewing the witnesses to it about the testator's apparent capacity and understanding; and by means of other relevant evidence extrinsic to the document – evidence that is more often from friends and relatives than from psychiatrists. Most wills are also discussed with and reviewed by attorneys at some point before, during, or shortly after their making. This affords the attorney an opportunity to assess the testator's capacity according to the cited definition, as well as to improve the testator's decisionmaking.

Advance directives can provide similar assurances of capacity. Most directives are witnessed and notarized to conform with state law; a properly validated directive provides evidence that the writer was capable of appreciating the necessary formalities, and of course the witnesses may be called upon to give their impressions of the writer's state of mind. The terms of statutory directives are sketchy and may not in themselves offer much proof of capacity; but the makers of directives very often enlarge on the statutory forms, adding detail and specificity, enumerating decisions, or even starting from scratch, writing a document meant to express personal philosophy. Such emendations, while recommended for other reasons, are also useful in supporting the presumption of capacity.

The capacity problem with advance directives persists because it is possible to make a perfectly good directive without consulting with anyone – family or friends, doctor or lawyer. You do not need a lawyer, and you may not have friends or family or even a doctor at the moment. Everyone is presumed to have capacity until *proven* otherwise; thus, the lack of evidence of any such discussion and consultation cannot itself give rise to a determination of incapacity (and therefore invalidity of the directive). Writers of directives can help to ensure that their capacity is clearly apparent by having such consultations – which also have the very valuable results that their directives may be improved in content and expression, and will be better understood by family and physician and thus more likely to be obeyed. For those who have no regular physician when the directive is written, the best alternative is to bring up the directive during later encounters with caregivers. This opportunity to reaffirm the directive before others accomplishes all of the same goals that can be achieved by discussing it when first written. Of course, there will still be instances when a directive has not been discussed with anyone. The question of implementing such directives is the subject of a later chapter.

When the patient cannot directly contest others' determinations, as is the case when an advance directive is brought into play, the 'future factor' does present a problem. Does its prospective character imply that there is anything special about the capacity to write an advance directive? In this respect, advance directives are not like wills, even though wills are also prospective decisions, for in a will you can only give away property you have to people who exist – you do not need to imagine what it would be like to have more money, or to have to divide your estate among different children. Because prospective health care decisionmaking seems to labor under special handicaps of anticipation and imagination, it might be thought that making good advance directives requires a supercapacity.

A bad decision does not necessarily indicate decisional incapacity. Nor is it necessarily the case that a decision later rejected by its maker was incompetently made. The possibility that a different choice could have been made should not invalidate a directive by itself. Besides, we do not really know what *is* a bad decision about future treatment. None of us, not even physicians, can imagine the future well enough to know with certainty each time anyone else is doing so poorly at such imagining to be judged incapable of it. We may be able to recognize some bad choices, and when we do we must try to correct them. That is not the same as declaring someone incapable of choosing because we believe the choice was wrong. We should certainly ensure that writers of advance directives know that the future is uncertain and contains unknowns. Much more than that seems impossible to ask. (The 'future factor' will be considered at greater length in Chapter 3).

Decisional capacity is a conundrum because it must be both described and detected, and because the description and means of detection we choose are chosen, at least in part, according to our moral judgments about individual freedom and responsibility, about right choices and what it is to be human. 'Competence' is a value-laden label that only pretends to scientific objectivity and attempts to deny the reciprocal relationships between patients and physicians, tests and standards, individuals and societies.

Clinicians should examine the tools and information they and their colleagues use to determine the decisional capacities of patients whose mentation has been questioned. There is a vast array of evidence and test instruments that are regularly used by clinicians to make such judgments, and the relevance and weight of these data must always be carefully considered.[10] We presume all adults to be capable of free and responsible choices. The correct question to ask is whether there is any reason to suspect that this person is not choosing freely and responsibly. Then, what are these reasons? Can we eliminate these obstacles to free and responsible decisionmaking? This is the sort of inquiry that seems to me most fruitful. Some of the reasons for not deciding freely and responsibly may correspond with what we would currently call 'incapacity'; some will not. Some of them may be remediable, and others may not be. Capacity is no special hurdle in health care decisionmaking. If physicians and others act on the presumption that all advance directives can be freely and responsibly made, advance directives will be better supported by caregivers and thus will become better documents, more thoughtful and more often honored.

Notes

[1] In fact, the only reported criminal prosecution of physicians to date for withdrawing life-sustaining treatment from a patient was initiated by one of the patient's nurses after the patient's family resisted continuation of what was considered by the nursing service to be standard comfort care (turning the patient in bed and humidifying the patient's airway with a misting device). The charges against the physicians were ultimately dismissed (*Barber v. Superior Court*, 1983).

[2] For example, the development of anesthesia made consultation with patients during surgery impossible, and incidentally caused many people to fear that physicians would perform procedures without their consent while they were unconscious (Pernick, 1982).

[3] For the most recent versions of the regulations, see Department of Health and Human Services (1989); Food and Drug Administration (1990). For their history, see Faden *et al.* (1986).

[4] For example, the Declaration of Helsinki's informed consent requirement was considerably relaxed for what the WMA described as "therapeutic research", in which benefit to subjects was anticipated (World Medical Assembly, 1964).

[5] Thus, until the mid-20th century (*Brown v. Hughes*, 1934; *Fortner v. Koch*, 1935), any treatment considered "experimental" carried grave liability risks for the physician (*Carpenter v. Blake*, 1871; *Slater v. Baker and Stapleton*, 1767), and even now it is not clear whether patient and physician may make a contract about unusual or unorthodox treatment – for example, to deliver cheaper, cost-saving care – because of the courts' desire to protect patients.

[6] The Supreme Court majority did not address the weight of the liberty interest assumed in *Cruzan*; Justice Brennan for the dissent did, however, assert its fundamental character (*Cruzan v. Director*, 1990, p. 4927), and other courts have likewise done so (*In re A.C.*, 1990).

[7] constitutional rights differ from common law rights in another important way. State law may change or replace common law rights by legislation (if the legislature is clear and explicit about its intent to do so). Constitutional rights cannot be affected by statute, only by constitutional amendment. The *legal* meaning of state statutes that provide "living will" forms or otherwise address end-of-life decisionmaking is thus colored by the backdrop of common and constitutional law. This legal issue is discussed further in Chapter 4.

[8] See Areen *et al.*(1984) pp. 1112-1117; Burt, (1979). See also the two films made about Dax Cowart's experience, *Please Let Me Die* and *Dax's Case* (made by Cowart himself), both available from Concern for Dying, 250 West 57th Street, New York, NY 10019.

[9] When the patient refuses treatment, the integrity of the medical profession cannot require that treatment be continued. The issue is more complex whenever caregivers feel morally and professionally uneasy about continuing requested supportive care in the face of the patient's refusal of definitive treatment. Finally, when the patient requests particular treatments that the physician believes are not medically justifiable, the conflict of values is clearly drawn. Chapter 6's discussion of "Request Directives" and "Medical Judgment and Advance Directives" addresses this conflict in more detail.

[10] Of necessity, many determinations about a patient's capacity are made at the bedside by physicians – sometimes but not always with the assistance of psychiatric, neurological, or psychological expertise. Because decisional capacity is task-specific, a global determination of lack of capacity, such as that provided by a mental status examination, cannot necessarily show that the patient cannot make a given decision – especially if the determination of incapacity is made before the need for decision arises. Therefore, global determinations of incapacity should be considered preliminary, and should either be reexamined at the time a decision is needed or used to provide evidence in a judicial proceeding to determine the patient's capacity (except where the emergency exception applies). Though some commentators have argued that the courts should always be consulted for determinations about patients' decisional capacities, except where statutes permit otherwise, by custom many such determinations are made by attending physicians without judicial review.

In essence, decisional capacity – 'competence' – in the context of health care decisionmaking means the ability to give an informed consent: that is, the ability to give a consent that is intentional, based on understanding, and free from control by others. Setting the standards for understanding, voluntariness, and intention means determining how much of those attributes is necessary. Legally, decisional capacity is a minimal threshold standard, below which it is not reasonable to honor the patient's choices because the patient is not sufficiently capable of making them. Moreover, decisional capacity is task-specific – that is, patients may be competent in some ways and not in others, and therefore capable of making health care choices but not financial decisions, or capable of making minor or familiar decisions but not of grasping complex technical information for other decisions. Finally, decisional capacity is not fixed, but may wax and wane with the patient's condition. Decisions made during a "window of capacity" should be honored during incapacity.

Thus, standards of capacity must establish minimum threshold levels of decisional ability and must be specific, both temporally and in the ability being measured. Testing for that capacity takes many forms, each of which has some weaknessess and some strengths.

The *presence of decision* is sometimes offered as a test of decisional capacity. This test requires only the expression of assent or dissent. Such a test is insufficient, because it does not necessarily reflect the patient's ability to understand and to decide freely. It may mask any number of cognitive or psychological disorders, and is likely to result in many "false positive" determinations of capacity. It can even give rise to false negative determinations, where anything from language barriers to massive motor-neural disorders could prevent the communication of a decision.

The patient's *understanding* of the decision faced is sometimes tested as a way of gauging capacity as well as a way of determining whether the patient has grasped the basic issues disclosed by the caregiver and has some sense of why they, and the decision faced, are important. The most common means of testing understanding is to ask the patient to repeat information back to the caregiver "in your own words." Sometimes more standardized written multiple-choice questionnaires are used.

There is a risk of false negatives in this test, because it is unavoidably biased in favor of the caregiver's definition of "understanding." Moreover, it must be carefully done to ensure that it does not become a test of the patient's recall. However, since this test deals only with understanding and not also with the patient's reasoning process, its principal risk is that caregivers may overestimate the degree of understanding that is actually sufficient for patients to make informed choices. It is probably the best test, if carefully used.

Another test, frequently used, is examination of the patient's *decision-making process* – that is, asking patients to explain the basis for their choices, and evaluating their reasons and their reasoning. If a patient has not considered a decision fully enough or taken all of the important considerations into account in making it, the patient will be judged lacking in decisional capacity. This test runs a high risk of false negatives, as it clearly favors decisionmaking processes that resemble those of whoever is evaluating the process in question, and thus may be biased against cultural, social, and religious differences in decisional priorities.

Finally, the *decision* itself has been known to serve as a test of decisional capacity. This test is also substantially biased. Whether the patient makes the 'right' choice may be as much a matter of legitimate differences in viewpoint as of defects in decisional capacity, resulting in false negatives caused by value conflicts. Like the test for presence of a decision, this test could also give rise to false positives, since a patient with no capacity to understand the situation could still announce the 'right' choice.

Chapter Three

The "Future Factor":
The Conceptual Foundations of Advance Directives

> [O]n occasions of momentous choice we are in the
> position of carrying forward a pattern of self that is, in
> the nature of things, necessarily understood only with
> imperfection. Occasions of such choice are occasions
> of judgment and discernment, not occasions of
> algorithmic calculation. (Churchill, 1989, p. 177)

In Chapter 2 it was argued that patients' own contemporaneous health care choices should be honored so long as they have sufficient decision-making capacity, even when those choices are viewed by caregivers and others as not in the patient's best interests.[1] The patient's autonomy thus serves as the foundation for contemporaneous treatment choices. Advance directives are not contemporaneous decisions, however. Whether they take the form of instruction directives, which list decisions about various interventions and various circumstances, or proxy directives giving to a named individual the power to make decisions for the patient, or a combination of the two, all advance directives announce decisions that are to be carried out in the future, at a time when the patient does not have the capacity to discuss or change them. This chapter addresses two central concerns about the moral validity of this *prospective decisionmaking*.

First, do patients really have the capacity to make autonomous prospective decisions about future medical treatment, despite the uncertainties and unknowns involved, including the likelihood that such decisions will take effect when they themselves are mentally and physically changed? Can the future be adequately anticipated? Some caregivers and scholars believe that patients' advance directives simply cannot be sufficiently informed about the future to be practically meaningful.

Second, even if such decisionmaking is possible given its uncertainties, are incapacitated patients so different from their former selves and so lacking in the attributes that characterized their former selves that it does not make sense to treat their former choices as binding, or even relevant? Some caregivers and scholars believe that the interests and concerns of the writers of advance directives are so far different from their needs and interests when severely incapacitated that it is wrong to view patients' autonomy as having any application when they are severely incapacitated. In a sense, they claim, such patients must have changed their minds about their wishes.

Both of these concerns raise important questions worthy of careful consideration, but neither is ultimately persuasive. They suggest, however, that our understanding of autonomy, and of who the patient is, need a richer exploration in order to understand how autonomy and respect for persons serve as the foundations for advance directives. This exploration should enable clinicians to think more carefully about the nature of advance directives and how best to accomplish their purposes.

Appreciating the "Future Factor"

Part of what distinguishes humans from other animals is our ability to live in a way that encompasses not only present but also past and future. Many of us spend a good part of our lives planning for our own and others' futures. We are accustomed to making resolutions, promises, and agreements that we intend to have a binding effect on our future actions. Continuity of personal identity, of self, is thus in some practical sense both assumed by and necessary to human living.

In addition, we are accustomed to making resolutions, promises, and agreements to change ourselves and others in the future. We send our children to school to assist in their becoming good people and good citizens; we rehabilitate drug abusers and lawbreakers; we vow to change our type A behavior, to lose weight, to learn gardening, to study Eastern philosophy; we decide to become parents, or to undertake the search for faith. Thus, we recognize change – sometimes great change – as falling within the continuity of an individual self. We look back and acknowledge how differently we viewed life when we were young, or before we were married, or while we were still in school. Nonetheless, we know that although in one sense we are no longer "the same person" as we were then, we are still the same person in some deeper sense.

Two principal questions arise with respect to people's attempts to write advance directives expressing choices about future actions affecting themselves: First, have they sufficiently anticipated what may come to pass in the future? And second, what if they change their minds? Both these questions have great significance for advance directives. 'Appropriate anticipation', though not part of the minimal standard of decisional capacity, is clearly desirable in decisionmaking. We would not decide, for example, that a person who does not know what he really wants to do as a career is therefore not able – and should not be permitted – to choose a job. Still, appropriate anticipation becomes a pressing concern as soon as one attempts to write an advance directive. There is enormous difficulty entailed in specifying particular decisions for particular circumstances in advance, especially for patients who do not currently suffer from or anticipate a particular disability. There are many possible decisions, many potentially relevant circumstances, and many unknowns.

It is possible that the breadth of the problem accounts in part for the popularity of sweepingly general directives like those promulgated by some patient advocacy groups. General, exhortatory directives may contain no real instructions, and may not intend to; the writer may simply want caregivers to be aware of a general wish to avoid a prolonged dying. On the other hand, many patients may be unaware how difficult these broad directives can be to apply.

Advance directives of either the instruction type, which enumerates the writer's wishes in particular circumstances or about particular procedures, or the proxy type, which names a substituted decisionmaker, require the writer to consider and decide about a vast array of possible conditions and events. When the writer prepares an instruction directive, these decisions appear in the body of the document itself. In a proxy directive, these decisions ordinarily must be discussed with the proxy holder even though they need not appear in the document. Both types of directives are extensively described and discussed in Chapter 4.

Although it is difficult to anticipate all of the circumstances necessary for the best possible prospective decisionmaking, that does not mean that 'appropriate anticipation' should be an additional requirement for assessing the ability to write an advance directive. The reason is simple: it is a requirement impossible to measure fairly. Like other, similar requirements for decisional capacity that have been proposed but discarded – 'maturity,' for example – it is hard to measure such a standard and even harder to test for it, in light of the value judgments it would impose and the variety of ways people actually make decisions. All tests of decisional capacity run the risk of setting unrealistically high standards, standards that promote the values of the person applying the test and that treat other ways of reasoning as less valid. An anticipation component would increase this risk even more, and therefore would be undesirable unless we are prepared to declare many people who wish to write directives incapable of making prospective decisions at all. Such determinations mean that the power to decide for these people must be given to someone else.

For example, imagine two nursing home patients with similar health histories: arthritis, diabetes, and one mild stroke. Grace Bowman has spent many hours thinking about her advance directive and has written a document that exhaustively considers the possibilities if she should have another stroke or experience any of the serious possible complications of her diabetes. She decides she does not want mechanical ventilation, because she hates her memory of the experience of being intubated briefly after her stroke. In contrast, Robert Fielding's advance directive is short and sweet: "No hospitalization."

How are we to judge these two patients' capacities to write their directives in terms of their anticipation? Naturally, the best thing that can happen is that their own caregivers will discuss their directives with them as soon as they know of their existence. That way, it might be noticed that Grace has not said anything about whether she might agree to *temporary* ventilation if her life could be saved thereby, or whether she would agree to forms of respiratory support that are less uncomfortable and burdensome, though perhaps less effective. Robert, on the other hand, might convince a clinician that his dislike of hospitals is unshakable. In both cases, any factual misconceptions that might form the basis for their decisions could be uncovered and corrected.

Even when patients can talk with their physicians, and their mental state, level of information, and understanding can be assessed, how can anticipation be measured? Suppose Grace's actual health crisis, when it comes, stems from a wholly different cause – a traffic accident on an outing. Must her directive be invalid because she did not anticipate all possible health problems? Or suppose you ask Robert – whose directive does in fact cover every medical crisis imaginable (except those not requiring hospitalization) – what would happen if he changed his mind and he says "But I won't! That makes no sense to me! I've never set foot in a hospital and I never will and I'll *sure* never change my mind about *that*!" Should his directive later be treated as invalid because he has written off the possibility that he could change his views?

No! Both directives should stand as valid – but not because Grace and Robert should be penalized with the consequences of their decisions. The argument that would include appropriate anticipation as necessary to a valid directive would also devalue many patients' ways of making decisions, without necessarily helping to encourage better decisions. Moreover, the remedy is Draconian. There are ways of tackling some of the problems of the 'future factor' that do not require that the whole directive be discarded – and that can help to encourage better decisions.

Improving Awareness of the Future Factor

Decisionmaking in circumstances of inherent uncertainty can be improved, yes, but the uncertainty can never be eliminated. So long as patients understand that the uncertainty exists, they should be allowed to live or die with it if they so choose. But they can be encouraged (or even required) to do some things that will reduce caregivers' discomfort about that uncertainty and help others to extract the most guidance (imperfect though it may be) their directives have to offer.

The potentially massive undertaking represented by writing an advance directive can be bounded in two standard easy ways, which directly address the practical aspects of the problems of anticipation and change of views. First, virtually all statutory advance directives contain clauses making them very easy to revoke, at any time, in any intelligible manner and regardless of whether the patient is otherwise decisionally capable at the time of revocation. Thus, anyone able to formulate a change of mind and express it in any way should be able to revoke a directive.[2] Even when a patient is no longer able to revoke the directive 'formally', by destroying it or defacing it, revocation can be effective in many ways. Any interested caregiver, family member, or friend may elicit the patient's response to the directive and thereby witness the revocation.

Second, the possibility of a change of mind can be considerably reduced if the authors of directives would periodically reexamine, update, and reaffirm their advance directives. Though bearing superficial resemblance to the updating of a last will and testament, updating an advance directive serves some additional and different purposes. It permits the authors of directives to keep up with increases in their knowledge of their own conditions and with advances in medical treatment, both of which may affect future choices as reflected in the directive. Moreover, periodic updating encourages regular assessment of one's own views and preferences as they may change with time and as a result of other changes, medical advances aside. Because we know that our views on many things may change, we would without question be remiss in failing to acknowledge the need for at least occasional reassessment of an advance directive.

Personal Identity and Advance Directives

The question of changing one's mind also has deeper ramifications. Regardless of the frequency with which we update directives, they still set out decisions, made at one time, that are intended to govern actions at another time, a time when revocation may well be impossible. If we do not make these decisions for ourselves, someone else will have to make them for us, without benefit of our guidance. Other examples of prospective decisionmaking – a last will and testament or statement authorizing organ donation – are more readily accepted than advance directives. Why? Because they take effect only after death, and anticipated death or disability is separable from their subject matter. Advance directives are capable of hastening death, rather than simply altering its consequences. When patients are fully capable of making decisions, reasoning about their views, changing their minds, and understanding the relationship between their past and present choices – yet at some remove from the circumstances under which the decision will actually be made – can they make valid decisions that if honored may result in death?

It is important to see that this question is very different from asking whether patients have the legal right to make medical choices resulting in death. That question has already been answered: Patients do have the right to refuse any medical treatment regardless of whether death will result.

But that question was discussed assuming the chooser was capable of decisionmaking at the time of the choice. The advance directives scenario seems different at first because it implies an enlargement of the circumstances under which we were initially willing to permit choices leading to death. We might be prepared to acknowledge that a competent person could decide to refuse a treatment that was painful or burdensome, or even to refuse treatment in order to end a life felt to be painful, limited, and degrading, but some of us might also feel that to prefer death to being permanently unconscious or severely demented is somehow wrongly devaluing life (Dresser, 1986).

There are two related types of argument that are made in support of the position that patients should not be able to write advance directives, at least in certain kinds of cases. Both these arguments "work" by asserting that decisionally capable persons do not have the power to make certain kinds of decisions that will take effect when they are no longer decisionally capable.

The "Black Box"

This argument holds that no one should be permitted to make a decision about treatment under circumstances entirely beyond our experience. No matter how carefully writers of advance directives anticipate and imagine their future medical circumstances, it is impossible to experience a permanent coma, persistent vegetative state, or irreversible dementia. If we try to imagine such a state, by making use of knowledge of apparently similar states like temporary coma and acute delirium or psychosis, we can only get to an approximation at best. Technical knowledge of brain functioning in different states is imperfect and cannot really provide understanding. Indeed, this argument goes, it is possible, and cannot be ruled out, that patients in these demented states experience an inner life to which we can have no access. How can we know that Karen Quinlan did not have some kind of 10-year-long vision? We cannot.

And therefore, we also cannot accept the decision of the decisionally capable person who purports knowingly to reject the possibility that demented life has value. It is not possible to reject something about which we are – inevitably – too ignorant.

The black box argument is currently empirically supported by our still-great ignorance about the relationships among brain function, consciousness, and experience. The argument does not depend upon that ignorance, however, unless we agree that internal experience corresponding with minimal selfhood must be perceivable and demonstrable empirically. Our increasing technical knowledge is likely to squeeze the possibility that such patients partake of some intangible experience into a vanishingly small corner. However, another aspect of the black box argument does not rest on the unknown character of the demented patient's experience, but proceeds to remove all arguments against continued existence for these patients. According to this reasoning, the kinds of arguments adduced for withholding or withdrawal of treatment have to do with physical pain, discomfort, and burden, and also with their psychic counterparts (e.g., concerns about dignity and degradation). This argument holds that, given what we know about brain function, consciousness, and experience, we can tell when pain is a problem and we can then eliminate it. In the many cases in which physical pain is not a problem, because it is not perceived by the patient, there is no 'merciful' reason to terminate treatment.

And as for psychic pain, the black box argument maintains that it is even less likely that patients in demented states can sense any loss of dignity or experience their existence as degraded. These psychic pains are felt only by conscious, decisionally capable persons who imagine themselves in such conditions; they cannot be a real thing, cannot matter, for unconscious and severely demented patients.[3]

By removing most of the justifications for treatment termination in unconscious and demented patients, and leaving either existence alone or existence with the unknowable possibility of great value, the black box argument seems to seek to give life itself an overriding value by defining away the costs of preserving it. This is little different in effect from prohibiting nontreatment of unconscious demented patients who are not terminally ill.

The Stranger

Picking up from where the black box left off, the stranger argument holds that what writers of directives count as significant reasons for treatment termination cannot be reasons in the experience of patients at the time a directive would be invoked. Therefore, the argument goes, those reasons (privacy, dignity, the risk of suffering, concern about being a burden to family, or a personal definition of what makes life worth living) cannot be the basis for advance directives. People who write directives are different people from their incapacitated selves, with different needs and interests, and it is not necessarily in the best interests of the incapacitated patient to be bound by the advance directive written by that patient when decisionally capable (Dresser, 1986; *Evans v. Bellevue Hospital*, 1987).

Both of these arguments would disqualify patients from making their own choices about their future health care precisely *because* those choices involve important values. It is claimed that the values that influence patients to refuse treatment are incompatible with the needs and interests of persons who have lost the higher brain capacity to affirm those values. Thus, decisionally capable persons are no closer than strangers to the unconscious patients they will become. In fact, true strangers should make better decisions for decisionally incapable patients than their advance directives make. Someone who knows only the impaired patient will not be tempted to compare him or her with a functioning person or with prior wishes, focusing only on current needs (Dresser and Robertson, 1989).

These arguments thus replace advance directives with a strictly contemporaneous best interests assessment. Because the present interests of the incapacitated person – avoiding pain, experiencing pleasure, and recovery of capacity (Dresser, 1986; Dresser and Robertson, 1989; Feinberg, 1984) – simply do not include privacy, dignity, and the other concerns of the directive writer, incapacitated persons are not better off if these particular strangers, the former selves, control their care than they would be if any other strangers, such as caregivers, appointed guardians, or courts, were the decisionmakers.

The Continuity of A Life

These arguments presume a radical discontinuity in the selfhood of patients in severely demented states. Essentially, these arguments hold that at least some incapacitated patients currently would disagree with the decisions in their advance directives, but cannot say so. Either the patient would be experiencing value from continued existence and therefore would not wish to die, or the patient's current inability to experience value would make him or her indifferent to dignity considerations as well as to most other justifications for preferring death. The arguments postulate two different 'personhoods', with a disjunction occurring with the onset of permanent serious loss of mentation. Why should we accept such a break? Why cannot decisionally capable persons seek to direct their future lives until death, so long as they understand how radically their circumstances may change?

There are strong practical arguments against postulating a point beyond which an individual no longer has the right to control his or her life. Most obvious is the difficulty of finding such a point. If permanent serious loss of mental capacity is to be the point of disjunction, there must be both an agreed-upon standard of irreversible dementia that places the patient in this category and an agreed-upon test for determining whether that standard has been met. Our current scientific ignorance alone should be enough to make sufficient agreement impossible.

There are significant moral difficulties with picking such a point, of course. How different is different, when the difference between any two points is so clearly on a continuum (Rhoden, 1990)? Perhaps the point should be placed at the patient's loss of decisional capacity – that is, exactly where an advance directive should take effect. But this could be a point where many patients, though profoundly incapacitated, have memories, desires, values, and interests that link them much more deeply with their former selves than persons in permanent coma or persistent vegetative state could be linked. Perhaps, then, the point should be moved back, in which case we could have a paradoxical result: patients who are incapacitated but still responsive could have their advance directives honored but the profoundly demented could not. If that seems troubling, it is probably because at bottom the 'stranger' argument is more about what decisions ought to be made than it is about how we should regard the relationship between past and present selves.

There is the additional difficulty of persuading people – especially patients and their families – to see this discontinuity between 'selves' and act in accordance with it. For those who did not know the patient before he or she became incapacitated – caregivers, for example – this may seem less a problem than it does for family members and others who know more of the patient's history. And there are additional reasons to resist discontinuity between persons with decisional capacity and their permanently demented selves. The effect of such a discontinuity is to deny people the right to envision, and treat, their lives as wholes – to deny them autonomy in the Kantian sense while they are alive – and this is wrong. It is not the presence or absence of 'value', 'humanity', or 'personhood' in permanently unconscious or demented patients that should determine whether their prior decisions should be valued. We already agree that decisionally capable individuals, who clearly have value, may decide to refuse treatment. Thus, we agree that competent individuals may determine their own value for themselves, even if that determination results in treatment refusal and death. How decisions should be made about demented patients who did not make prospective decisions while they had the capacity to do so is a vitally important issue, but it is not at all affected by the determination that patients who choose to direct their own lives until death should be permitted to do so.

Rebecca Dresser, an articulate proponent of the 'stranger' argument, nonetheless has acknowledged that patients have some interest in having their choices applied to their future selves:

> Incompetent patients...fail to retain an interest in having their former treatment preferences honored. Competent patients, however, can have an independent interest in directing their future care...that can survive the alteration in an individual's interests or identity that accompanies the onset of incompetency and serious illness.
>
> Joel Feinberg has explained how persons can possess interests that survive their deaths....In Feinberg's view, the...thwarting of [a future-oriented] interest harms the person before death, even though the harm does not become obvious until later, when the person no longer exists.
>
> Similarly...honoring...past preferences demonstrates respect for patients in their former competent states. The past preferences principle... embodies a...choice to protect this interest of competent patients in controlling their future treatment, rather than a decision to protect any such interest incompetent patients possess in their incompetent states. (Dresser, 1986, p. 393-394 (footnote omitted); Feinberg, 1984, p. 92)

Saying that the patient's interest in having an advance directive runs from the past to the present but not from the present to the past seems to be a distinction without a difference, if the effect is the same. Dresser argues that the effect is not exactly the same, because the patient's interest in advance directives is not as strong as an interest in making contemporaneous decisions, but is more like the interest in organ donation or property distribution after death. Ronald Dworkin gives the patient's interest greater weight, however:

> A competent person's right to autonomy requires that his past decisions, about how he is to be treated if he becomes demented, be respected, even if they do not represent, and even if they contradict, the desires he has when we respect them, provided he did not change his mind while he was still in charge of his own life....For competent people, concerned to give their lives the structure integrity demands, will naturally be concerned about how they are treated when demented. Someone anxious to insure that his life is not then prolonged by medical treatment is anxious exactly because he thinks the character of his whole life would be compromised if that life were prolonged in that way. (Dworkin, 1986 p. 13)

Dworkin admits that his argument "has austere consequences", and admits that we may be unable to follow it in some cases, but asks us to recognize that whatever good reasons we have for failing to honor past choices, we nonetheless violate the patient's autonomy in so failing. Loss of decisional capacity to many people means the complete devaluation of personal dignity, concern for family, control over one's life, and many of the other values and interests that we customarily consider significant in planning our lives and futures (Cantor, 1990). Surely, many of us would feel injured and affronted now if we were told that after we lose capacity our choices for ourselves will have no meaning.[4]

Of course there will be troubling cases, in which caregivers may find themselves reluctant to implement some directives. The patient whose directive refuses all treatment "if I become irreversibly incompetent" may not simply become unconscious. Instead he may have a drastically reduced IQ and impaired memory, and spend his days sitting in a wheelchair – perhaps making sounds or performing sterotyped movements, but still apparently extracting something from life that is positive to his current self. These troubling cases suggest that there are times when the patient's autonomy must bow to the good-faith concerns of the community and its valuation of the patient's current needs and interests (Rhoden, 1990). Such cases call for a sensitive balancing of autonomy and beneficence, with proper weight given both to the advance directive and to current circumstances. They should be a warning to doctors and patients to think carefully, and to talk together, when writing directives. But they should not be taken to invalidate directives.

To argue that advance directives lack value because incapacitated patients are not capable of finding value in their earlier expressed concerns for their own privacy and dignity is to claim that the interests of the incapacitated patient can be defined and given value only by someone other than that patient when decisionally capable. But there is little reason to suppose that anyone else will be better at doing that than the patient, especially if the patient considers carefully the questions involved. It is true that the particulars of the patient's condition are best appreciated by someone who is on the scene at the time (Buchanan and Brock, 1986), but that person is not really any closer to being inside the patient's current experience than a well-informed patient was when writing the directive.

Most significantly, patients clearly have by far the best grasp of their own values. If the current interests of decisionally incapable patients are determinative of treatment, then the value placed by others on the patient's current state, rather than the value placed on that state by the patient in the past, is determinative. This disregard for the autonomous choices made by patients themselves is an injury to their autonomy even though they may be unaware of it.

Granted, there is no means of perfectly ascertaining what is best for decisionally incapable patients; but we accept decisionally capable patients' choices not because they are perfect but because they are *theirs*. Conscientiously made advance directives can reflect patients' decisions in this way without offending our sense of what is ours the way these discontinuity arguments do. Patients who choose to direct their entire lives should indeed have the right to do so – *right* in the sense that no propositions about selfhood should be able to interrupt the continuity of a life by invalidating prospective decisions about it. This is only the right to have one's life treated as a whole. Such a right can be exercised by means of many different kinds of health care decisions, and other interests may still prove able to override particular choices, *but not* by replacing the individual's valuation of his or her own life with some other valuation.

If advance directives carry less weight than contemporaneous choices, as some would have it, then they could potentially be outweighed – by the present interests of the patient, or even by family interests or those of society. How those interests are valued is critical.

For example, incapacitated patients have an interest in recovering capacity, if indeed that is a possibility. How the possibility of recovery should be valued then becomes a central concern. If the patient, when decisionally capable, expressed a desire to terminate treatment "unless I am substantially certain to regain my decisional capacity", or "after I have been in a persistent vegetative state for six months", or in some other way assigned a value to the possibility of recovery, there appears little if any justification for using anyone else's valuation of the possibility of recovery to determine whether the directive should be honored. But a less explicit directive might make it harder to determine what value to give to the chance of recovery, and then it might be necessary to use someone else's evaluation. Essentially, then, if advance directives do count for less than contemporaneous decisions, that is because they cannot always be made more precise by discussion at the time. However, if a directive is always the basis for treatment choice, and a guide for determining the best choices, the better guidance a directive offers the more weighty it should be. This returns us to the practical questions of how directives should be used – and how they should be written if they are to be used well.

Patients have an interest in having their lives treated as continuous, but the real issue lies in what the continuity of a life implies about the degree of reflection that should be part of the writing of an advance directive. This is where a relationship arises between our prudential interest in writing directives that give good guidance to others about our future selves (Cantor, 1990) and others' duties to honor our directives in good faith, insofar as they can be honored.

Others' Obligations Regarding Directives

Although others have duties to the persons who write directives, they may also feel obligations toward the often drastically changed and limited selves we are in the future, when they must be honored. Naturally, the duties involved may be different if their objects are different. Naturally, also, the appropriate objects may be different for different duty holders. Does the physician have a duty to the former, decisionally capable person, the present, incapacitated person, or both? How about a spouse, or a sibling, or a child, or a court? To whom are their duties, if any, to be directed?

Honoring a directive essentially means agreeing to recognize the life continuity envisioned by its writer. This is not exactly the same as recognizing the past but not the present self; it is the more difficult task of giving the present self a continuity with its past, and it includes recognizing the decisionally capable patient's own valuation of incapacity, as well as gaining some experience of the incapacitated patient.

Caregivers have a relationship to the incapacitated patient with a directive that is different from that of the patient's family and friends. The health professional-patient relationship gives rise to an obligation of service to the patient that is strongly grounded in the caregiver's role. This role is likely to be more clearly delineated and better defined than are the manifold obligations felt by the friends and family of the patient. Yet caregivers, like others, may represent a wide range of involvement with and commitment to the patient – they may have helped the patient to write the directive, or they may meet the patient and learn of the directive while the patient is still decisionally capable, or they may admit the patient to the emergency room and discover a "living will" card in the patient's wallet. Is there a way to talk about the caregiver's obligations that covers all these cases?

The relationship between health care professional and patient creates a duty in the caregiver to exercise his or her skill, knowledge, and judgment in the patient's best interest. As we saw in Chapter 2, this duty includes the obligation to obtain the patient's informed consent before performing any procedures. Through informed consent, then, the caregiver's duty to act in the patient's best interests is shaped by the patient's choices and preferences. Similarly, when the patient's wishes are captured in a paper from the past and the caregiver is faced with an incapacitated patient, it is the duty to treat in accordance with the patient's informed choice that knits the patient's present and past into a single life.

When it comes to contemporaneous informed consent, the caregiver has no power to act against the decisionally capable patient's will, except in a few very narrowly drawn instances. Yet many caregivers may believe they have good reasons to avoid the daunting task of discovering and acting in accordance with the patient's choice in the case of advance directives. Let us evaluate the possible reasons a caregiver might offer for failing to implement a patient's advance directive.

Time

Emergency circumstances can be a real barrier to the implementation of advance directives. The emergency room physician treating an accident victim is not really in a position to halt things immediately when a nurse, looking through the patient's wallet for people to contact, finds a "living will" card. Yet in a great many cases, lack of time is much less of an excuse than it is made to appear. Sometimes it may be very clear that an advance directive is valid, applicable to the current situation, and unequivocal. For example, suppose a person with a known, particular, progressive condition has written an advance directive refusing respiratory support, or dialysis, or some other treatment that the progression of this illness renders foreseeable. If there is time to ascertain that, there is time to implement it. If there is not time to avoid initiating treatment, there is *always* time to gather more information and withdraw treatment later.

One of the most important things about time is that spending some early always saves some later. Many caregivers, out of a reluctance to broach sensitive issues with patients and families, fail to raise discussion of patients' preferences, or to suggest that patients write advance directives, at times when there is more leisure to do so. Even when directives are discovered at the bedside, there is often enough time to read them reasonably carefully and discuss them with the patient's family and friends.

Quite a bit of information-gathering takes place in the emergency room, whenever there is any time to do so; it is part of good health care. Most of what we need to know about an advance directive can be sought and obtained in a comparable amount of time, if it becomes similarly ingrained as a part of good care to seek it.

Confusion

Uncertainty about the meaning and application of a directive is the next reason for not implementing it, once it has been found and examined. As we shall see in Chapter 4, directives take many forms, and some confusion is virtually inevitable. Many directives are couched in terms that are reasonably clear but global and unexplained. This produces uncertainty about whether the particular decisions at issue are addressed by a directive's general pronouncements. Alternatively, directives that list many specific decisions may not provide many clues as to how a decision not listed should be treated. Caregivers may also have concerns about the decisions of a named proxy when the basis for the proxy's decisionmaking is not made explicit in the directive. Finally, changes in state law may create ambiguities, when patients add their own more liberal provisions to restrictively worded statutory directives.[5]

When there is any time available at all to talk with family, get a history, and the like, there is time to gather information that can at least begin to allay the confusion. Except in emergencies, caregivers always have opportunities both to ask patients whether they have written a directive and to resolve potential confusion about the application and scope of an advance directive. The caregivers who know of the document should discuss it with the patient in order to understand it as thoroughly as possible and to help clarify it if necessary. The patient's primary physician bears the additional responsibility of informing other caregivers about the document and its meaning, especially if the physician knows the patient well and has discussed the directive with him. Many times, the primary physician will have helped to draft it.

Most of the possible confusion about a directive's application and scope can be readily resolved by discussion with the patient, if possible, and if not, with others. For example, sometimes when patients' directives refuse a particular treatment or technology, the physician may be uncertain whether the patient meant also to refuse a trial of that treatment or temporary dependence on that technology. Discussion can easily clarify this. If doubt still remains after discussion, declining to honor the directive most certainly does not dispel that doubt. It is the physician's duty to make an effort in good faith to apply an advance directive to the decisions faced regarding the directive's author. A caregiver who feels unable to apply a directive to a decision because the directive seems ambiguous or unclear must take the directive elsewhere, outside of the family and friends, for further scrutiny or action: to a new caregiver who feels able to act, to a hospital ethics committee, or to a court for interpretation.[6]

Avoiding the Issues

Another reason that can keep caregivers from implementing directives is their fear of unpleasantness, which can arise from a number of sources: family infighting; publicity; the disapproval of institutional administration; and the spectre of the law.

The problem is undeniable; everyone tries to avoid unpleasantness, and health professionals one way or another face more of it than anybody else at the best of times. It is small wonder that all of us should wish to avoid making the most painful circumstances even more painful. There is a powerful and hard-to-overcome impulse in health care to avoid asking certain questions and raising certain issues. Failing to raise those issues and ask those questions can give rise to serious problems, however. When physicians do not know their patient's wishes they have no guidance for the decisions that will need to be made. Especially in crisis, this lack of knowledge can seriously complicate decisionmaking. In addition, when the physician knows a patient's wishes but does not have the patient's directive, it may be difficult to convince family members to abide by those wishes, or even to persuade a cautious institution that implementing those wishes is legally permissible. Discussion is therefore important because of the increased pain and difficulty that can be avoided by means of advance directives.

The desire to avoid difficult questions is an untenable reason for failing to implement existing advance directives. The informed consent doctrine establishes honoring the patient's wishes as both a moral and a legal imperative; living will laws convey support for caregivers who implement them in good faith; and the courts make it clear that careful documentation of the decision made and the reasons for it will, in the great majority of cases, protect caregivers from liability by offering explanations of their actions. Failing to implement a directive out of fear (whether fear of lawsuits or fear of upsetting families), or out of reluctance to complicate matters, is a serious and unacceptable breach of duty. As time passes, more directives are honored, and talked-about cases become means of educating caregivers, institutions, and the public to view implementing directives as a familiar routine, avoiding the issue will come to be recognized as less and less desirable.

Questions of Capacity[7]

Legal fears, though not sufficient to justify failing to honor directives, are nonetheless reason to proceed circumspectly in implementing them. One legal (and moral) concern that deserves attention is the eternally recurring problem of the patient's decisional capacity at the time of writing a directive. Caregivers who know patients before they become obviously incapacitated are able to ascertain their capacity to write and to reaffirm advance directives for health care decisionmaking by talking with them then. But suppose a caregiver who was not able to do that has concerns about the directive. Is the possibility of the patient's incapacity when the directive was written a reason not to honor it?

The answer is no. As discussed in Chapter 2, ordinary "soundness of mind" is something that everyone is capable of evaluating, and most health professionals are no more nor less expert in ascertaining it than anyone else. Advance directives usually demonstrate that the writer's mind is 'sound' in this sense in two ways. The directive itself is intended to be a coherent statement that exhibits self-awareness, gives reasoning and argument, and states values and preferences, so that simply having thought about these decisions and written a directive is proof of soundness of mind. Many directives are not actually written by patients, however – they are merely adopted as is and signed. Still, witnesses are usually present, and they sign the document attesting to their belief that the writer is rational and serious about the directive. That is what the witnesses are there for; it is unnecessary for a caregiver to hold back from implementing a directive because *he or she* was not a witness.

Suppose the caregiver's concern is a little different – not merely for the patient's 'soundness of mind' but for the patient's foresight and imagination. Suppose the directive provides for the refusal of any treatment that can save the patient's life but will result in severe intellectual impairment. Suppose further that the patient has suffered a massive stroke and needs surgery to reduce pressure on the brain, but the location of the clot guarantees permanent brain injury nonetheless. And suppose finally that the caregiver believes that with proper foresight and understanding, the patient would not have decided to forgo treatment under these circumstances, because stroke victims have valuable abilities in addition to their considerable weaknesses. The caregiver reasons that ordinary witnesses cannot know whether the writer of a directive is deciding on the basis of accurate knowledge and appreciation of the situation, but experienced caregivers can.

The flaw in this well-meaning argument lies in the assumptions it makes about how patients should make decisions. The argument is correct in proposing that one who writes a directive should have good information and should carefully consider it. However, it does not follow that a decision with which the caregiver disagrees is necessarily "incompetently" made. It is not fair for caregivers to discard directives made without their counsel because they suspect they were not made from the best possible knowledge, in the caregiver's estimation.

But suppose that a heart disease patient's directive categorically states, "If I should become incapable of making my own health care choices, I wish to be allowed to die with dignity. Therefore, I refuse all cardiopulmonary resuscitation and all ventilatory assistance." The patient develops a severe pneumonia, is demented from fever and medication, and needs to be placed on a respirator temporarily to return her to the level of capacity, health, and function that preceded the infection. Her physician is concerned about whether, in writing her directive, this patient had thought about possibilities like this one; concerned that the directive does not reflect an informed choice, the physician decides not to honor it.

The same result – temporary use of the respirator to return the patient to relative health and decisional capacity – can be reached by *interpreting* the directive rather than rejecting it. As we shall see in Chapter 4, most directives are intended to apply only when there is little or no possibility that the patient's decisional capacity could be restored by treatment. Of the four model directives set out in Chapter 1, only two say this in so many words. Yet it is so much a part of the basic idea of advance directives that it would be reasonable for any physician in this position to infer, in good faith, that a directive that does not explicitly contradict this limitation probably includes it. The best solution would be to read the patient's directive and discuss this very point while the patient is decisionally capable. The next best solution is to interpret this directive as applying only when the use of support would be permanent or when the patient's capacity and function cannot be restored, unless the directive explicitly states that the patient refuses even temporary support or that she refuses support regardless of whether she can be restored to "meaningful quality of life", or "a cognitive, sapient state." Family members and friends may of course also be asked whether they can shed light on how the patient intended this directive to be read.

The point here is simple but central: the caregiver who harbors a legitimate concern about the meaning of a directive, and therefore about the completeness of the information on which the patient based the directive, does not always have to discard the directive and start from scratch. Instead, whenever possible, the directive can be interpreted in good faith, so that all of the directive's contents are still available to help guide decisions.

No directives are made from perfect knowledge. Many are made from nearly perfect knowledge, with the close advice and counsel of another caregiver; and most are made from enough knowledge and consideration that they make sense when caregivers attempt in good faith to implement them. If a directive can be implemented and there is no reason to think it was not competently made, it is not fruitful to require further demonstrations. The clinician's interest in discussing a directive further with a still-capable patient, in order to improve the patient's deliberations, does not extend to the power to discard directives that are clear enough to implement after the opportunity for improving them is past.

There are already many proofs of validity and patient capacity in most advance directives. To require more than the amount of knowledge, consideration, and safeguards sufficient to enable others to implement a directive[8] may really amount to something else. Caregivers who have a very high level of concern about the patient's information and deliberation may sincerely believe that any patient who considered the question carefully and properly would not refuse treatment. To these caregivers, it may seem that the only effective proof of autonomous *decisionmaking* would be *a particular decision*. Yet it is very clear that "making the right decision" is a *wrong* standard by which to judge decision-making capacity (Faden *et al.*, 1986; Roth *et al.*, 1977).

This brings us to the remaining reason caregivers have for refusing to honor directives. If concerns about decisional capacity are examined carefully, sometimes a more basic issue is unearthed.

Dislike and Discomfort

The bottom line is that many caregivers are uneasy about the decisions that advance directives represent. Directives refusing care go against professional imperatives; they appear to disvalue the impaired lives that health care professionals strive to preserve; they can seem to represent immaturity and cowardice; and they may offend the religious and moral sensibilities of some. These concerns are real, and call for sensitive exploration and discussion. But none of them can override the patient's moral claim of self-direction and decision-making freedom and responsibility.

The time to engage these issues is with the decisionally capable patient. Caregivers should discuss all of these issues with patients – should argue, persuade, and engage the patient in the important process of making, examining, and confirming choices. But the comatose patient with a new doctor should not suffer because the doctor could not talk with him a month ago. The caregiver must attempt to understand the directive, with whatever help necessary; and a directive understandable enough to be implemented must be implemented. If the caregiver will not honor it, the patient must be transferred to the care of someone who will obey it. To fail to do so would be to abandon a patient in need of assistance. Caregivers can choose not to implement all or any directives, so long as they give patients or their proxies ample notice and help them to make alternative arrangements.

With advance directives, decisions must sometimes be quickly made. It is possible that caregivers sometimes may have to act against their own wishes in order to avoid putting patients at the mercy of those wishes. Because the obligation to honor patients' wishes is so strong, caregivers with strong moral views may need to consider ways of making their views known to patients as early as possible and to establish pathways for arranging alternative caregivers who will implement directives.

Emergencies, Opportunities, and the Quality of Life

It is easy to exhort caregivers to honor directives and respect the choices they embody. Some directives will always be especially difficult to implement, however – for instance, directives that ask others to refrain from action in certain situations where the window of opportunity for action is small.[9] A patient's request for a do-not-resuscitate order – whether the request comes from a person facing surgery, with its ever present risk of cardiorespiratory arrest, from a patient whose particular condition makes an arrest a real possibility, or from one who is simply hoping for a way to die – is really an advance directive. It will go into effect when the patient is experiencing cardiorespiratory arrest and thus is incapable of making a decision at that time.

When a decision about resuscitation is necessary, patients must either be resuscitated or not. It is not possible to take a little more time to decide, as it may be when the decision in question is whether to continue dialysis or mechanical ventilation. When patients specifically refuse the *institution* of a particular procedure, caregivers may feel more pressured, and more inclined to refuse to honor directives that place them under that pressure.

Nonetheless, directives about events that call for quick action and decision by caregivers are just as valid as those that allow for more leisurely deliberation. The circumstances under which advance directives are to take effect cannot be required to be serene and pristine. Moreover, the need for quick response to a directive need not preclude taking the time to make a thoughtful decision whether to implement it, and to have thoughtful conversation about it with the patient and others.

The DNR request is an example of a directive where the patient explicitly refuses intervention regardless of the possibility of a 'good' outcome. Clearly, without such an explicit statement, the caregiver could not be expected to refrain from all resuscitations. But just as clearly, explicit directives to this effect must be considered thoughtfully, and caregivers do need to understand them in order to honor them.

Conversation about do-not-resuscitate orders is likely to address why the patient has decided to refuse resuscitation. In a recent article in the *New England Journal of Medicine*, Tomlinson and Brody have usefully divided no-codes into three categories: medically futile (i.e., probably unsuccessful) resuscitations; resuscitations that are undesirable because if successful, they are likely to result in an unacceptable quality of life for the patient; and those that are undesirable because the patient's present quality of life is unacceptable (Tomlinson and Brody, 1988). It is the latter two types of refusals that are hardest for caregivers to accept, because they are refusals of genuinely lifesaving or life-prolonging treatment.

Yet all that has been said so far in this volume supports the patient's right to say "Doctor, I don't want you to save my life." Patients have that right just as they have the right to sign out of the hospital against medical advice or to refuse to go in the first place. However difficult to accept, this is so.

The patient who refuses to accept the initiation of lifesaving or life-prolonging treatment thus may present a situation not unlike the Jehovah's Witness, who is willing to undergo surgery, but only "bloodless" surgery.

The limitation placed by the patient on the physician's exercise of skill and judgment seems very great; but advance directives are, after all, essentially intended to guide and limit the physician's discretion in various ways. There should be time and opportunity made to discuss these limitations with the patient, and the physician is always free to refuse them so long as someone else is found who can accept them. But every physician has a responsibility to consider very seriously all advance directives, even these, and no physician may undertake the patient's care without the intent to honor them.

Reasons or Justifications?

What of the patient's reasons for refusing treatment? An advance directive refusing a procedure may give a 'good' reason (*e.g.*, unacceptable quality of life after the procedure) or a 'poor' reason (*e.g.*, unacceptable quality of life now) or no reason at all. How do any of these reasons matter?

The reasons patients have for making advance directives have a limited place in the clinician's assessment of a directive. The right to refuse treatment does not depend on reasons. The patient's capacity to make decisions about medical care is often displayed through reasoning, but the standard used to measure that capacity is a minimal standard, and the right of the patient to make decisions for good, bad, or no reasons is well established so long as the patient is *capable* of reasoning.[10]

And yet, throughout this book it has been emphasized that comprehensive explanation of the values underlying treatment choices is the best assurance the patient has of writing a directive that can be followed. How is that not the same as saying to the patient "You must justify yourself to me or I cannot implement your wishes"? How is that different from requiring good reasons?

Though the difference is subtle, the clinician who understands it can elicit the patient's reasons while still avoiding the temptation to ask patients to *justify* their choices. Reasons help caregivers to know what the patient wants – what the choices are. When a patient writes a comprehensive directive, reasons and explanations of underlying values enable caregivers to apply the directive to situations that include decisions not precisely specified in the directive; explanations help caregivers determine what the patient would have done (Cantor, 1990). In contrast, a directive that says nothing but "I refuse resuscitation in the event of arrest during surgery" is clear enough on the question of cardiac arrest during surgery but no help on anything else. Inclusion in the directive of reasons for the patient's choice could suggest to a clinician that broader application is desired, or that further discussion with the patient is needed. The patient who cites the risk of an unacceptable quality of life after resuscitation as the decisive factor in her decision has broadened the clinician's understanding of her choice in a way that may make it easier to follow it. Perhaps she is not yet fully informed about the magnitude of the risk, and would choose differently if she were. Or perhaps her choice suggests that other procedures and treatments that incur similar risks should be discussed with her as well.

These uses of the patient's reasons help the clinician to answer the question "*How* can I know and do what this patient sees as best for her?" They are not intended to answer the question "*Why* should I do what this patient thinks is best?" Reasons are not meant to be justifications for the patient's choices; advance directives need not be justified to be implemented.

In his remarkable book, *The Silent World of Doctor and Patient*, Jay Katz discusses a patient of Dr. Mark Siegler, Mr. D. (Katz, 1984, pp. 156-160), who refuses diagnostic tests without explanation but is perceived by all concerned to be rational and autonomous in his refusal of these interventions. Without this additional diagnostic guidance, his condition worsens; he refuses to go on a respirator, suffers a respiratory arrest, and dies.

Katz gives an eloquent account of what he would have done differently if he had the opportunity to speak with Mr. D. about his refusals. He says he would tell Mr. D. that he could not honor Mr. D.'s wishes until he understood the basis for them, for lack of explanation might conceal serious misconceptions or grave disorders of thinking and feeling that would indicate an unsound decision. He would tell Mr. D., "[Y]ou must not hide behind silence" (Katz, 1984, p. 159). In short, Katz claims the right to know *why* Mr. D.'s choice should be honored.

In a thoughtful rejoinder to Katz, Charles Baron points out that:

> the sort of doctor-patient conversation which Professor Katz offers us....is one in which the patient is made to feel that the doctor carries the ultimate authority. The doctor has merely conceded to the patient some portion of the decision-making authority subject to the condition that the patient pass some test by giving the 'right' answers concerning the reasons for refusing treatment. (Baron, 1987, p. 39)

Baron argues that it is physicians' uncertainty, rather than patients' lack of decision-making capacity, that moves physicians to treat patients over their objections when they do not explain their refusals well enough. He suggests that caregivers

> make clear that what they need is to be reassured by their patients that the patient's refusal to accept treatment is not the result of some failing in the doctor's handling of

the case and its presentation. Patients thus realize that they are not...being put through
some test by those in authority before they can get what they want. Rather, one human
being [the physician] is asking another human being [the patient] to do the first...a
favor....Is it likely that any patient would refuse such a request? (Baron, 1987, p. 40)

Baron, who is not a physician, puts the matter of equality in the physician-
patient relationship quite baldly by stating that the patient does the doctor a
favor by explaining. Katz speaks like a physician, declaring that he could not
let Mr. D. die because he did not understand his choice. Katz is right to
assert as strongly as he does that continuing conversation between caregivers
and patients almost always succeeds in establishing a mutual understanding.
But when it comes right down to it, patients do not owe doctors explanations,
and Baron is right.

This sensitive issue has special significance for advance directives,
because they do not represent contemporaneous decisions. If explanations are
required but not supplied by a document, there is no opportunity for further
discussion: the document may be invalidated. On the other hand, if
explanation is desirable but not mandatory, the document will be considered
valid and applied insofar as is possible. Explanations will simply assist in its
interpretation.

Baron suggests that no patients who understand why the caregiver wants
to understand their choices would refuse to give an explanation. Naturally,
then, a patient's refusal to explain could still suggest that the patient is being
unreasonable in a way that calls his or her decision-making ability into
question. The difficulty cannot be avoided: The patient can refuse the
doctor's care without explanation, but the doctor must fear that the patient's
refusal to explain is pathological. There is no way out of this. Yet caregivers
can and should control their fears about the patient's decisional capacities.
Clinicians who talk with patients about their choices and elicit reasons for
them in order to increase their understanding of their choices will rarely face
a patient who will not explain.

Only if lack of explanation makes it excessively difficult to interpret and
apply a directive in good faith should a clinician feel justified in not honoring
it. Explanations are not owed, but freely given, and understandings are
shared. The caregiver who feels that he or she cannot follow advance
directives that do not sufficiently explain their choices must converse with
their authors while that is still possible. If it is not, the caregiver must pass
such directives on to others who will follow them, or to an ethics committee
or other body that will attempt to interpret them.

Advance Directives in the Ideal World

The conceptual foundations of advance directives are first, autonomy, and second, community. Advance directives are documents that both preserve and foster autonomous individual choice. They preserve autonomy by their mere existence: they declare choice. They foster autonomous choice by requiring those who write advance directives to think about what they want and to explain that to others. Because the making of an advance directive requires a reasoned, articulable attention to one's own wishes, it can be said to foster autonomy by encouraging more thoughtful choices, much in the same way as the legal doctrine of informed consent has been said to promote rational decisionmaking because it requires that the patient hear – though not necessarily use – information and reasons about medical treatment choices.

In the law of informed consent, however, an informed decision need not display its reasoning in order to be valid. Yes or no will suffice (except insofar as the patient may need to be determined capable of reasoning). This is because – in theory at least – the process of informing for decision has given the patient and physician some opportunity to understand each other's goals. However, advance directives do not have the same luxury of simply declaring themselves. There is often little connection between the reasoning process of the patient-writer and the involvement of the caregivers, friends, and family who must act to implement the directive – no exchange on which to build any assessment of the decisional process, and no chance for the further exchange that may be necessary once the directive is implemented. Yet in many instances, the involvement required of those implementing a directive is profound. Thus, it is reasonable to require that advance directives explain themselves to a degree necessary to enable others to follow them. The problem lies in determining what minimal level of explanation is sufficient.

In treatment decisionmaking where the patient is currently decisionally capable – the run-of-the-mill informed consent case – direct exchange between caregiver and patient is essential and continued exchange is possible. Moreover, in many instances, the patient is able to exercise the option of just shutting the relationship down and getting another doctor. In the case of advance directives, however, continuing exchange is unavailable and the patient cannot leave the relationship. The patient has no other choices. To be fair, then, we should not substantively limit the validity of well-conceived advance directives by honoring them only when the patient is "ill enough" or by permitting them to express decisions about some treatments but not others. Nor should we set an excessively high standard of autonomy or decisional capacity that invalidates directives not containing indicia of sophisticated, comprehensive examination of all possible future scenarios.

We should nonetheless be demanding of persons writing directives, but in a different way. We should make certain specific assumptions about the thinking of persons who write directives unless we have evidence that is clearly to the contrary. We should assume that writers of directives have used foresight and carefully considered the implications of their choices, and we should honor and interpret directives on that basis. We should not be tempted to second-guess the authors of directives, to argue that they could not really have anticipated what their circumstances would be like and might have changed their minds. We must instead assume that they were autonomous agents who considered these possibilities in reaching their decisions. To do otherwise would reduce many advance directives to frustrating ephemera impossible to obey, impossible not to second-guess. And concomitantly with this move to assume a high degree of moral agency in writers of directives, we must endeavor to make that assumption a reality.

Advance directives are valid expressions of patients' medical treatment choices. As such, they should be presumed to reflect a high degree of commitment to the choices they express, resulting from thoughtful and circumspect consideration of relevant medical and nonmedical circumstances and future probabilities – including the possibility of the unexpected and the chance of a change of views. Thus, a directive should be followed unless genuine reason to doubt it appears from the document itself or from surrounding circumstances (*In re Westchester County Medical Center (O'Connor)*, 1988). Doubts should immediately be discussed with the patient's family and friends and with other caregivers, or taken before an ethics committee or even a court.

However, directives can only be implemented insofar as they instruct. Whenever a directive does not speak directly to the choice at hand, caregivers will have to treat it not as the embodiment of the patient's choice but as evidence of the patient's likely choice. Because the course of life is so unpredictable, many directives will be honored primarily or only in this special evidentiary sense. When a directive does not speak about the particular decision at hand, it must provide a basis for determining what the patient would have chosen, if it is to be useful as evidence.

Caregivers have, and whenever possible should exercise, the right to ask the patient for an accounting, either at the time the directive is made or when it is later presented and discussed. The caregiver may require the patient to articulate as fully as possible his or her choices, the basis for them, the priorities the patient has identified and their weights, preferences in specific situations, awareness of family feelings and views, and awareness of the possibility that unanticipated things might happen and of the possibility that a change of mind might result at a time when it cannot be expressed. The patient can then go on record – in the document itself or in discussion with physician or family – about issues of particular importance. In addition, the patient can designate the physician or another person as decisionmaker, to choose when there is no direct guidance from the directive, learning as much as possible about the patient's views and desires. The reason clinicians may require this from patients is not because patients must explain and justify themselves to satisfy their doctors, but because both patient and doctor have a duty, whenever they have an opportunity, to make the patient's directive good guidance for others. The difference may be subtle, but it is fundamental.

Patients have an obligation to make their advance directives good guidance for others. The consequences of failing to do so are simple. You may not get what you want, because nobody is sure what that is – not because they have a technical excuse to fail to honor your directive, or because they do not like the idea of it, but because the process of trying to imagine what you would have said about X is not aided by what you said about Y. The patient who wants a directive followed may need to be overwhelmingly thorough and clear: in writing, in conversation with his or her own physician, in conversation with friends and family or with the person designated as surrogate decisionmaker. Simply put, as much as they may seek firm and direct control of their health care choices, patients with directives are patients in search of an advocate. And it is neither effective nor fair to call upon an advocate who is unprepared and ill-armed for the role. The directive acts as the advocate's ammunition. Or, less dramatically, the directive enables the caregiver to know the patient's interests, without which knowledge the caregiver cannot follow them.

This view grounds advance directives in autonomy while acknowledging that discussing, interpreting, and applying them takes place in a community. Such a view encourages sophistication and foresight in the writing of directives, without requiring it – without imposing criteria for validity that would be likely to invalidate many carefully and deliberately executed directives. This view also holds patients to what they say in their directives, thereby both encouraging them to take directives very seriously and reducing the concern that whatever they direct will be second-guessed or ignored. It encourages physicians to discuss their patients' directives with them extensively, so that directives can give the best possible guidance. Finally, it provides physicians with a plan of action to deal with what is currently the most common advance directives scenario: a new admission, an unknown and unconscious patient, with a directive.

That plan is this: If the directive meets state validity criteria (see Chapter 4) or appears otherwise to have been thoughtfully conceived, prepare to honor it insofar as you can confidently apply it to the problems at hand. Consult with the patient's own physician, family, and/or friends for information that sheds light on the directive, whether it is information that could overcome your presumption that the directive is valid, or information that will provide additional guidance about the patient's thinking and preferences for any decisions the directive cannot entirely answer. If questions become unanswerable or the answers become contradictory, consult your institutional ethics committee or some equivalent; if necessary, seek a court's interpretation.

The caregiver must presume that a coherent set of values and opinions underlies every directive.[11] To look for that underlying meaning makes it easier to recognize it, and to expect it means that the caregiver is not required to make it up if the patient did not put it there. In this way, the patient's autonomy is protected and encouraged, but it is also directed by patients' obligations to facilitate the work of the moral communities who must act on their behalf.

Notes

[1] The only exception is when a choice directly and unavoidably injures others, so that this *may* not be true in some instances when the patient is pregnant.

[2] But see also Chapter 5's discussion of the possibilities of limiting the power to revoke directives, if the writer so chooses.

[3] For an answer to this argument, see the dissenting justice's opinion in the Conroy case (*Matter of Conroy*, 1985).

[4] It seems safe to assert that most people who plan for their aging and retirement think a great deal about maintaining their own sense of dignity during the changes of circumstances that accompany aging – including the possibilities of diminished income, social contact, activity, mobility, and health. Because concerns like dignity are so important to our planning for the future, it seems fundamentally wrong to deny their validity where the future holds extreme disability. See Dworkin's (1986) discussion of "precedent autonomy." See also Cantor's parallel legal arguments (1989, pp. 403-404).

[5] For example, many statutory directives are written to apply only in terminal illness. Such language does not, however, make it "illegal" to honor a directive by a patient who is not terminally ill (see discussion in Chapters 2 and 4). Many patients add to statutory directives their own additional special provisions about withholding or withdrawal of treatment in permanent coma, persistent vegetative state, advanced Alzheimer's disease, and other conditions that may not technically be 'terminal', without realizing that these additions raise a problem of

interpretation when the general statement of the directive purports to apply only to terminal illness.

[6] Other difficult questions of interpretation can arise when the patient's reasons for refusing particular treatments are not known, making it problematic to apply a directive to circumstances not specifically mentioned in it. Knowing the basis for the patient's refusal is important and may be very enlightening (Roth *et al.*, 1977). Nonetheless, it is always hard to be certain you have enough information to make an appropriate decision, and the resultant ambiguity may be most troubling. See Chapter 5 for further discussion of the problems of honoring patients' choices.

[7] See also the discussion of decisional capacity in Chapter 2.

[8] For further discussion of how much knowledge, consideration, and safeguards might be enough, see Chapter 4.

[9] A surprisingly common scenario arises when a patient facing surgery seeks the surgeon's agreement to withhold or curtail emergency treatment if complications arise during the procedure (Lederer and Brock, 1987).

[10] See the discussion of competence in Chapter 2; see also Faden *et al.* (1986).

[11] As Eric Cassell (1985) points out, patients nearly always make sense, even though the sense of what they say is not always readily apparent to doctors.

Chapter Four

Advance Directives:
Current Forms, Legal Fears, Moral Goals

> Legislation has many advantages, not the least of
> which is clarification of the law on a particular subject.
> But it is a serious error to assume either that in the
> absence of legislation there is no law, or that
> legislation will solve the myriad of personal and
> emotional factors that control the way both physicians
> and non-physicians deal with difficult issues. (Annas,
> 1988, p. 366)

There are two basic forms that advance directives may take. Commonly used
names for these two forms are "instruction" directives and "proxy" directives:
directives that give caregivers instructions about the patient's choices, and
directives that name a proxy to make choices on the patient's behalf and
convey them to caregivers (President's Commission, 1982, pp. 156-166).
Many directives combine these forms in various ways. In this chapter, we
examine the characteristics of these two types of directives, and some of the
statutory directives that display these characteristics, in order to familiarize
caregivers with the many forms directives take and to assist them in
interpreting and honoring directives in whatever forms they take.

No attempt is made to generate a new model directive or to promote any
of the existing models. Nor is any attempt made at a comprehensive
discussion of state law – it changes too fast in this area for any such
discussion to be valuable. However, an Appendix containing the citations to
all state living will and health care proxy statutes as of 1990 is included in
this book for reference purposes.

This book does not avoid a statutory catalogue for reasons of convenience.
Instead, it reflects the understanding that state laws can assist patients in
refusing treatment but do not create their right to do so. Therefore, one of
this chapter's goals is to get away from the idea that there is a best way to
write a directive, and move toward the idea that advance directives, in

whatever form, are valid so long as they are based on thoughtful consideration and give clear guidance to those who are to honor them.

A crucial question, then, is what constitutes "clear guidance" in an advance directive. All directives need to answer, in some way, certain questions for caregivers and others who are to implement them. Many different kinds of answers to these questions may be acceptable. Therefore, model directives, with their single set of possible answers, are invariably too narrow to recommend as best for all patients.

Some refusal of treatment decisions may be recognized as generally acceptable in any properly executed directive, such as any of the state statutory "living wills." Other, more controversial decisions (for example, refusing artificial nutrition and hydration, or refusing treatment for a potentially reversible life-threatening condition) are likely to be acceptable *only if* they have been explained satisfactorily, to someone who can implement the directive (e.g., the patient's physician), to someone who can explain it in turn to the one who will implement it (e.g., a named proxy), or in extensive commentary in the directive itself (e.g., Cantor, 1990). Thus, some directives can only provide clear guidance if patients, caregivers, family, and friends can discuss things beforehand and if someone can be available at the right time. The directive that adds a request to call the patient's personal physician for verification is most likely to be honored, for this reason. The directive that is most likely to be honored when no one who knows the patient well is available will be one that is less bold in its choices, unless it can explain itself persuasively and in detail.

The questions directives must answer include the following:

When does the directive take effect? (Must the patient be decisionally incapacitated only, or also terminally ill?) To which health care decisions would it apply? (To all decisions, to life-and-death decisions, to decisions about certain interventions only? Which interventions?)

What decisions should be made, or who should make those decisions, or both? (Is treatment refused? On what basis? Is a philosophical statement included, or just a "laundry list"? Can other decisions be discovered from these general rules or are only the explicitly mentioned choices intended? Has a proxy been named? On what basis should such a proxy decide?)

A second, different set of concerns must be answered by the directive as well: Is the patient serious? Is s/he sufficiently informed? Has s/he been thoughtful? Is there any reason to suspect lack of decisional capacity? These questions too are best answered by persons with knowledge of the patient. But in order to serve patients' choices fairly, advance directives themselves need to be able to answer them when no other advocate is available.

Advance Directives as Legal Documents

Many people – caregivers and patients included – regard advance directives in a kind of narrow, legalistic way. They treat them as orders from patients to doctors, orders that are binding only if they conform strictly to what a law has said they should say and how a law has said they should say it. As a result, patients often prepare, and are advised to prepare, advance directives that bristle with notary seals and witness signatures and with clauses that match word-for-word with the terms of all the living will statutes in all the states in which they are most likely to fall ill. More important, physicians and hospital administrators often look for these things in the directives they encounter and, if they are not all there, refuse to honor the directive because it is "not legal."

Without a deeper understanding of advance directives, it is hardly surprising that caregivers should have a high degree of concern both for preserving the lives of their patients who have written directives and for their own potential liability for not doing just that. Yet in this light, advance directives appear as documents that must be obeyed if they are airtight and cannot be obeyed if they are not. Should caregivers want directives to be "airtight"? And what should be done if they are not?

It is important to recognize that there are two different kinds of legal concerns that caregivers may have about advance directives. The first concern is that a directive is not valid if it does not match the "living will" given in state law. This view is contradicted by the language of the great majority of "living will" laws, which commonly begin with a statement like "This statute provides an optional and nonexclusive procedure by which patients can exercise their rights." Thus, most state laws explicitly acknowledge that other versions of advance directives – other written forms and even evidence of oral statements – may also provide patients with the means of exercising their rights.[1] Therefore, directives that do not conform precisely to the form prescribed by state law may well be valid, and cannot be dismissed out of hand because they are "nonconforming."

There are two general ways in which a directive can fail to match state law. First, it may fail to fulfill all of the state's indicia of reliability – witness statements, notary seals, physician certifications, and the like. This *formal* nonconformity might be minor (for example, one witness rather than two) or it might be major (for example, the entire document is a barely legible handwritten sentence in pencil on a sheet of notebook paper with no signature). With assistance from the patient's family and, if necessary, from the institution's administrative and legal representatives, the caregiver must decide whether such nonconforming directives contain sufficient other indicia of reliability – that is, whether it is clear from the directive itself that the patient understood the import of the directive, believed it important, and took it seriously.

Such seriousness of purpose can be shown by the patient's having added language to the directive that explains the reasons for it, adds lists of procedures and treatments or conditions covered, or names a proxy decisionmaker. It can be shown if the document has been periodically reaffirmed by initial and date. It can also be shown by extrinsic evidence, such as affirmation by family members or notes in the medical record indicating that the patient discussed the directive with other caregivers. The key to evaluating directives that do not conform formally to state statutes is to remember that the patient must somehow show seriousness about the directive. A directive that only lacks one witness is likely to show sufficient seriousness in some way, while one that is substantially nonconforming in this formal sense is highly likely to fail reasonable scrutiny.

The second way in which a directive can fail to conform to state law is more difficult, because it represents a *substantive* non-conformance – for example, directives intended to apply when the patient is not terminally ill (as in a persistent vegetative state) or directives seeking to refuse artificial nutrition and hydration when the state statute attempts to preclude such refusals. A few states have written directives purporting both to narrow the broad common-law right to refuse treatment and to challenge the proposition that all treatment refusals are constitutionally protected.

The rights upon which treatment refusal are based are of two types: the American "common" (court-made) law supporting the rights of informed consent and refusal of treatment, and an American constitutional right, sometimes labelled privacy for intimate personal and medical decisionmaking,[2] and more recently left unspecified (*In re A.C.*, 1990) or denominated a liberty interest in freedom from bodily intrusion (*Cruzan v. Director*, 1990). All states, even those few that still do not have "living will" statutes, acknowledge the common law basis for advance directives. Thus, advance directives will be treated as evidence of the patient's wishes even in states without such statutes, and "nonconforming" directives, in all states except those few attempting to narrow the common law, will also always constitute evidence of the patient's wishes.

The constitutional right that forms the basis for advance directives has been imperfectly articulated in case law. As discussed in Chapter 2, most treatment refusal cases have viewed the common law and constitutional rights of refusal as essentially coextensive, without much analysis. Not long ago, a federal district court in Rhode Island became the first federal court to hold that the right of privacy encompasses the right to refuse medical treatment, including artificial nutrition and hydration (*Gray v. Romeo*, 1988). At about the same time, in a highly controversial and much-criticized opinion, the Missouri Supreme Court came to the opposite conclusion (*Cruzan v. Harmon*, 1988). Early in 1990, the District of Columbia Court of Appeals firmly acknowledged a constitutional right of bodily integrity "to accept or refuse medical treatment" (*In re A.C.*, 1990, p. 1130/slip op. 26), without further specifying its nature or origins, and suggested that U.S. Supreme Court precedent assumed the existence of such a right (*In re A.C.*, p. 1125/slip op. 21). Then, at the end of its 1990 term, the Supreme Court, in deciding the case from the Missouri Supreme Court (*Cruzan v. Director*, 1990), asserted that a decisionally capable patient has "a constitutionally protected liberty interest in refusing unwanted medical treatment", and assumed that this constitutionally protected right would encompass the refusal of "lifesaving hydration and nutrition" (p. 4920). The Court named as the source of this right not a generalized right of privacy but a "Fourteenth Amendment liberty interest" (p. 4920, n. 7).

If there were no constitutional basis, but only a common law basis, for advance directives, then states would be free to pass statutes that greatly changed the common law. The many statutes that establish "optional and nonexclusive procedures" for advance directives are specifically saying that they do not intend to change the common law; instead, they will recognize any directive that accords with common law, and simply offer one suggested form for directives. A very few states – Missouri included – have written statutes purporting to prohibit patients from writing certain kinds of directives; usually these statutes state that patients may not refuse artificial nutrition and hydration.[3]

In order to narrow the common law in this area, where it is deeply rooted and of long standing, states must be explicit in their intent and persuasive in their reasoning, and must not exceed the limitations posed by the Constitution. Moreover, no state can hope to preclude private decisionmaking by patients, their families, and their physicians without applying criminal sanctions. Caregivers should remember that no criminal charges have been successfully brought against anyone for honoring patients' or families' requests for withdrawal of treatment,[4] nor has civil liability successfully attached.[5] Caregivers implementing written advance directives, even those not conforming precisely to state law, are very unlikely to be at risk, even now that *Cruzan* (1990) appears to have given the states the ability to require directives to be "clear and convincing." Indeed, the risk may lie in the failure to honor directives (see Chapter 6).

In its decision on the *Cruzan* case (1990), the U.S. Supreme Court did not directly address the constitutionality of Missouri's "living will" statute. Instead, it found a constitutional right to refuse medical treatment, while allowing the Missouri *courts* to require that a decisionally incapable patient's desire to refuse artificial nutrition and hydration be shown by "clear and convincing evidence." In that case, the Missouri Supreme Court had found that Nancy Cruzan's parents did not meet that standard with evidence about her general character and about several conversations she had with friends and family members.[6] Written directives of the types advocated by this book, including durable powers of attorney and thoughtfully composed "nonconforming" directives, would certainly meet such a standard. It is more difficult to predict what other indications of a patient's wishes might meet that standard, and in states choosing to apply the standard, it could become riskier to proceed without a directive in the absence of specific legislation authorizing treatment withdrawal. Nonetheless, informal evidence about the patient will always be available to assist physicians (and, if necessary, courts) in interpreting existing directives.

Importantly, even Missouri does not require that all decisions to implement advance directives be reviewed by a court (*Cruzan v. Director*, 1990, p. 4930, n. 15, Brennan, J., dissenting). Thus, caregivers need not fear that judicial bottlenecks will preclude the implementation of patients' directives. And most important of all, this decision allows, but hardly requires, other states to follow Missouri's lead. Essentially, the *Cruzan* decision requires states to recognize "nonconforming" directives, and permits them to test the validity of such directives by a relatively high standard. Only three states have embraced this clear and convincing evidence standard. The rest of the states whose courts have ruled in treatment refusal cases have emphasized common law and constitutional commitments to flexibility and individual freedom.

There are still not many cases on advance directives or even on treatment refusal, so it is impossible to say that there are many settled issues in the field. Even the Supreme Court ruling leaves many issues unresolved. However, the clear majority of states and state courts that have dealt with treatment refusal view advance directives as capable of having many valid forms and containing many different valid choices (Legal Advisors Committee, 1983). The *Cruzan* decision does not change this (Annas, 1990; Annas *et al.*, 1990; Weir and Gostin, 1990). Importantly, physicians and their institutions should understand that they need not await definitive judicial

pronouncements in their states before acting in good conscience to implement "nonconforming" directives. If that were so, no law could ever be interpreted or challenged.[7]

A second type of legal concern about advance directives is the fear of "guessing wrong", the concern that after a directive is implemented someone will claim it should not have been. (Under some circumstances, caregivers may also fear that their decision *not* to implement a directive, out of concern that it is not clear enough or not well-informed, could be challenged in court. Failing to implement a directive has thus far been viewed both as less legally consequential and less morally problematic, though this is changing, as we will see in Chapter 6.)

The fear of guessing wrong, or, more properly, *second*-guessing wrong, about advance directives tends to lead to conservatism in their interpretation, so that the result may be the effective invalidation of directives that do not closely match state statutory forms. In addition, however, caregivers may feel that even the statutory form does not help them to know whether patients really knew what they were doing, so that they may be reluctant to implement directives anytime the family indicates disagreement with a directive. These concerns are not illegitimate, but can easily grow far out of proportion to the real issues behind them and the real risks to caregivers from implementing directives.

The central point is this: advance directives – like any product of law or policy – have to exhibit a balance between the interests of the patients writing them and the interests of those who are to honor them, between fairness and faithfulness to moral goals on the one hand and clarity, certainty, and convenience on the other. An advance directive serves as *evidence* of the patient's choice – good evidence or poor evidence, depending on what it is able to say about the decision at hand.[8] Because every directive will be judged legally – if it *is* judged – on its own merits, and the actions of caregivers will similarly be judged individually, the outcomes of such judgments (or even whether judgment will occur) cannot be predicted. This prospect of individual judgment by the courts carries with it both an obligation of individual judgment, by every caregiver, of every directive, and a promise that it is very likely that a caregiver's good-faith, conscientious judgment about a directive, when explained in court and supported by the record, will be protected from liability. This is as firm a promise of legal support as can be given for any activity that has not been granted immunity from prosecution. Good faith decisions, carefully made and fully explained, may be challenged and tested but will rarely be found wanting.

One of the reasons people incorrectly believe that advance directives must agree with statutes before they may be implemented is that all "living will" statues contain a provision stating that good-faith obedience to a directive conforming to the statue shall not be grounds for civil or criminal liability. These provisions lead caregivers and their institutions to conclude that good-faith obedience to directives *not* conforming to their state statutes will be grounds for liability.

There are several reasons why this is not true. First, the liability protection given to physicians who honor statutory directives is very limited.[9] It does not preclude suit, but instead provides the physician with a very good defense, all but guaranteeing that unless evidence other than the directive itself is introduced, the case will be disposed of at an early stage and the physician will win. However, any evidence that the physician did not act in good faith or that the directive was not valid could eliminate even the limited protection offered by the 'right' kind of directive. For example, a patient's family could claim that the patient was tricked into signing the directive or that the physician knew the patient was mentally incompetent at the time of signing.

The liability protection offered by statutory directives is thus more like 'preapproval' than real legal insulation. Statutory directives are assumed to be trustworthy and reliable, but this presumption may be overcome by evidence to the contrary, and then the matter is reopened and the physician's protection gone. At this point, the physician must prove that he or she was right to implement the directive. To do so, the physician may simply show (1) that the patient's wishes were discussed and recorded in the chart, along with the physician's impressions of the patient's decisional capacity and understanding of the meaning and implications of the choices expressed; or (2) that the directive was discussed with the patient's friends and family, who verified that it appeared consistent with views the patient had expressed to them when he or she still had capacity; or (3) that the directive itself expressed clear wishes, appeared to be based on good information and written to express personal values, could be reasonably applied to the decision at hand, and gave no indications for suspicion that it ought not to be implemented.

Even a physician who honored the 'wrong' kind of directive, or no written directive at all, is nonetheless very likely to win any lawsuit challenging end-of-life decisions for a patient – and preclude the filing of most such lawsuits – by following the same good standard practice of knowing the patient and family, thoroughly documenting all discussions about treatment choices, and giving compassionate and responsible care. These things are enough to

protect the physician when it comes to advance directives, as with all aspects of caregiving.[10] Because this kind of discussion and documentation is good medical practice and the physician should be doing it whether or not an advance directive is involved, the written directive itself is, at best, confirmatory of this other, equally good or better evidence of the patient's wishes and the doctor's actions.

Sometimes, directives that follow statutory models can make it harder for physicians to discover and do what their patients really want. Such directives often give poor evidence of what the writer wanted. Statutory models are all-purpose, least common denominator, compromise directives (President's Commission, 1983). They contain only what *everyone* is prepared to agree is inoffensive, and are usually very generally worded, leaving little opportunity for writers to make known strong particular preferences of any kind. The treatment decisions faced by a patient's family and physicians do not always fall squarely and clearly within the vague, narrow bounds of such directives; a caregiver who has only such a directive to rely upon is likely to find it little help for many decisions.

It is paradoxical that these statutory directives provide some legal protection, even though the decisions protected by such statutes are more likely to be poorly guided than if there were a fuller directive. Many caregivers will be more comfortable, legally and morally, if they supplement the contents of a bare statutory directive with additional evidence of the patient's wishes. A caregiver who wishes to be sure of acting responsibly will interview family and friends and do whatever else is necessary to increase his or her knowledge of the patient and the patient's wishes. The patient who writes a thoughtful and thorough advance directive can convey that same evidence to caregivers more efficiently, fully, and accurately. However, most bare statutory directives are not extensive enough to do that without modification.

Some caregivers may feel that the existence of a 'legal' statutory directive gives them permission to seek real evidence of the patient's wishes on this sensitive subject, and that therefore they are best off with such a directive in hand – giving them the maximum legal protection, slight though it is – and nothing else in writing. Even when there is no directive, however, physicians are still bound to seek evidence of the patient's wishes for all medical treatment decisions, and to honor the patient's wishes if the evidence of them seems sufficient. Since written statements from the patients themselves will always be better evidence, in every respect, than the same statements repeated to caregivers by others, there is no ground for preferring a 'legal' directive if a more detailed version is available or could be written.

Many advance directives advocacy groups, whose target audiences are patients and families, recommend that writers of directives complete the directive prescribed by their state of residence and attach supplementary documents that set forth their treatment choices with more accuracy and detail. This can be somewhat problematic advice, however, when the statutory directive is narrowly drawn but the patient wishes to refuse treatment under broader circumstances – for example, if the statutory directive is limited to terminal illness (as most are) but the patient wishes to refuse treatment in the case of severe chronic illness and irreversible loss of mental capacity. Patients writing these "double-barreled" directives must be aware of the confusion that could ensue when the clinician tries to reconcile the directive's two parts, and should state specifically and clearly that their supplementary, non-statutory directives are intended to have priority. If no such statement is included, clinicians should be sure to clarify these patients' wishes whenever possible. Some model directives now contain priority statements. (See discussion in "Combining the Forms", below.)

A Florida decision illustrates the problem of the "double-barreled" directive well. Estelle Browning was an 88-year-old nursing home resident in a persistent vegetative state, maintained by means of a nasogastric tube for several years since a stroke despite an advance directive executed in accordance with Florida law, because the Florida statutory directive authorizes termination of treatment only when death is "imminent." Ms. Browning had supplemented her directive with strong, clear verbal statements and discussions with the witnesses to her directive, her named guardian, and her physician. She had much experience visiting incapacitated friends and believed that artificial support, including artificial feeding, was an intolerable indignity. Nonetheless, the medical director of the nursing home in which she resided ordered the institution of artificial feeding and antibiotics, over the objection of her treating physicians, because of the limiting language in her statutory directive.

As a result, the court concluded that Ms. Browning's directive could not serve as the basis for withdrawal of the tube, but held that her guardian could assert the right to make the withdrawal decision based on her constitutional right of privacy. Thus, the temptation that may exist to prepare a statutory directive but reach a private understanding with family, friends, and caregivers about what really should happen can give rise to problems when not all parties agree. In this case, the difficulty probably stemmed from liability fears on the part of the institution. If Ms. Browning had put her full wishes in writing as a supplement to the statutory directive, it might at least have been a little easier for her guardian and her physician to assert her interests in the face of the nursing home's concerns, and perhaps it would even have been possible to stay out of the judicial forum entirely, which the Florida Supreme Court acknowledged to be preferable (*In re Guardianship of Browning*, 1990).

On the other hand, clinicians should not *require* patients to write these double-barreled directives in order to gain the liability limitation of the statutory directive. The concern of physicians, friends, and family – the legal concern, as well as the moral and even the professional one – is being able to determine what the patient wanted, or would have wanted.[11] The usefulness of a directive depends only upon whether it provides sufficient evidence of that. Caregivers should require good evidence, that is, enough evidence on which to act, in whatever form it appears. The patient's own self-conscious writing is best. If a directive fails to match a statute because it gives more detail than the law requires, the failure is very unlikely to matter. There is no airtight advance directive and there cannot be. The only guarantees that can be had by physicians and other caregivers are substantive, rather than formal: Rely on directives that guide you well; and help your patients to write them that way.

Clinicians who recognize the importance of viewing patients' directives as legitimate guidance rather than legal orders will also see that a viewpoint that encourages patients to write directives and express their wishes is a viewpoint not precisely compatible with many institutions' legal and policy perspectives on termination of treatment. Focusing on patients' choices bypasses, for those patients who express choices, a network of treatment policies, patient protocols, and legal procedures reflecting the legitimate but sometimes short-sighted goal of limiting institutional liability. It is within this institutional context that the concern that directives be 'legal' has flourished.

For example, it is often not caregivers but their institutions who are reluctant to accede to patients' wishes to withhold or withdraw treatment. Hospitals may fear criminal prosecution for the removal of a feeding tube even though all of the patient's family and caregivers seek the tube's removal. Nursing homes may establish policies requiring transfer of patients to a hospital whenever treatment is necessary, thus requiring families to obtain court orders to enforce advance directives refusing hospitalization and life-sustaining treatment.

Although institutional concerns in this area are understandable, it is nonetheless burdensome to families to seek court endorsement of all advance directives. Institutions need to be shown that, regardless of the perceived risks of honoring patients' treatment refusals, the presence of a written document supporting the withholding or withdrawal of treatment makes successful prosecution even less likely. (See Chapter 6 for further discussion of this issue.) Even though there might be no case law on advance directives or treatment refusal in a particular state, this absence of precedent does not signal the necessity of prior court approval for implementing a directive. Instead, caregivers and institutions should feel able to guide the courts by example, making thoughtful good-faith choices based on directives. More and more courts are coming to recognize that end-of-life decisions are private ones, to be made privately unless there is significant reason to doubt their validity. This is especially true when an advance directive evidences the patient's prior reflection about the decision that must be made.

Avoiding the consequences of an unnecessarily conservative institutional perspective is not necessarily difficult, but requires interested clinicians to do more than simply request that the hospital administration or the hospital attorney develop a clear policy on advance directives. A more effective approach would probably be for clinicians to draft a statement explaining their viewpoint and asking for discussion about how institutional policy can best reflect the real value and purpose of directives, respect patients' choices, and support clinicians' conscientious efforts to honor those choices without unduly compromising the institution's concerns. In this way, advance directives policy can be developed, as are other institutional policies, as part of the institution's attempt to support the delivery of good medical care.

The remainder of this chapter is devoted to assisting clinicians in developing a sense of how to strike the necessary balance between fairness and certainty, both in helping patients to write directives and examining and interpreting directives after patients have lost decisional capacity. It will also help persons wishing to write directives in their consideration of how to make their directives flexible and clear.

The following discussion of various forms of instruction directives and proxy directives is intended to illustrate various problems within the balance of fairness and certainity, and to suggest possible solutions. This is not a comprehensive inventory of law on the subject. Many such inventories exist, published in legal and medical literature and by patient advocacy groups (Cohen, 1987a, 1991; Concern for Dying, 1986b; President's Commission, 1983; Society for the Right to Die, 1985, 1988; see also Meisel, 1989).

Instruction Directives: Living Wills

Instruction directives, popularly known in the United States as "living wills" (Kutner, 1969), are probably the most familiar as well as the most common of advance directives.[12] The name "living will" conveys the solemnity of the document, gives it a legal flavor, and suggests something about its format: a list of instructions akin to a testamentary disposition of assets. But "living will" is a misleading term as well (Francis, 1989); it suggests that advance directives are only legal documents and it too often consigns them to the company of other legal documents in the safety deposit box, rendering them undiscoverable, and therefore useless, when they are needed.

The Testamentary Model

Instruction directives are based on a "testamentary" model, which is to say that in their form and scope, they resemble a "last will and testament". The model contains the following elements: a statement by the writer affirming the seriousness of the declaration ("I, being of sound mind..."); a list of instructions, which can be detailed and specific, brief and general, or anything in between; and usually, the signatures of disinterested witnesses and some official acknowledging stamp or seal.

Scope
Advance directives become effective only when (1) the writer is no longer capable of making medical care decisions, and (2) a decision covered by the directive is called for. It is immaterial which of these two conditions triggers inquiry into the other, but the two determinations must be made or reconfirmed as close together as possible to ensure that both conditions exist. Directives usually say very little about the first condition, relying instead upon our hazy but somehow commonly held notion of "competence", or decisional capacity.[13] The determination is more difficult when the patient is impaired or demented but not entirely unresponsive (e.g., patients with mental illness, stroke victims, etc.), so that "decisions" are indeed offered but appear ambiguous or untrustworthy. When there is an advance directive in existence and the patient's ability to make a critical decision is in question, the directive can help guide the physician's assessment of the patient's decisionmaking capacity, if used to elicit the patient's current choices and reasoning.

The key component of an instruction directive is the decisions it covers. As we have already seen, an advance directive may apply to any and all health care decisions the writer wants it to apply to, from life-and-death decisions to less consequential personal preferences. To establish which decisions are covered, instruction directives generally consider two parameters: "When I am in X condition, I want/do not want Y treatment." (For example: "When I am terminally ill, I do not want to be placed on a respirator." "When I am permanently unconscious, I wish to be given food and water by whatever method necessary." "If I should have another stroke and later contract pneumonia, I do not wish to be treated with antibiotics").

There is no inherent limitation upon the range of conditions that can bring a directive to bear. Of course, because people want directives in order to preserve the choices they believe important, directives will most typically be applied to life and death choices, circumstances of grave illness or debility, and strong personal preferences. Most directives, then, will have to do with terminal illness, permanent unconsciousness, and major interventions like respiratory support and resuscitation. But amputations and other major surgery, dialysis, cancer therapies, and artificial nutrition and hydration have all been the subjects of treatment refusals and have become important subjects for advance directives as well. In short, the range of conditions and decisions about which an advance directive may be written is not inherently limited except that it applies to medical treatments and procedures when the patient is not able to make a choice.

Another way of delineating which decisions are covered by a directive is to specify what treatment should be withheld "if there is no reasonable possibility of recovery" of "if I cannot return to a cognitive, sapient state." This kind of statement in an instruction directive helps to make clear what is important to the patient and what underlies the patient's mention of specific treatments and specific circumstances. It also, inevitably, introduces highly subjective and value-laden terms, which some caregivers consider inappropriate. It is vital to recognize that subjectivity is absolutely appropriate in an advance directive; only genuine ambiguity represents a problem of interpretation.

Most statutory living wills and even some model directives by their own terms limit their applicability much more than does the law of treatment refusal. They usually apply only when the patient is "terminally ill." This is because living will statutes contain only what is viewed as generally agreed upon and not too controversial. Such statutes cannot limit patients' constitutional right to refuse treatments even when they are not terminally ill. However, this terminal illness limitation does avoid many of the most difficult and controversial treatment refusal scenarios and much of the interpretive difficulty of advance directives.

Weaknesses

The potentially great scope of advance directives generates a problem: How can the authors of directives best address all the decisions and conditions they wish to address in their directives?

The "laundry list" approach that is characteristic of instruction directives has an obvious weakness. It is rarely possible to construct a specific and inclusive list of conditions and decisions to cover every contingency. If the author of a directive has a single overwhelming preoccupation, it may indeed be possible to isolate the condition(s) and decision(s) applicable to it. But many writers of directives will begin with a short list and find that it rapidly expands as they consider small alterations in circumstances, wondering whether these changes affect their choices and whether specificity about them is necessary.

Anticipation of every contingency is impossible. There will always arise circumstances and decisions not directly addressed by a directive. The problem is what to do when the directive does not address the circumstances at hand. A good directive can give clues that can help others reconstruct the author's preferences. This means, in turn, that caregivers must attempt to look for such clues. For example: On the one hand, a situation similar to one addressed in the directive should perhaps be treated the same way. On the other, since it was not named, perhaps the author did not perceive it as similar. If in a deliberately narrow directive the author felt strongly only about the situations named, what sort of standard should be used to make other presumably less important decisions that were not addressed?[14]

The nature of the testamentary model comes to the rescue here. The last will and testament is traditionally viewed not just as a laundry list disposing of assets but as a kind of life statement, expressing the deceased's philosophy, style of life, attachments, ties to friends and family, and the like. It is relatively common and very easy to write a will that is an explicitly personal statement, conveying the deceased's views and explaining bequests in light of those views.

Similarly, instruction directives can, should, and often do contain some form of general personal statement which serves to help explain and reinforce the decisions listed. (See, e.g., Cantor, 1990.) Such statements may be brief and sweeping or very detailed, and they may stand virtually alone in the directive or accompany an extensive laundry list of do's and don'ts. Three examples of suggested advance directives of the instruction type serve to demonstrate the range of possibilities.

(1) The Uniform Rights of the Terminally Ill Act (1990) is a model statute designed to be adopted or adapted in state law. It is narrowly drawn, stating only:

If I should have an incurable or irreversible condition that, without the administration of life-sustaining treatment, will, in the opinion of my attending physician, cause my death within a relatively short time, and I am no longer able to make decisions regarding my medical treatment, I direct my attending physician, pursuant to the Uniform Rights of the Terminally Ill Act of this State, to withhold or withdraw treatment that only prolongs the process of dying and is not necessary to my comfort or to alleviate pain.

Signed this _____ day of _____, _____.

Signature _____

Address _____

The declarant voluntarily signed this writing in my presence.

Witness _____

Address _____

Witness _____

Address _____

The only cues here for clinicians are contained in the language at the end of the body of the directive, which describes in general terms the treatments that are to be withheld or withdrawn. "Terminal condition" and "life-sustaining treatment" are defined in the statute, though not in the directive itself. (The definitions are narrow, calling for a medical opinion that death will occur "within a relatively short time" without life-sustaining treatment, which, in any event, "serves only to prolong the process of dying.")

(2) In contrast, Concern for Dying's model directive (1990), also discussed in Chapter 1, makes an explicit philosophical statement about the acceptance of death:

**To My Family, My Physician, My Lawyer and
All Others Whom It May Concern:**

Death is as much a reality as birth, growth, and aging – it is the one
certainty of life. In anticipation of decisions that may have to be made
about my own dying and as an expression of my right to refuse treatment,
I,_____ , being of sound mind, make this statement of my
wishes and instructions concerning treatment.

By means of this document, which I intend to be legally binding, I direct
my physician and other care providers, my family, and any surrogate
designated by me or appointed by a court, to carry out my wishes. If I
become unable, by reason of physical or mental incapacity, to make
decisions about my medical care, let this document provide the guidance
and authority needed to make any and all such decisions.

If I am permanently unconscious or there is no reasonable expectation of
my recovery from a seriously incapacitating or lethal illness or condition,
I do not wish to be kept alive by artificial means. I request that I be given
all care necessary to keep me comfortable and free of pain, even if pain-
relieving medications may hasten my death, and I direct that no life-
sustaining treatment be provided except as I or my surrogate specifically
authorize.

This request may appear to place a heavy responsibility upon you, but by
making this decision according to my strong convictions, I intend to ease
that burden. I am acting after careful consideration and with understanding
of the consequences of your carrying out my wishes. *List optional specific
provisions in the space below.*

This Living Will expresses my personal treatment preferences. The fact
that I may have also executed a declaration in the form recommended by
state law should not be construed to limit or contradict this Living Will,
which is an expression of my common-law and constitutional rights.

The philosophy expressed in this model directive's first sentence may help
clinicians to determine what a "reasonable" expectation of recovery is for a
patient who has signed it. Concern's model directive leaves space for the

author to add provisions, and in addition to listing witness names, it lists all persons to whom copies of the directive have been given, thereby facilitating communication among all interested parties.

(3) Finally, the Society for the Right to Die's model directive (1990), also discussed in Chapter 1, similarly encourages instructional specificity:

Living Will Declaration

To My Family, Doctors, and All Those Concerned with My Care
I, _____ , being of sound mind, make this statement as a directive to be followed if I become unable to participate in decisions regarding my medical care.

If I should be in an incurable or irreversible mental or physical condition with no reasonable expectation of recovery, I direct my attending physician to withhold or withdraw treatment that merely prolongs my dying. I further direct that treatment be limited to measures to keep me comfortable and to relieve pain.

These directions express my legal right to refuse treatment. Therefore I expect my family, doctors, and everyone concerned with my care to regard themselves as legally and morally bound to act in accord with my wishes, and in so doing to be free of any legal liability for having followed my directions.

I especially do not want: _____ (Cardiac resuscitation, Mechanical respiration, Artificial feeding/fluids by tube)

Other instructions/comments:(You may want to add instructions or care you do not want – for example, pain medication; or that you prefer to die at home if possible.)

This Living Will Declaration expresses my personal preferences. The fact that I may have also executed a document in the form recommended by state law should not be construed to limit or contradict this Living Will Declaration, which is an expression of my common-law and constitutional rights.

This directive can be quite specific and detailed, but it should be noted that confusion and ambiguity, though reduced by listing specific refusals, are not always entirely eliminable.[15]

Note the different ways in which these three model directives state their goals. Goals are distinguishable from the conditions and decisions to which directives apply, but they are important for understanding why those particular conditions and decisions are significant. The first directive seeks only "the good death"; the second chooses a good and peaceful death instead of life without a reasonable expectation of recovery; and the third looks to comfort and pain relief in the dying process. These goals help to give the directives more meaning. Yet it is also apparent that amplifying statements like these could expand and proliferate just as much as the laundry lists of conditions and treatments can.

Strengths

It is easy to appreciate the problem of how to convey treatment choices in the form of an instructional directive: just try to write one yourself. The ambiguities of interpretation that attend position statements like those shown above are matched by the difficulties of making lists that are relevant and manageable in size. Yet the combination of position statements and lists of preferences and choices can paint powerful, clear, and compelling portraits of patients and their treatment decisions. Despite the near-certainty that instruction directives will not be easy to apply to all the situations that will arise, their great strength is that they actually put choices on paper. Well-written instruction directives exist as evidence of, and guides to, patients' wishes. In general, their usefulness increases with their detail. They may be endlessly argued over, but they are accessible to all concerned with the patient's care, and what they say cannot be hidden.

State Variations on the "Living Will"

"Living will laws" now exist in most states of the Union.[16] They are regularly considered by the legislatures of all states in which they are not yet law, and existing laws are frequently amended. The discussion of state laws that follows is not intended to be comprehensive, nor to provide legal interpretation of individual statutes. Instead, it is hoped that an overview examination of American law in this area will enable all clinicians to recognize what is viewed as important about advance directives, and, where necessary and desirable, to distinguish those things from the things that should be important about directives.

Like the model acts discussed above, statutory living will-type advance
directives almost always deal only with the refusal of treatment.[17] Living will
laws came into existence for several reasons. First, they provided state
legislatures with the opportunity to declare sympathy with the "death with
dignity" movement. These statutes thus provide a measure of support for
those who promote patients' rights and encourage caregivers to recognize
treatment refusals. In many states, living will laws were passed before state
appellate courts had ever issued an opinion in a treatment refusal case. The
existence of such a statute is considered likely to "spill over" and influence
a court to give some support for nonconforming directives. It is also likely
to cause more people to write directives, conforming or not, since they are
perceived as approved by the state.

Second, such statutes are often sought by the medical profession.
Physicians with concerns about liability and a lack of confidence in the legal
process naturally seek as much protection as they can for what they perceive
as risky choices.[18] These statutes really offer little more protection than the
courts would provide without them, but they are down on the books in black
and white, which helps to reduce the clinician's uncertainty and increase
institutional acceptance of directives.

Third, living will statutes spell out the decisions with which a legislature
is willing to acknowledge agreement: a sort of least common denominator of
treatment refusal. Most of these statutes declare themselves to establish an
"optional, nonexclusive procedure." The message that this conveys from the
legislator to health professionals and the public is, "We are sure about these
provisions, so we will specify them; others may be all right too, but we will
not automatically approve them."

It is important to establish that common agreement, for the reasons given
above; yet it has a serious risk, as was already noted. Too often, statutory
living wills are perceived as going as far as the law will allow; variations on
the statutory form are viewed as unreasonable and suspicious. Thus, the
appropriateness of treatment refusal ends up being measured by a legislative
majority standard – what most people would feel right about doing. This
majoritarian approach, though very easy to fall into and something of a
natural mistake, is a mistake nonetheless.

Standard Statutory Forms

State natural death acts, medical treatment decision acts, death with dignity
statutes, or whatever else they may be called, for the most part share a
common set of features. In addition to (1) a model directive, they contain: (2)
purpose declarations, which recognize the patient's right to make treatment

decisions; (3) definition sections which, by defining key terms like "life-sustaining procedure", "extraordinary means", or "terminal illness", help to specify the decisionmaking limits given by the model directive; (4) specifications about how the directive should be witnessed and solemnized; (5) liability protection for persons honoring a valid-appearing directive in good faith; and (6) provision for revocation of the directive, which is usually made very easy. Most statutes also provide that (7) an attending physician's refusal to honor a validly executed directive, or to transfer the patient into the care of a physician who will honor it, shall be considered "unprofessional conduct." And many statutes provide that termination of treatment according to a valid directive can neither be considered suicide nor required as a condition of insurance.

There are many different varieties of statutory instruction directive schemes, but many of the variations between statutes are minor. There is no efficient way to talk about all of the current instruction directive statutes – now in place as of late 1990 in 41 states and the District of Columbia and subjected to frequent amendment – and interested clinicians ought simply to read the complete statutes in their states.

A model directive, drafted some time ago in a legislative services project at Yale Law School, has found its way into a great many state statutes. It is usually adopted not quite verbatim, and many small variations may be found, some of which may have great significance.

Yale Model Act Variations
The Yale model act's directive is reproduced in Chapter 1. It is operable only when the patient is terminally ill, and applies to all "life-sustaining procedures." The directive is procedurally very specific about terminal illness, specifying who must certify the patient's illness as terminal, but "terminal" is not defined at all. Instead, "life-sustaining procedure" is defined as any medical intervention which prolongs dying; physicians must determine that "death will occur whether or not life-sustaining procedures are utilized." There are *two* declarations of decisional capacity made by the author in the directive, and one by the witnesses.

Some of the variations of this directive are given below. There are others.

Arizona (Arizona Medical Treatment Decision Act, 1986).

DECLARATION

Declaration made this _____ day of _____ (month, year).
I, _____, being of sound mind, willfully and
voluntarily make known my desire that my dying not be artificially
prolonged under the circumstances set forth below and declare that:

If at any time I should have an incurable injury, disease or illness certified
to be a terminal condition by two physicians who have personally
examined me, one of whom is my attending physician, and the physicians
have determined that my death will occur unless life-sustaining procedures
are used and if the application of life-sustaining procedures would serve
only to artificially prolong the dying process, I direct that life-sustaining
procedures be withheld or withdrawn and that I be permitted to die
naturally with only the administration of medication, food, or fluids or the
performance of medical procedures deemed necessary to provide me with
comfort care.

In the absence of my ability to give directions regarding the use of life-
sustaining procedures, it is my intention that this declaration be honored
by my family and attending physician as the final expression of my legal
right to refuse medical or surgical treatment and accept the consequences
from such refusal.

I understand the full import of this declaration and I have emotional and
mental capacity to make this decision.

Signed _____
City, County and State of Residence _____
_____

The declarant is personally known to me and I believe him to be of sound
mind.

Witness _____
Witness _____

Note how the Arizona statutory directive differs from its model. First,
Arizona has tried to redefine "life-sustaining procedures" by stating that the
directive applies if death will occur "unless" they are used (instead of
"whether or not"). Is the meaning clearer here? Is it the same meaning as in
the model directive? Because the directive goes on to say, as does the model

directive, that it applies when life-sustaining procedures "would serve only to artificially prolong the dying process", the answer to both questions is "maybe."

Second, the legislature has added food and fluids to the things that may be deemed necessary to provide comfort care. Is this, too, a clarification merely? Or does it change the meaning of the comfort care provision to imply that food and fluids *must* be deemed comfort care and must be provided?

Indiana (Indiana Living Wills and Life-Prolonging Procedures Act, 1989). Indiana's statute contains *two* model directives, one for refusing treatment and another for requesting it.

LIVING WILL DECLARATION

Declaration made this _____ day of _____ (month, year). I, _____, being at least eighteen (18) years old and of sound mind, willfully and voluntarily make known my desires that my dying shall not be artificially prolonged under the circumstances set forth below, and I declare:

If at any time I have an incurable injury, disease, or illness certified in writing to be a terminal condition by my attending physician, and my attending physician has determined that my death will occur within a short period of time, and the use of life-prolonging procedures would serve only to artificially prolong the dying process, I direct that such procedures be withheld or withdrawn, and that I be permitted to die naturally with only the provision of appropriate nutrition and hydration and the administration of medication and the performance of any medical procedure necessary to provide me with comfort care or to alleviate pain.

In the absence of my ability to give directions regarding the use of life-prolonging procedures, it is my intention that this declaration be honored by my family and physician as the final expression of my legal right to refuse medical or surgical treatment and accept the consequences of the refusal.

I understand the full import of this declaration.

Signed _____
City, County, and State of Residence _____

The declarant has been personally known to me, and I believe (him/her) to be of sound mind. I did not sign the declarant's signature above for or at the direction of the declarant. I am not a parent, spouse, or child of the declarant. I am not entitled to any part of the declarant's estate or directly financially responsible for the declarant's medical care. I am competent and at least eighteen (18) years old.

Witness _____ Date _____
Witness _____ Date _____

....

LIFE-PROLONGING PROCEDURES DECLARATION

Declaration made this _____ day of _____ (month, year). I, _____ , being at least eighteen (18) years old and of sound mind, willfully and voluntarily make known my desire that if at any time I have an incurable injury, disease, or illness determined to be a terminal condition I request the use of life-prolonging procedures that would extend my life. This includes appropriate nutrition and hydration, the administration of medication, and the performance of all other medical procedures necessary to extend my life, to provide comfort care, or to alleviate pain.

In the absence of my ability to give directions regarding the use of life-prolonging procedures, it is my intention that this declaration be honored by my family and physician as the final expression of my legal right to request medical or surgical treatment and accept the consequences of the request.

I understand the full import of this declaration.

Signed _____
City, County, and State of Residence _____

The declarant has been personally known to me, and I believe (him/her) to be of sound mind. I am competent and at least eighteen (18) years old.

Witness _____ Date _____
Witness _____ Date _____

The Indiana refusal directive only requires *one* physician to certify the patient's terminal condition – but it requires that the certification be in writing. It defines "terminal" as "within a short period of time." (Is that helpful or redundant?) Third, it too adds "nutrition and hydration" to the list of care that should be provided – *without* calling it comfort care, but allowing for the possibility that it might not be "appropriate" in all cases. Fourth, Indiana seems a lot more concerned about providing assurances of the disinterestedness of witnesses, limiting considerably the class of potential witnesses by age and relationship.

One of only a few states to do so, Indiana also provides a model directive for patients who want their lives prolonged in the face of terminal illness. But this second declaration does not require as much of its witnesses as does the first. Because the prospect of continued existence is less likely to give rise to *financial* conflicts of interest in witnesses, the qualifications for witnesses to this model directive are minimal.

Maryland (Maryland Life-Sustaining Procedures Act, 1988).

DECLARATION

If any time I should have an incurable injury, disease, or illness certified to be a terminal condition by two (2) physicians who have personally examined me, one (1) of whom shall be my attending physician, and the physicians have determined that my death is imminent and will occur whether or not life-sustaining procedures are utilized and where the application of such procedures would serve only to artificially prolong the dying process, I direct that such procedures be withheld or withdrawn, and that I be permitted to die naturally with only the administration of medication, the administration of food and water, and the performance of any medical procedure that is necessary to provide comfort care or alleviate pain. In the absence of my ability to give directions regarding the use of such life-sustaining procedures, it is my intention that this declaration shall be honored by my family and physician(s) as the final expression of my right to control my medical care and treatment.

Declaration made this _____ day of _____ (month, year). I, _____, being of sound mind, willfully and voluntarily direct that my dying shall not be artificially prolonged under the circumstances set forth in this declaration.
I am legally competent to make this declaration, and I understand its full import.

Signed _____

Address _____

Under penalty of perjury, we state that this declaration was signed by _____ in the presence of the undersigned, who, at _____ request, in _____ presence, and in the presence of each other, have hereunto signed our names and witnessed this _____ day of _____ 19___, and declare: The declarant is personally known to me, and I believe the declarant to be of sound mind. I did not sign the declarant's signature to this declaration. Based upon information and belief, I am not related to the declarant by blood or marriage, a creditor of the declarant, entitled to any portion of the estate of the declarant under an existing testamentary instrument of the declarant, financially or otherwise responsible for the declarant's medical care, or an employee of any such person or institution.

Address _____

Address _____

The Maryland directive defines "terminal" by requiring that death be imminent, and adds "food and water", as Indiana added "appropriate nutrition and hydration", to the category of comfort care. It also provides greater assurance of the solemnity of witnessing a directive and the disinterest of witnesses, but in a manner a little different from Indiana's.

Interestingly, the Maryland statute contains an additional provision specifically stating that additions to this directive will be recognized as valid. The State Attorney General has declared that specific refusals of nutrition and hydration will therefore be honored, but that the statutory directive alone cannot be interpreted to permit nutrition and hydration to be withheld or withdrawn. This statute also contains a section authorizing the execution of an "affirmative" directive requesting life-sustaining treatment, but no suggested form is given.

New Hampshire (New Hampshire Terminal Care Document Act, 1988)

DECLARATION

Declaration made this _____ day of _____ (month, year). I, _____, being of sound mind, willfully and voluntarily make known my desire that my dying shall not be artificially prolonged under the circumstances set forth below, do hereby declare:

If at any time I should have an incurable injury, disease, or illness certified to be a terminal condition by 2 physicians who have personally examined me, one of whom shall be my attending physician, and the physicians have determined that my death will occur whether or not life-sustaining procedures are utilized and where the application of life-sustaining procedures would serve only to artificially prolong the dying process, I direct that such procedures be withheld or withdrawn, and that I be permitted to die naturally with only the administration of medication, sustenance, or the performance of any medical procedure deemed necessary to provide me with comfort care.

In the absence of my ability to give directions regarding the use of such life-sustaining procedures, it is my intention that the declaration shall be honored by my family and physicians as the final expression of my right to refuse medical or surgical treatment and accept the consequences of such refusal.

I understand the full import of this declaration, and I am emotionally and mentally competent to make this declaration.

Signed _____
State of _____ County _____

We, the declarant and witnesses, being duly sworn each declare to the notary public or justice of the peace or other official signing below as follows:

1. The declarant signed the instrument as a free and voluntary act for the purposes expressed, or expressly directed another to sign for him.

2. Each witness signed at the request of the declarant, in his presence, and in the presence of the other witness.

3. To the best of my knowledge, at the time of the signing the declarant was at least 18 years of age, and was of sane mind and under no constraint or undue influence.

_____ Declarant

_____ Witness

_____ Witness

Sworn to and signed before me by _____, declarant

_____ and _____, witnesses

on _____ .

_____

Signature

_____

Official Capacity

New Hampshire provides us with yet other ways to emphasize the same issues: "sustenance" instead of "food and water", and an even more elaborate witnessing statement.

Tennessee (Tennessee Right to Natural Death Act, 1988)

LIVING WILL

I, _____, willfully and voluntarily make known my desire that my dying shall not be artificially prolonged under the circumstances set forth below, and do hereby declare:

If at any time I should have a terminal condition and my attending physician has determined that there can be no recovery from such condition and my death is imminent, where the application of life-prolonging procedures would serve only to artificially prolong the dying process, I direct that such procedures be withheld or withdrawn, and that I be permitted to die naturally with only the administration of medications or the performance of any medical procedure deemed necessary to provide me with comfortable care or to alleviate pain.

In the absence of my ability to give directions regarding the use of such life-prolonging procedures, it is my intention that this declaration shall be honored by my family and physician as the final expression of my legal right to refuse medical or surgical treatment and accept the consequences of such refusal.

I understand the full import of this declaration, and I am emotionally and mentally competent to make this declaration. In acknowledgement whereof, I do hereinafter affix my signature on this the _____ day of _____, 19 ___.

_____ Declarant

We, the subscribing witnesses hereto, are personally acquainted with and subscribe our names hereto at the request of the declarant, an adult, whom we believe to be of sound mind, fully aware of the action taken herein and its possible consequence.

We the undersigned witnesses further declare that we are not related to the declarant by blood or marriage; that we are not entitled to any portion of the estate of the declarant upon his decease under any will or codicil hereto presently existing or by operation of law then existing; that we are not the attending physician, an employee of the attending physician or a health facility in which the declarant is a patient; and that we are not a person who, at the present time, has a claim against any portion of the estate of the declarant upon his death.

_____ Witness
_____ Witness

Subscribed, sworn to and acknowledged before me by _____, the declarant, and subscribed and sworn to before me by _____, and _____, witness, this _____ day of _____ , 19 ____.

_____ Notary Public

Recall the different ways in which these directives have tried to describe and define a terminal condition. Our last example, Tennessee, also requires that the physician find that no recovery is possible. Note, however, that "certification" is not required; is this a change of substance or just a try at less pompous language? With "certified," "certified in writing," and "determined" all used in different statutes, what should physicians actually do to satisfy the conditions of directives from state to state?

Each of the state legislatures that produced these elegant variations upon the Yale Law School's model directive did so conscientiously and probably with good reasons in mind. It is not clear, however, why legislatures are tempted to do so much tinkering with statutory directives, since the statutes themselves usually specify that the model directive need only be "substantially" complied with in order to afford the statute's full protection.

Some state legislatures go in for short and sweet directives, modeling their statutes on the Uniform Rights of the Terminally Ill Act, both in its original 1985 form and, more recently, its 1990 revision (reproduced above), or Concern for Dying's model directive (reproduced in Chapter 1).

Connecticut (Connecticut Removal of Life Support Systems Act, 1989).

DECLARATION

If the time comes when I am incapacitated to the point when I can no longer actively take part in decisions for my own life, and am unable to direct my physician as to my own medical care, I wish this statement to stand as a testament of my wishes. I, _____ (NAME) request that I be allowed to die and not be kept alive through life support systems if my condition is deemed terminal. I do not intend any direct taking of my life, but only that my dying not be unreasonably prolonged. This request is made, after careful reflection, while I am of sound mind.

_____ (Signature)

_____ (Date)

_____ (Witness)

_____ (Witness)

Maine (Maine Uniform Rights of Terminally Ill Act, 1990)

DECLARATION

If I should have an incurable and irreversible condition that, without the administration of life-sustaining treatment, will, in the opinion of my attending physician, cause my death within a short time, and I am no longer able to make or communicate decisions regarding my medical treatment, I direct my attending physician, pursuant to the Uniform Rights of The Terminally Ill Act of this State, to withhold or withdraw such treatment that only prolongs the process of dying and is not necessary for my comfort or to alleviate pain.

Optional: I direct my attending physician to withhold or withdraw artifically administered nutrition and hydration which only prolongs the process of dying.

Signature: _____

Note: This optional provision must be signed to be effective.

Signed this _____ day of _____ _____.
              date   month   year

    Signature_____

    Address _____

The declarant voluntarily signed this document in my presence.

    Witness_____
    Address _____
    Witness _____
    Address _____

A few state statutes restrict the scope of instruction directives in a manner that is different enough to merit special consideration. Most state statutory directives may be written by any competent adult.[19] A few statutes, however, require that patients whose directives were written *before* they became terminally ill must reaffirm them after they have been diagnosed as in a terminal condition. And some statutes include required waiting periods before a directive may be honored.

California's Natural Death Act (1989), which was one of the earliest, enacted in 1976, has both of these qualifications. If it is not written or reaffirmed at least fourteen days after the patient's condition has been diagnosed as terminal, the directive has advisory power only, meaning that failure to honor it will *not* constitute unprofessional conduct. Colorado

(Colorado Medical Treatment Decision Act, 1989) has a waiting period but not a reaffirmation requirement. In Colorado, a directive only becomes effective when a patient has been diagnosed as terminal and has been incompetent for at least 7 days.

Summary

Instruction directives can take a variety of forms, with small but potentially significant variations appearing in uncountable profusion. When patients base their directives on state statutory forms, in order to know what each such directive means it is necessary to examine the whole of each statutory scheme – not just the model directive itself but also definitions, penalty clauses, and all of the other provisions meant to help specify how the directive should be read and where the limits of its interpretation should lie. Slavish devotion to statutory form is not necessary in order for a patient to write an instruction directive that can be implemented with a minimum of uncertainty. A caregiver who seeks honestly to evaluate the meaning and validity of such a directive will probably not be placed at legal risk in the great majority of cases.

Directives must provide evidence of their own validity. Solemn witnessing statements and notary seals are important but not indispensable indicators of validity. In an original directive that does not conform precisely to a statutory model, a statement acknowledging the importance of the decisions stated, specifically accepting their consequences, and listing both the date of writing and reaffirmation dates is likely to be viewed as providing comparable evidence of due execution.[20] To the extent that witness statements provide external evidence of the patient's mental state, such evidence could also be provided later by patients' physicians or attorneys.

Not only do most living will statutes themselves acknowledge that directives may be less than carbon copies of the model and still enjoy full statutory protection, but also, in their purpose statements, many statutes explicitly acknowledge that there are means other than directives whereby treatments may be refused (e.g., by oral statements to family, friends, or caregivers, as in most of the court decisions concerning treatment refusal). In light of this, the clinician's task is to examine a directive to see whether it provides good evidence of the patient's choice and thus can be implemented – *not* to implement a directive only if it substantially duplicates the statute.

The caregiver faced with helping a patient to write an instruction directive, discussing an already written directive with a patient, or interpreting a directive with the help of the patient's family, friends, personal physician, and history needs both to feel confident about taking action in response to the directive and also to be flexible in assessing the degree of imagination and forethought the patient needs to exhibit in the directive in order to inspire that confidence. The best directive to look for is one that contains a general statement of beliefs and preferences as well as specific instructions (in short, a directive of more substance than many of the statutory directives given above) and carries the same or similarly powerful assurances of solemnity, without necessarily carrying their restrictions. The writer's mental capacity is always presumed, and should need no special consideration unless some reason appears to question it.

Most important, the restriction of living will laws to instances of terminal illness is not necessary either morally or legally. The terminal illness limitation, while still defined and construed very narrowly by some legislatures and courts, has been recognized by others as impermissibly limiting patients' choices unless it is interpreted more broadly. Therefore, some courts have interpreted the statutory term "terminally ill" to mean that death will occur within a short time if treatments, *including artifical nutrition and hydration*,[21] are not given (*In re Greenspan*, 1990; *In re Guardianship of Browning*, 1990). Such an interpretation argues persuasively for the validity of nonstandard directives that explicitly refuse treatments without regard to any terminal illness limitation – for example, directives that refuse treatments if the patient becomes comatose or permanently demented. These directives should be implemented if there are other indications of the seriousness and thoughtfulness of the document, and if it is clear from the directive that the patient intended and understood the consequences of its broader applicability.

Proxy Directives: Durable Powers of Attorney

Proxy decision making in health care is hardly new. It takes place every time a patient is incapable of choice but a decision must be made; it is simply one way of describing the health care decision-making process under those circumstances. But there are two significant variables in this process: Who acts as proxy? And by what criteria does the proxy decide (Juengst and Weil, 1989)? Proxy directives, which name the patient's choice of person to act as decisionmaker and specifically grant decisional authority to that person, eliminate the difficulty of finding the right person – a difficulty that can be substantial when there is disagreement not only about who of several is the right person but also about the standards by which the "rightness" of the choice should be judged. The U.S. Supreme Court's decision in the *Cruzan* case (*Cruzan v. Director*, 1990, O'Connor, J., concurring) suggests that proxy directives merit recognition along with instruction directives, as a means of effecting patients' constitutional right to refuse treatment.

It is pretty generally agreed that when the patient's decision is unavailable, whoever decides must use what has been labeled the "substituted judgment" standard (*In re Quinlan*, 1976; *Superintendent of Belchertown State School v. Saikewicz*, 1977) – that is, must attempt to determine what the patient would have wanted. If enough direct evidence of the patient's preferences is not available, then the patient's general character, values, past choices, and so forth are examined, along with the caregiver's medical advice, to determine what decision the patient would have viewed as being in his best interests (*Matter of Conroy*, 1985). This standard expresses the recognition that, in making medical decisions, most individuals determine what they believe to be in their best interests by weighing medical advice along with their own values and many other nonmedical factors.

When a patient names a proxy decisionmaker, the nature of the proxy's decision-making method should be discussed between the proxy and the patient. Because the proxy is deciding in the patient's place, it is understood, unless otherwise specified, that substituted judgment is intended (see Chapter 5). If the patient so directed, however, a proxy could conceivably use any of many different decisional strategies, ranging from doing whatever the doctor says to refusing everything to making decisions based on finances or even to flipping a coin. Of course, unusual standards of decision must be carefully explained and justified in the directive in order to survive good-faith scrutiny by caregivers or courts.

Most of the time, courts that approve the appointment of proxy decision-makers specify a decisional standard like the following, from a decision of the Florida Court of Appeals: "The surrogate decisionmaker's function is to make the decision which clear and convincing evidence establishes that the patient, if competent, would make" (*In re Guardianship of Browning*, 1989). However, it is often difficult to distinguish decisions based on substituted judgment from decisions based on best interests considerations when the decisionmaker is a family member or friend, and proxies themselves may not be able to specify their decision-making process neatly. (See discussion in Chapter 5.) It should be acknowledged that friends and family acting as proxies may well be imprecise in their decisional standards, and that may be perfectly appropriate, since the named proxy is the patient's own choice. It is quite likely that some patients who name their spouses as proxies expect the spouse not to determine what the patient would have wanted, but to choose, based on their relationship, what the spouse thinks is best for the patient – which is a slightly different standard.

Proxy directives provide a neat and immediate solution to the instruction directive's central flaw, the impossibility of specifying a decision, in advance, on every conceivable occurrence. If an instruction directive fails to cover a particular set of circumstances, the language and outlook of the directive will be used as evidence by physician, family, and friends in the attempt to construct a consistent decision for the circumstances at hand. The addition – or substitution – of a proxy directive simplifies that construction process by handing it over to one designated individual.

The Agency Law Model

Proxy decisionmaking is a common concept in law, used primarily for business convenience. Most of us are familiar with the concept of voting by proxy at shareholders' meetings, and with the general idea that one person can act as the agent of another for business transactions and other activities. Insurance agents, real estate agents, and the like are persons who act on behalf of, and in the name of, a "principal" – the insurance company or the homeowner. Agents have the power to do anything in the ordinary course of business in the principal's interest, and to "bind" the principal to the consequences of any such action. In short, the agent has the power to act as the principal.

This very great power is overseen and controlled by the principal in two ways: by limiting the scope of the agency granted, and by the power to terminate the agency relationship. Most agency relationships are clearly circumscribed in scope and given for a short, often self-limiting term: proxy voting during the annual meeting, real estate agency until my house is sold, managing property while I am away, etc. Moreover, the relationship between principal and agent is basically contractual and can be terminated by either party in appropriate contractual fashion. From this it follows that the authority of an agent to act for his principal terminates when the principal is no longer able to act, or to scrutinize the agent's actions, or to revoke the power. Therefore, ordinary agency terminates upon the death or incapacity of the principal.

Although terminating agency upon the principal's incapacity is consistent with most common uses of agency law, there are many other valid transactions that are made impossible by that restriction. In an attempt to strike a balance between the desire to facilitate transactions that would otherwise be impossible and the risks of permitting agents to act when they cannot be closely watched by the principal, the durable power of attorney was created. "Power of attorney" is a general term for the grant of agency power, since an attorney is an agent for the principal in legal matters. "Durable" denotes a power that survives – or, very often, does not take effect until – the incapacity of the principal.

When patients name someone to make health care decisions on their behalf should they become incapacitated, they are essentially giving to the chosen decisionmaker a durable power of attorney for health care decisionmaking. Recognizing this, patient advocacy groups often suggest that persons wishing to name a decisionmaker use the statutory durable power of attorney, which is available in some form in every state, in order to add whatever formality and legality it has to offer to the grant of authority.

All states have durable power of attorney statutes; most of these are based on or very similar to the Uniform Durable Power of Attorney Act (1982), which defines the power this way:

Section 1. [Definition]

A durable power of attorney is a power of attorney by which a principal designates another his attorney in fact in writing and the writing contains the words "This power of attorney shall not be affected by subsequent disability or incapacity of the principal," or "This power of attorney shall become effective upon the disability or incapacity of the principal," or similar words showing the intent of the principal that the authority conferred shall be exercisable notwithstanding the principal's subsequent disability or incapacity.

Section 2. [Durable Power of Attorney Not Affected by Disability or Incapacity]

All acts done by an attorney in fact pursuant to a durable power of attorney during any period of disability or incapacity of the principal have the same effect and inure to the benefit of and bind the principal and his successors in interest as if the principal were competent and not disabled.

Both ordinary and durable powers of attorney, as treated in these statutes, deal primarily with the principal's property and financial concerns; thus, statutes generally require that a document granting a durable power be registered with the local Registry of Deeds, that the agent make periodic accountings before an officer of the court, and other such provisions that seem far removed from the content of health care decisionmaking. Here is an example of a standard form for the grant of a durable power of attorney from the statutes of North Carolina (North Carolina Durable Power of Attorney Act, 1987):

KNOW ALL MEN BY THESE PRESENTS, that I, (name), the undersigned, resident of (name) County, State of North Carolina, hereby make, constitute and appoint (name) as my true and lawful Attorney-in-Fact for me and in my name, place and stead, giving unto the said Attorney-in-Fact full power to act in my name, place and stead in any way which I myself could do if I were personally present with respect to the following matters as each of them is defined in Chapter 32A of the North Carolina General Statutes to the extent that I am permitted by law to act through an agent:

(1) real property transactions: _____

(2) personal property transactions: _____

(3) bond, share & commodity transactions: _____

(4) banking transactions: _____

(5) safe deposits: _____

(6) business operating transactions: _____

(7) insurance transactions: _____

(8) estate transactions: _____

(9) personal relationships & affairs: _____

(10) tax, social security & unemployment: _____

(11) benefits from military service: _____

(initial line opposite those which you desire to give attorney-in-fact authority and strike through those which you do not give attorney-in-fact authority)

This instrument is executed pursuant to the provisions of Chapter 32A of the General Statutes of the State of North Carolina and shall not be affected by my subsequent incapacity or mental incompetence. The provisions of Section 32A-9 of the General Statutes relating to registration in the office of the Register of Deeds of _____ (name) _____ County of this power of attorney shall be strictly complied with. However, it is my intention that no filing of this instrument and/or filing of any accountings with the Clerk of Superior Court shall be necessary.

My Attorney-in-Fact shall keep full and accurate records of all his/her transactions as my agent and of all my property which may come into, be in, or have been in said attorney-in-fact's possession. Annually or more often s/he shall render a full accounting of any and all transactions conducted by him/her in my behalf and list therein all of my property then in his/her possession. Such accountings and inventories shall be rendered to me if I am still mentally capable, otherwise to _____ (name).

It is my hope and expectation that my Attorney-in-Fact will not, except at my request, exercise the authority granted by this instrument unless and until I become incapacitated or mentally incompetent.

And, in general, my said Attorney-in-Fact is given full power and authority to do and to perform all and every act or thing whatsoever requisite or necessary to be done for my upkeep, care and maintenance and for the management of any property owned by me, as fully to all intents and purposes as I might or could do if personally present, and I hereby ratify and confirm all that my said Attorney-in-Fact shall lawfully do or cause to be done by virtue hereof, it being my intent and purpose to confer upon my said Attorney-in-Fact the broadest possible powers to be used and exercised in the discretion of my said Attorney-in-Fact for my use and benefit.

The powers herein granted shall be deemed continuing and relate as fully to any property which I may hereafter acquire as to any property which I may now own, and the powers herein conferred may be exercised repeatedly.
IN WITNESS WHEREOF, I, the said (name) have hereunto set my hand and seal, this the _____ day of _____, 19_____.

Formally naming an individual to make one's health care decisions is a good idea; yet using one of these durable powers of attorney to do it can be a somewhat uncertain proposition. It is not clear whether statutes providing for this grant of a standard, all-purpose durable power intended to contemplate grants of medical decision-making power, which are much more intimate than most grants of authority to make business decisions and require an utterly different expertise. The question of whether a general durable power may be used for health care decisions is still an open one in nearly every state, but a rapidly growing number of state legislatures has added provisions for appointment of a proxy to their living will laws or provided a separate Durable Power of Attorney for Health Care.[22] The easiest thing to do, of course, is just to add the name of a proxy to an instruction directive. This is from Texas' statute (Texas Natural Death Act, 1989):

(e) The directive may include other directions, including a designation of another person to make a treatment decision in accordance with Section 4A of this Act for the declarant if the declarant is comatose, incompetent, or otherwise mentally or physically incapable of communication.

The Uniform Rights of the Terminally Ill Act (1990), recently amended, includes a health care proxy clause in its model declaration. Its language parallels that of the declaration itself, reproduced above, and also permits designation of the attending physician as proxy if the appointed person cannot or will not serve. Maine's new statute, based on the Uniform Act, goes it one better by including an optional nutrition and hydration withdrawal clause in its proxy designation as well as its declaration.

Utah's method, which is part of a complex statutory scheme including two different kinds of suggested directives (Utah Personal Choice and Living Will Act, 1986), is more elaborate:

75-2-1106. (1) A person 18 years of age or older, the "principal," may designate any other person 18 years of age or older to execute a directive under Section 75-2-1105 on behalf of the principal after the principal incurs an injury, disease, or illness which renders him unable to make a directive, by executing a special power of attorney before a notary public, which shall be in substantially the following form:

SPECIAL POWER OF ATTORNEY

I, _____, of _____, this _____ day of _____ , 19____ , being of sound mind, willfully and voluntarily appoint _____ of _____ as my agent and attorney-in-fact, without substitution, with lawful authority to execute a directive on my behalf under Section 75-2-1105, governing the care and treatment to be administered to or withheld from me at any time after I incur an injury, disease or illness which renders me unable to give current directions to attending physicians and other providers of medical services.

I understand that "life-sustaining procedures" do not include the administration of medication or sustenance, or the performance of any medical procedure deemed necessary to provide comfort care, or to alleviate pain, unless my attorney-in-fact specifies these procedures be considered life-sustaining.

I have carefully selected my above-named agent with confidence in the belief that this person's familiarity with my desires, beliefs, and attitudes will result in directions to attending physicians and providers of medical services which would probably be the same as I would give if able to do so.

This power of attorney shall be and remain in effect from the time my attending physician certifies that I have incurred a physical or mental condition rendering me unable to give current directions to attending physicians and other providers of medical services as to my care and treatment.

_____ Signature of principal

STATE OF _____)
                                                    : ss.
County of _____)

On the _____ day of _____, _____, personally appeared before me _____, who duly acknowledged to me that he has read and fully understands the foregoing power of attorney, executed the same of his own volition and for the purposes set forth, and that he was acting under no constraint or undue influence whatsoever.

_____ Notary Public

My Commission Expires: Residing at: _____

The Scope of Proxy Directives

Obviously, the purposes for which a durable power of attorney is granted must be enumerated. The scope of a general durable power may be very broad, but only if it is specified as such. A general power can probably not be read to cover health care decisionmaking without a specific indication that such coverage was intended, but it appears that the grant of power can specifically be made to include health care decisionmaking even when that does not seem to be contemplated by the general statute. In other words, it is necessary to say, in or accompanying a proxy directive, that the grant includes the power to make health care decisions. It is possible to add such language to the form provided by a state statute. However, it is still not absolutely certain that all courts will recognize such a designation, though support for it is growing (Cohen, 1987; *Cruzan v. Director*, 1990, pp. 4923 - 4924, O'Connor, J., concurring).

The scope of special durable powers of attorney that specifically address health care decisions might logically be broad, covering all health care decisions when the principal is incompetent. Such a proxy directive would operate like the appointment of a guardian for an incompetent patient.[23] With so broad a grant of guardianship, the agent, or attorney-in-fact, would be consulted on every decision just as the patient would have been.

Informally, of course, family and friends fill precisely this role all the time; it is only when refusal of life-saving or life-prolonging treatment is contemplated that formally recognizing a proxy decision-maker is seen as necessary. In fact, it could be argued that a general grant of health care decisionmaking power should not include end-of-life decisionmaking. Such decisions are not ordinary for patients, and therefore end-of-life decisions may need more and different knowledge of the patient than do routine authorizations of treatment. It may appear that, for a variety of reasons, the person who routinely authorizes treatment for an incompetent patient is not the right person to make a decision to terminate care.

It is good advice to patients, therefore, that in order to be unambiguous their directives should give their proxies power to make "all health care decisions *including* refusal of treatment", or to make "*only* health care decisions involving the withholding, withdrawal, institution, or continuation of life-sustaining treatment (including artificial nutrition and hydration)." However, in the absence of such specificity it would be wrong for caregivers to read a grant of authority to make health care decisions too narrowly, so as to preclude a proxy from making these most important decisions. Most patients do want their named proxies to make these decisions, even if they have failed to say so explicitly, since the central purpose for writing an advance directive is to have those very important decisions made according to one's own wishes.

Providing for the appointment of a proxy specifically, and only, to refuse treatment seems to be the goal of statutory proxy designations like those from Utah and Texas (reproduced above). They grant authority to the proxy to execute statutory instruction directives on the patient's behalf, and the statutory directives, as we know, focus on refusal of life-prolonging treatment. It is perhaps more realistic, however, to avoid giving proxies partial decisional authority, good for some health care choices but not others.

The proxy's involvement should be what the patient's would otherwise have been. It makes sense, therefore, for the patient to use a durable power of attorney to identify a proxy for all health care decisions, including refusal of treatment, as in the "proxy designation clause" in the Society for the Right to Die's model instruction directive (1990):

PROXY DESIGNATION CLAUSE

Should I become unable to communicate my instructions as stated above, I designate the following person to act in my behalf:

Name _____

Address _____

If the person I have named above is unable to act on my behalf, I authorize the following person to do so:

Name _____

Address _____

The Concern for Dying model directive (1990) has a slightly more detailed "Durable Power of Attorney for Health Care Decisions":

Durable Power of Attorney for Health Care Decisions

To effect my wishes, I designate _____,
residing at _____, (phone#)_____,
(or if he or she shall for any reason fail to act, _____,
residing at_____, (phone #) _____)
as my health care surrogate – that is, my attorney-in-fact regarding any and all health care decisions to be made for me, including the decision to refuse life-sustaining treatment – if I am unable to make such decisions myself. This power shall remain effective during and not be affected by my subsequent illness, disability or incapacity. My surrogate shall have authority to interpret my Living Will, and shall make decisions about my health care as specified in my instructions or, when my wishes are not clear, as the surrogate believes to be in my best interests. I release and agree to hold harmless my health care surrogate from any and all claims whatsoever arising from decisions made in good faith in the excercise of this power.

Strengths of Proxy Directives

There are two very great advantages to proxy directives, from the caregiver's point of view. First, there is no need for the caregiver (with or without the help of the hospital legal department) to puzzle out the import of an instruction directive that does not precisely apply to the decision at hand. The proxy directive provides not decisions but a decisionmaker, and it is *that* individual's job to make and justify decisions in light of the patient's preferences and values. The availability of a proxy can ease the uncertainties and burdens of these decisions for caregivers.

Second, the appointment of a decisionmaker means that decisions can be made concurrently rather than prospectively, by someone who can see the situation and discuss it with the physician instead of having to imagine and anticipate it. Thus, someone other than the physician is involved *at the time of decision*. This should help ease the concerns of those who hesitate to credit decisions made by patients when they are far removed from experiencing the disease and disability about which they are deciding by directive (Buchanan and Brock, 1986). The proxy does not directly experience the patient's condition, but then no one does – not even the caregiver. The proxy does, however, know the patient well, and can engage in contemporaneous discussion with caregivers, thus providing them with a better opportunity to respond to the patient's desires in light of the patient's condition than is offered by many instruction directives.

Weaknesses of Proxy Directives

What is gained by not having to specify instructions in an advance directive is an advantage only at one end of the process: in the document itself. The process of choosing and informing a proxy can be subject to the same challenges as writing an instruction directive: it is difficult to anticipate everything you should, and explain everything you need to explain to give meaning to your choices, regardless of whether you are putting it on paper or talking with someone chosen as your proxy.

In order for a proxy to represent the patient's wishes in health care decisionmaking, the proxy must know as much as possible, both about the patient's specific instructions and desires and about the personal values, preferences, past experiences, and current circumstances that form the basis for them. In some instances, the process of informing a chosen proxy may be minimal. For example, a patient who generally follows his physician's recommendations could have as proxy his physician, knowing that the physician's decisions would be based on his best medical judgment. Or a patient might name a spouse or child and say "Do what you think best", relying on good knowledge of the proxy's own views as well as his or her acquaintance with the patient's views. Both of these designations are based on extensive prior knowledge of the chosen proxies and their decision-making patterns. In other cases, patients must do more to establish the proxy's decision-making patterns, by giving the proxy information about themselves.

For many writers of advance directives, the naming and education of a proxy may be particularly difficult. Many writers of directives have strongly held views that they cannot be certain are shared by family and friends. Family members who would not hesitate to refuse treatment for themselves are often nonetheless reluctant to refuse it for a loved one. As treatment refusal is a highly controversial issue, there are certain to be many families divided about it. Patients who cannot be sure that proxies share their views cannot be sure that even a proxy who is trying hard to do what the patient wants either will know what the patient's choice would have been in a given set of circumstances or, knowing it, will be able to advocate effectively for it. This is a question of both uncertainty for the patient and burden on the proxy. Asking a loved one to act as your advocate under difficult circumstances such as these is a lot to ask, even though the burden is even greater on patients who cannot get proxies to honor their choices.

The case of Brenda Hewitt is a thought-provoking example of this complex problem. Although Brenda Hewitt's story, described by her common-law husband, Dr. Engelbert Schucking (1985), in the *Village Voice* and later in the journal *Law, Medicine, and Health Care*, is important for many reasons, one of its most moving and tragic aspects was Dr. Schucking's loving inability to comply with Brenda's wishes at a crucial point.

Brenda Hewitt was a diabetic with many attendant chronic problems. She was wheelchair-bound, a home dialysis patient, and in constant severe pain. She had drawn up many legal documents and statements expressing her intention to refuse treatment, and even to refuse hospitalization, if complications of her chronic illnesses arose. Dr. Schucking held her durable power of attorney and had promised to do as she wished. But when she became semiconscious, apparently as a result of a blood infection, and refused hospitalization, saying, "I want to die at home", her physician, though he also knew her wishes, refused to prescribe antibiotics unless Ms. Hewitt was hospitalized.

Dr. Schucking reluctantly agreed to take her to a hospital. Though in his account of her death he goes on to describe a horrible hospital experience, Dr. Schucking fixes his own guilt upon that decision: "I shall regret that yes till I die....I knew what I was doing was wrong. I had betrayed her" (Schucking, 1985, p. 268). Later he describes Ms. Hewitt's proxy directive in this way: "What it said, in effect, was: 'I am all yours: *you* decide how much I shall suffer, *you* judge what will be done to me. Let me live if you want me to, let me die if you think it is time'" (Schucking, 1985, p. 268).

If a proxy directive has this meaning, then its weaknesses are clear. There are many independent individuals who do not wish to be "all" anybody's; they would like to be more certain that their own choices are implemented. And even patients who feel confident about their proxy's ability to support their choices may understandably be reluctant to impose upon a loved one the burden of advocacy, which may be emotionally overwhelming – may be, for many reasons, simply too much to ask of the person who knows you best.

And, finally, there may be no one to do it. More and more adults in American society find themselves in comparative isolation after death and mobility have diminished family connections. Even people who live socially involved lives may lack friends and family close enough to agree to take on a proxy's responsibility. Many of those who feel most strongly about their health care choices may be in this position. Of course, if there is no one to designate, a proxy directive cannot even exist.

If proxy directives are used in lieu of instruction directives rather than to supplement them, it can be questioned whether they accomplish the same goals as instruction directives: presentation of the patient's prior choices. Unless we know that patients have made decisions when still decisionally capable or at least discussed their values and preferences with their proxies, the durable power of attorney preserves the patient's own self-determination only nominally. For this reason, it could also be argued that proxies ought not to be permitted to make decisions other than those named in standard statutory living wills unless they can produce evidence (such as a letter of instruction) to show that such choices accord with the patient's wishes. It may thus be best, in order to achieve the greatest certainty and give caregivers the best guidance, to combine both types of advance directive.

Combining the Forms

The strengths and weaknesses of the two prevalent models of advance directive – instruction directives and proxy directives – should now be easy to see. Those weaknesses and strengths tend to complement each other; thus, some combination of the two models may be the best choice for clarity and certainty. A directive that contains a statement of values and preferences, specific instructions, a proxy designation, and a statement indicating the basis for the choice of proxy (e.g., "I have discussed my wishes extensively with so-and-so and name her as my attorney-in-fact in the full expectation that she will act in accordance with them") has many advantages. (See, e.g., Emanuel and Emanuel's Medical Directive (1989), set out in Chapter 1.)

Such a combined directive gives specific instructions and a statement of values that will enable caregivers to make decisions immediately, should there be delay in involving the proxy or if the proxy is no longer available. The proxy designation makes it easier to assign authority for decisions falling within the cracks of the directive's specific instructions. The directive itself contains information about the patient's values and preferences; this helps to support the credibility of both the proxy and the specific instructions and helps to establish the patient's seriousness and thoughtfulness about the directive. In addition, these features ensure that the proxy knows at least something about the patient's wishes, though it is far better for the patient to discuss the designation extensively with the proxy as well. Finally, the proxy is a live and articulate person whose reasoning may be scrutinized by caregivers and who is available for discussion of the patient's options. The proxy thus is an important source of ratification of the validity not only of the directive but of the decisions made for the patient through the directive.

Concern for Dying, an organization dedicated to promoting advance directives, advises readers of its newsletter to use a "three-pronged strategy" to ensure that their advance directives will be honored (Concern for Dying, 1986a). This strategy is designed in order to make a directive as "airtight" as possible. It succeeds not because it results in "airtight" directives but because it emphasizes the underlying seriousness and coherence of the writer's wishes – which is precisely what makes a directive morally and legally persuasive.

Concern for Dying suggests the following: (1) Make your instruction directive as specific as possible in light of new treatment technology (e.g., artificial nutrition and hydration) and your own medical history. (2) Execute a proxy directive as well; use your state's Durable Power of Attorney, made as specific as possible to health care decisions, linked with your instruction directive, and based on full and frank discussions with the named proxy about your wishes and the reasoning behind them. (3) Also execute the statutory living will of your state, even if its scope is limited, stating clearly that you knew of the statutory version and specifically wrote your own directive to include choices not covered in the statute. (Both of the Concern for Dying/Society for the Right to Die model directives have been newly revised to include such a 'priority statement'.) Copies of all three documents should go together to personal physicians, family, friends, attorneys, proxies, and institutions where the patient resides or will be admitted.

A Patient Proxy Office?

This good advice cannot be followed completely, however, by a person who has no one to designate in a proxy directive. Courts often appoint guardians (including, sometimes, caregivers) to act on behalf of incompetent patients who have neither directives nor relatives to act as proxies. The same guardian appointed sooner, through a proxy directive, could learn much more through conversations with the patient, so that better decisions could be made.

Since the 1960s and 1970s, many proposals have been made for the establishment of patient advocates in hospitals and other institutions. The roles of such advocates are described in a variety of ways (Kayser-Jones and Kapp, 1989), but one advocacy role that has not yet been much discussed is that of proxy decisionmaker. Though obviously this would be only a partial solution to the problem, patient advocates could be made available within a hospital, nursing home, retirement community, etc., so that everyone coming into the institution capable of writing an advance directive could have conversations with an advocate and ultimately name the advocate as a proxy. Then the advocate would be called upon to make decisions for that person as necessary, based on any instruction directive written by the patient and on the conversations they have had about the patient's wishes and rationale for them.

Of course, it is difficult for strangers to gain much knowledge of the patient within a short time. Nonetheless, the neutral, official, advocacy function of these proxies should increase the likelihood that express wishes will be obeyed and implied wishes discerned. An institution-based advocate would have to be credible within the institution but supported independently of it, so that there would be no risk that the advocate's proxy decisions would reflect the institution's interests rather than the patient's. The size of the "case load" that such an advocate could handle is not clear. Nor is it known whether the time it would take a newly institutionalized patient to go through this process is too long for it to be effective before incapacitating illness strikes. But it is a partial answer.

Postscript: Reading Directives

It is easy to make a persuasive case for the superior validity and guidance of a very complex, multifunctional advance directive. People who want to control their own medical decisions through advance directives are well advised to prepare comprehensive directives reflecting their preferences and reasoning. But this book is directed also to physicians and other caregivers who must interpret and implement directives. What help is knowing what a really good directive is if you are likely to see directives that are not so comprehensive?

First and most important, caregivers have a vital role to play with all of their patients, in advising them, before they are incapable of decisionmaking, about making good advance directives – or, at the very least, advising them to begin thinking about what they might want to happen if they become gravely impaired.

Second, both in giving that advice and in reading directives, caregivers must think beyond the advance directive forms given by statutory models. In a sense, caregivers attempting to interpret and honor advance directives are acting as proxy decisionmakers for their patients, attempting to use all they know of their patients to interpret and apply their directives fully and fairly. They should advise patients to do more than what is found in statutes, and more importantly, they should not read and judge directives by statutory models. Directives that do not look the way living will statutes prescribe may nonetheless be perfectly valid for all intents and purposes. The fear of liability for implementing "nonconforming" directives is largely unfounded; so long as the directive gives its readers adequate guidance and assurance that it was written with understanding of its gravity and its consequences, most "nonconforming" directives will not even be challenged, and those that are stand a good chance of being found valid.

Recognizing that the model directives contained in living will statutes not only are never free from problems but also invite excessively legalistic thinking about treatment refusal, the Legal Advisors Committee for Concern for Dying – an extremely accomplished and distinguished collection of legal scholars and practitioners – some years ago drafted a model Right to Refuse Treatment Act (Concern for Dying, 1986, pp. 57-61; Legal Advisors Committee, 1983), which does *not* contain a model directive. Instead, after defining some of the key terms it employs, the Act simply and clearly sets out the scope of the patient's power to write advance directives of both the instruction type and the proxy type and specifies very general minimum requirements for a directive's validity:

Section 2.

A competent person has the right to refuse any medical procedure or treatment, and any palliative care measure.

Section 3.

A competent person may execute a declaration directing the withholding or withdrawal of any medical procedure or treatment or any palliative care measure which is in use or may be used in the future in the person's medical care or treatment, even if continuance of the medical procedure or treatment could prevent or postpone the person's death from being caused by the person's disease, illness or injury. The declaration shall be in writing, dated and signed by the declarant in the presence of two adult witnesses. The two witnesses must sign the declaration and by their signatures indicate they believe the declarant's execution of the declaration was understanding and voluntary.

Section 5.

A declarant shall have the right to appoint in the declaration a person authorized to order the administration, withholding or withdrawal of medical procedures and treatment in the event that the declarant becomes incompetent. A person so authorized shall have the power to enforce the provisions of the declaration and shall be bound to exercise this authority consistent with the declaration and the authorized person's best judgment as to the actual desires and preferences of the declarant. No palliative care measure may be withheld by an authorized person unless explicitly provided for in the declaration. Physicians and health care providers caring for incompetent declarants shall provide such authorized persons all medical information which would be available to the declarant if the declarant were competent.

The straightforward, nonformulaic approach of this model act helps to make clear that a directive can take any form that makes the patient's wishes known and appears to have been prepared voluntarily and with understanding.[24]

Most of the time caregivers face advance directives they will be simple statutory model directives, because that is still what people think they have to write. These directives can present guidance problems for clinicians because they often say very little. When a directive can be applied to the decision faced, there is of course no problem; nonetheless, the clinician acting in good faith should try to supplement the directive's guidance with all of the usual means of learning about the patient, including conversation with family and friends, consultation with the patient's other physicians, complete familiarity with the patient's medical history, and the like.

These same means of learning about the patient must also be used, and are of considerably greater importance, when the directive does not appear to apply directly to the decision faced. A directive that seems to give little guidance must become the basis for the clinician's attempt to find decisional guidance – not the excuse for a failure to ascertain or to honor the patient's wishes.

How shall the clinician know when a directive should be honored? Perhaps it is easier to say when directives should not be honored. First, if after the clinician makes a good faith effort to interpret it in the light of all other information, the directive does not provide reasonably clear guidance for the decision faced, it will not be possible to implement it.

Second (which is related), if it is so incomplete or radically inconsistent as to call into question the presumption that the patient had decisional capacity and deliberately intended it to be effective, it should not be implemented.

Third, if persuasive external evidence (from family, friends, etc.) is so in conflict with the directive as to raise serious doubts about its validity when written, then it ought not to be implemented.[25]

In each of these situations, when the directive cannot simply be honored, the caregiver should use the directive as some evidence of the patient's wishes to come to a decision based on the patient's wishes and medical judgment, with the help of the patient's family and friends or of a hospital ethics committee, or turn the problem over to another authorized decisionmaker (e.g., to a court or a legal guardian). Every directive must be taken as far as it can be taken in good faith to discern the answers it is trying to provide. See Chapter 5 for further discussion of this problem.

Notes

[1] As of 1987, 29 living will statutes (of the 42 currently on the books) explicitly provided that they were intended to supplement, rather than to replace or curtail, the common law (Gelfand, 1987, p. 784 n. 202). Moreover, unless a statute or its legislative history explicitly provides that the legislature's intent was to change and to narrow the common law in this area, the chances are great that it would *not* be found to do so by a court, because the common law in this area is so well-developed (see, e.g., *In re A.C.*, 1990, pp. 17-20). Several courts have so ruled, even without an explicit statutory provision to that effect.

[2] See Chapter 2's discussion of the legal basis for directives.

[3] As of late 1989, legislatures in a handful of states – Colorado, Connecticut, Florida, Georgia, Idaho, Maine, Missouri, Oklahoma, Wisconsin – had amended their living will statutes to exclude nutrition and hydration from the list of treatments that may be withheld or withdrawn. In several of these states, patients and their families have successfully challenged this limitation; the courts in these decisions declare that a living will statute cannot restrict the right of treatment refusal available to patients under the Constitution. See, for example, *Corbett v. D'Alessandro* (1986); *In re Rodas* (1987).

The state of Oklahoma went further in 1987, however, when it passed the Hydration and Nutrition for Incompetent Patients Act, which is separate from its living will statute. The Act attempted to prohibit courts from honoring a patient's request for withholding or withdrawal of nutrition and hydration unless the patient was facing imminent death (Scofield, 1987). This limitation was clearly an impermissible restriction on the patient's constitutional right to refuse treatment (*Cruzan v. Director*, 1990).

In 1990 the statute was amended to establish a presumption that all patients want nutrition and hydration, which may be rebutted by means of clear and convincing evidence, when death is imminent, or when the administration of artifical nutrition and hydration will cause severe pain and is not medically possible (Oklahoma Hydration and Nutrition for Incompetent Patients Act, 1990). Despite these changes, this statute is still drawn so narrowly as to be problematic. Nonetheless, more statutes separately addressing refusal of artificial nutrition and hydration may be expected, and more statutory directives are likely to be amended to incorporate separate clauses refusing these treatments (e.g., Colorado, Maine, and others), as societal consensus about their provision begins to shift ground.

[4] See the Barber case's discussion of the role of the criminal law in this area (*Barber v. Superior Court*, 1983).

[5] In *Randolph v. City of New York* (1986), a Jehovah's Witness had refused blood transfusions and subsequently undergone a Cesarean section. During an emergency hysterectomy that became necessary when the placenta could not be removed, an accidental laceration caused a massive hemorrhage. After unsuccessful efforts to control the hemorrhage, the physicians requested legal authorization for a transfusion, but it came too late to save the patient. When her husband brought suit for negligence, the court held that the patient's right to decide about her care outweighed the doctor's obligation to give necessary treatment, stating that it was unfair to penalize the physician for not ignoring the patient's wishes at the first sign of hemorrhage. It is hard to imagine a stronger case than this for upholding the validity of an advance directive (which this patient's refusal of transfusion essentially was), even when the family disagrees.

[6] After the United States Supreme Court's decision was announced, the Cruzan family sought a new hearing before the trial judge to offer new evidence of their daughter's wishes. The state of Missouri then sought and received dismissal as a party in the case, expressing confidence that the remaining parties, namely the Cruzans and Nancy Cruzan's court-appointed guardian, would properly apply the clear and convincing evidence standard (Gianelli, 1990). Because the new evidence was to consist of testimony from several of Nancy's former coworkers regarding oral statements she had made to them, the state's posture can be interpreted as conceding that oral statements can meet the standard. The hearing on this new evidence was held November 1 (Gianelli, 1990).

On December 14, 1990, in a brief opinion and order, Jasper County Probate Judge Teel found that Nancy Cruzan's prior oral statements to coworkers constituted clear and convincing evidence sufficient to support removal of her feeding tube. Judge Teel is the same judge who had originally ordered removal of Nancy Cruzan's feeding tube, which decision was challenged by the state of Missouri and resulted in the U.S. Supreme Court's ruling. This time, however, the state of Missouri did not challenge the court's decision, and state health department officials promised to comply with the order; 90 minutes after it was issued, Nancy Cruzan's gastrostomy tube was removed. She was expected to die within two weeks, while receiving comfort care and pain medication if necessary.

Nancy Beth Cruzan died peacefully in the early hours of December 26, 1990, amid a flurry of protests and last-minute legal efforts by right-to-life organizations. All of these efforts were rejected by both state and federal courts on the grounds that the petitioners had no "standing", or legal interest, in Ms. Cruzan's case and presented no substantive grounds for intervention. An emergency petition was to have been submitted to the U.S. Supreme Court on the day she died.

Judge Teel's December 14 decision and its aftermath have made clear that in Missouri the clear and convincing evidence standard in this context may be met by oral statements, thus reducing the potential burden of such a standard on victims of sudden illness and injury and others who have not prepared written advance directives. Similarly, the Illinois Supreme Court has recently interpreted its own "clear and convincing evidence" standard as being met by oral statements (*In re Greenspan*, 1990). Needless to say, in the vast majority of jurisdictions, which do not apply this high evidentiary standard, prior oral statements continue to be a principal means of assertaining a patient's desires and views.

[7] Many institutions and their legal advisors take a very cautious posture in this and other areas, and would prefer that patients and their families seek prior court authorization for "nonconforming" directives. This is an unreasonable posture (see articles collected in Gostin (1989) on the Linares case). Truly definitive judicial authorization is hard to come by, since the United States Supreme Court cannot hear all the cases we want it to hear, and certainly cannot hear them all in time for it to matter in many cases. Besides, when caregivers, patient, and family are in agreement except for "legal concerns", there is no reason in good conscience to indulge such disembodied concerns – especially because the moral underpinnings of advance directives are so strong. Finally, there is no justifiable assumption that a state law, especially in this controversial area, is constitutional unless proven otherwise. Legislatures often pass laws that they suspect or know are unconstitutional. Recall former Massachusetts Governor Michael Dukakis' 1988 refusal to sign a state statute prohibiting flag desecration because his legal staff advised him it was unconstitutional. He was widely criticized for failing to pass a statute that he knew would not withstand scrutiny. Critics reasoned that it was not the Governor's job to make such judgments, and denounced him for failing to "send a message" about what the Constitution *ought* to say. Thus, to assume that a state legislature has made a correct constitutional judgment is problematic (though of course legislatures must be regarded as having acted in good faith unless there is evidence to the contrary).

[8] To say that advance directives evidence rather than constitute choice is not to weaken their moral or legal force; on the contrary, it affirms their flexibility and suggests ways of strengthening their effectiveness. But compare Buchanan and Brock (1986, pp. 56-67).

[9] Most statutes provide that the withholding or withdrawal of treatment according to a directive that substantially conforms to their terms shall not be considered the cause of a patient's death. This is also true for any valid treatment refusal under common law or the Constitution. Therefore, most state statutes go on to offer physicians limited liability protection. Many provide that physicians and facilities acting according to the statutory terms shall not be "subject to liability" or even "subject to any proceeding". This sounds like broad immunity until it is realized that nearly all states qualify that immunity by offering it only to physicians who act "in good faith" or "in accordance with reasonable medical standards". Thus, physicians accused of bad faith or bad judgment or failure to meet the conditions of the statute are still required to defend themselves in court.

[10] Living will statutes themselves may acknowledge this by stating that their purpose is "to establish an optional and nonexclusive procedure" by which patients (or their proxies) may exercise their rights. See, e.g., the North Carolina Right to a Natural Death Act (1985, § 90-320), which also goes on to state, even more explicitly, "Nothing in this Article shall impair or supersede any right or legal responsibility which any person may have to effect the withholding or withdrawing of life-sustaining procedures in any lawful matter." A number of states – even those attempting to restrict patients' power to refuse nutrition and hydration by means of directives – include in their living will statutes elaborate preamble statements acknowledging patients' rights to refuse treatment.

[11] This is the "substituted judgment" standard of decision-making discussed in Chapters 2 and 5.

[12] In Britain, by contrast, they are called "dying wills."

[13] See discussions of decisional capacity in Chapters 3 and 5.

[14] This question is discussed further in Chapter 5.

[15] A rather tragic example of confusion about advance directives terminology arose recently in New York, and may have occasioned the removal of the term "meaningful quality of life" from this model directive. New York is one of the few states remaining without living will legislation, but one that has been the source of many important treatment refusal cases. Its Task Force on Life and the Law, established to draft policy guidelines and recommend legislation, has developed Do Not Resuscitate legislation and a Health Care Proxy law, both of which have been adopted into law, the latter in 1990, clearly in response to the Supreme Court's decision in *Cruzan*.

Tom Wirth was diagnosed as having AIDS-related complex (ARC) and wrote an advance directive substantially identical to an earlier version of the Society For the Right to Die's model directive; a few months later, he was admitted to Bellevue Hospital in a stuporous condition and was found to have toxoplasmosis. His directive provided for withholding or withdrawal of all of the treatments listed in that version of the Society's model directive, including antibiotics, if "there is no reasonable possibility of recovering or regaining a meaningful quality of life." His directive also named his long-time friend and lover, John Evans, as his proxy; Evans attempted to refuse antibiotic treatment for the toxoplasmosis. The hospital resisted and a court agreed, reasoning that Wirth was expected to recover from the toxoplasmosis if treated, and that it was therefore not clear that he considered his pre-toxoplasmosis state not a meaningful quality of life just because he had ARC. Because of this ambiguity, the court refused to recognize his proxy's claim that Wirth had meant he wanted no treatment unless he could recover from ARC (*Evans v. Bellevue Hospital*, 1987).

The court's somewhat questionable reasoning on this and other issues in the case was not tested on appeal, because Mr. Wirth never regained decisional capacity, and treatment was eventually stopped, in accordance with his directive. To its credit, the court did ask that directives be as clear and specific as possible; in this case it is likely that if Mr. Wirth had added some explanatory material to his directive, making it more than just a copy of a model form, the disagreement that arose in this case might have been avoided.

[16] By 1990, 41 states and the District of Columbia had some form of living will statute.

[17] Indiana's statute is a conspicuous exception; see below.

[18] In this respect, living will laws resemble Good Samaritan statutes, which have been widely acknowledged as unnecessary to protect health care providers from liability for rendering emergency care but which nonetheless are ubiquitous (Annas, 1988, pp. 42, 271).

[19] In fact, only a few statutes provide that directives may be executed on behalf of minors (Society for the Right to Die, 1988). Presumably this indicates legislative recognition that treatment refusal, like all other major decisions made by minors, requires particularized attention

to whether the minor in question is capable of autonomous decisionmaking under the circumstances – not just a legislative determination that minors cannot write directives.

[20] In states without living will statutes, this much is probably much more than is necessary to meet the highest evidentiary standard (Cohen, 1991). Even New York's highest court, which requires "clear and convincing" evidence of a patient's views, has stated that a written document suggests seriousness of purpose and that someone who has put wishes in writing is more likely to be sure that any changes of heart are communicated to caregivers (*In re Westchester County Medical Center (O'Connor)*, 1988). Moreover, the United States Supreme Court's *Cruzan* decision (1990), which allows states to set a "clear and convincing" evidentiary standard, confirms the validity of written directives as strongly as was possible in light of the facts of the case before it.

[21] Along with newly expanded meanings of "terminal illness" and "life-sustaining procedures" comes the problem of determining whether artifical nutrition and hydration should be included within the latter or treated separately in statutory directives. As we have already seen, some states address this problem and others do not. Of those that do, no two treatments are alike. Some of the most intricate and detailed legal language in any statutory scheme is found in Okalahoma's treatment of nutrition and hydration (Oklahoma Hydration and Nutrition for Incompetent Patients Act, 1990; Oklahoma Natural Death Act, 1990), which sets up a presumption that all persons want to receive artificial nutrition and hydration unless they specifically declare otherwise in a directive or overcome the presumption by satisfying one of several other conditions. The thorough and repetitive language used in these statutes provides a good example of the failure of even the most exhaustively scrutinized statute to shut all possible legal loopholes, and could be taken as an object lesson in the desirability of good physician-patient communication and understanding as an alternative to exclusive reliance on the written word.

[22] About a dozen state living will statutes provide for the appointment of a proxy in their model directives (Society for the Right to Die, 1988). More and more states – five in 1989 alone – have specifically enacted durable powers of attorney for health care decisionmaking. New York, one of the few states still without a "living will" statute, enacted a Health Care Proxy act in 1990, in response to Justice O'Connor's concurrence in the *Cruzan* decision. See *Cruzan v. Director* (1990, p. 4923, n.3, O'Connor, J, concurring). Other states have included language in their durable powers to specifically include medical treatment decision making as one of the things proxies may do. Still other durable power statutes cover health care decisions by implication or interpretation (by a court or state attorney general) (Cohen, 1987). In 1989, the Uniform Rights of the Terminally Ill Act was amended to include authorization for the appointment of a medical proxy.

[23] Such court-appointed guardianships, often called "guardian of the person" (as distinguished from guardianships of property), are provided for by statute in every state and are often part of the duties of social services authorities, who take responsibility for incapacitated patients without families.

[24] For an interesting new model document meant to encompass some of the flexibility contemplated by this model Act, as well as to stimulate and guide patients in formulating their choices, see the "Medical Directive" reproduced in Chapter 1.

[25] This does *not* mean that a directive should not be honored if the family disagrees with it. See generally the discussion of this issue in Chapter 5. See also note 5 above.

Chapter Five

When Choices Fail

In a handbook that is about advance directives – written statements directly expressing patients' treatment choices – it may seem superfluous to spend time discussing what happens to patients without written directives. There are two good reasons to do so, however.

First, it helps those faced with writing, advising about, or reading and evaluating advance directives to know what would happen without them; it gives directives a context, which should make them easier to write as wanted and to read as intended.

Second, advance directives let loose in the world are not marching orders but documents of engagement. As discussed in Chapter 3, advance directives depend upon both the value of autonomy and the value of community – upon a respect for the legitimate concerns of others that governs both the writing and the application of directives. There will often be many people whose concern for the patient engenders their involvement when a decision needs to be made. There may be some patients whose directives are clear and perfect and whose family, friends, and caregivers all agree in their support of it. More often, perhaps, there will be questions. Clinicians should be prepared to contend with all the potential sources of evidence about the patients's wishes and best interests even in the presence of a directive. It will help, then, to know how much credit to give those sources.

The Context of Medical Choices

To make sense of advance directives, we need to understand the place they fill in the larger picture of medical decisionmaking, for no one can evaluate a directive without knowing both the consequences of honoring it and the consequences of determining it to be invalid.

Advance directives are often likened to wills – hence the popular name "living will."[1] But they differ from wills in crucial and little-noted respects (Francis, 1989).

Most of us know a few things about wills. Most importantly, if we die without one, the state will dispose of our property according to an "intestate succession" formula established by law. Even though we may not know what the formula is, we probably know that it exists; moreover, we can readily find out what it is. We can decide whether we want to do something different from the formula, and if we are willing to go to the trouble of writing a will about it. We know that the formula also tells us what the state will do if we do write a will and it is ruled invalid. So we know what we risk by making a will that does not provide all the necessary indicia of validity, or one that contains unconvential, challengeable dispositions.

We may also realize that the law of intestate succession is not an arbitrary formula. It names property dispositions according to a conventional social morality: parents, spouse, and children are the principal beneficiaries. If we realize this, we will know that individuals can do almost anything they want with their property, so long as they clearly explain what they want to do and give reasons for departing drastically from the social norm (for example, for disinheriting all one's children in favor of an obscure charity administered through a Swiss bank account). Two values are at work here: the strong pull of the social order as represented by the law that prescribed a formula for property distribution without a will, and against it great respect for individual choice, which must nonetheless prove its soundness by careful documentation. Everyone knows that many things can go wrong with a last will and testament; yet the overall scheme is simple and its rules are straightforward.

In contrast, it is a significant problem for advance directives that we do not agree what will happen if you do not have one. American society is in the midst of struggling toward a moral consensus on this very question, and we may never reach it. We are not even sure what sort of consensus we should seek. Suppose that you have not made an advance directive and, comatose and terminally ill, you face being placed on a respirator. Should you be treated because, without written evidence of your preferences, the only reasonable thing to do is to treat you? Should you be treated because you did not express a preference in writing for nontreatment and therefore you must want treatment? Should evidence of your values and verbal statements govern the decision? Or should only your "best interests" be considered?

Requiring a written directive in order to withhold or withdraw treatment gives caregivers a clear and unequivocal action plan that appears to be based on respect for autonomy. According to this reasoning, patients who are motivated to refuse treatment may do so readily, simply by making an advance directive; therefore, if there is no directive, there is no desire to limit treatment. But this is not a fair assumption. To presume that only people with living wills do not want treatment imposes upon all patients a degree of foresight that may not be available to many people with unexpected illnesses.[2]

We could perhaps force a flowering of foresight by legislating this scheme, mandating treatment if no directive exists; after all, it is true that knowing what will happen to your property without a will spurs people to make wills. But the law of intestate succession grew also out of a consensus about what most people wanted to do with their property, or at least a judgment about what good citizens ought to want – to give to the "natural objects of their bounty." Do we agree that people who have not made advance directives generally want treatment? Or that they should want it? It seems clear that we do not. We probably agree that in certain situations it is fair to presume that patients want treatment: for example, in the classic medical emergency. However, where serious disability and short-term continuation of life are common treatment outcomes, we cannot claim consensus yet as to what patients want (Danis *et al.*, 1988). If we were to decide to force consensus by legislative choice, such a policy could be legitimated only by careful, serious, and explicit consideration of the advantages and disadvantages of such a move and its effects on the right to refuse treatment.

A beneficence-based decision to treat persons without advance directives because treatment is in their best interests is at least as difficult to support as the assumption that not having a directive is an expression of preference for treatment. Although this view seems plausible and in accordance with the ethics of the health professions, on closer examination it is difficult to grasp its meaning. We cannot say with consistency whether determining the patient's best interests is a "medical" or "nonmedical" activity (Annas and Glantz, 1986; *Canterbury v. Spence*, 1972; *Cobbs v. Grant*, 1972). We cannot state with certainty and generalizability who should make this determination, or what should be considered in making it. Nor can we readily predict with certainty whether treatment or nontreatment will be the beneficent choice in a given case, however the prior questions have been decided.

Perhaps we should be able to agree on who should decide and on what factors should be considered. If so, patients without advance directives can have some idea of what will happen when a decision becomes necessary, even though they will still have no idea what will happen *to them*. Even the best possible knowledge, then, is precious little.

Moreover, patients who have written directives cannot necessarily protect themselves from being regarded as though they had not. Advance directives may not be discovered until it is too late, or may never be found at all. They may be "invalidated", or they may not give guidance for the decision for which they are needed, or their language may require interpretation. In all of these instances, patients' caregivers, friends, and family will be unable to rely exclusively on the directive and will have to make decisions based, at least in part, on other decision-making principles.

By focusing on written advance directives, this volume is tackling the easiest part of the problem of medical decisionmaking.[3] Any caregiver who regards the patient's autonomous choices and preferences as important will find advance directives to be, at the very least, important guidance. Advance directives policy will undoubtedly help – has already helped – to inform the larger policy discussion. However, because encouraging written directives cannot provide answers in every case, a brief discussion of decisionmaking in the absence of advance directives is appropriate here.

Reconstructing Refusal: Substituted Judgment

As we know from the emergency exception to the informed consent requirement (*Canterbury v. Spence*, 1972, pp. 788-789; Meisel, 1979), physicians are presumed to act in their patients' best medical interests in advising, ordering, and performing treatment. When patients are unable to consent to care, physicians are sometimes permitted to proceed on the basis of their judgment of the patient's best interests, or they may serve as medical advisors to a court, a court-appointed guardian, or family members charged with making a decision in the patient's best interests (Baron, 1978, 1979; *Superintendent of Belchertown State School v. Saikewicz*, 1977). Treatment decisionmaking thus appears to present a neat dichotomy: If the patient is decisionally capable, do as the patient says; if not, do what the doctor says.

Treatment refusal complicates this simple scheme, however. The controversial decisionmaking doctrine known as "substituted judgment" (Annas, 1978; Buchanan and Brock, 1986; *In re A.C.*, 1990; President's Commission, 1983; Ramsey, 1978), first developed to justify making disbursements of money from the estates of incompetents for the benefit of family members, came to be applied in cases where family members disagreed with medical decisions about treating incapacitated patients. According to this doctrine, a patient who cannot decide should be decided for by somebody else who acts as a true proxy, making the decision the patient would have made if able to decide.

On its face, this appears to be an entirely different standard from one that looks to the patient's best interests. The earliest medical applications of substituted judgment, however, explicitly pitted medical against psychosocial views of "best interests," giving court approval for subjecting retarded patients to the medical demands of major surgery to donate kidneys to siblings of normal intellect, on the basis that the retarded sibling would be more harmed by loss of a family member than by loss of a kidney (*Strunk v. Strunk*, 1969).

The first case to apply substituted judgment to treatment refusal was the celebrated 1976 *Quinlan* decision (*In re Quinlan*, 1976). Before her unexpected disability struck, Karen Quinlan had in casual conversation expressed opinions consistent with the desire to avoid life-prolonging medical treatment. Later, these statements appeared to have some relevance to the decisions at issue when she was no longer capable of decisionmaking; however, they were too vague for the *Quinlan* court to rely upon them as conclusive evidence of her treatment preferences. Thus, though the court reasoned that patients' treatment decisions were supported by the right of privacy, it could not find that Karen Quinlan had made a competent decision to refuse treatment.

In order to make a decision on her behalf now, the court had to declare that incapacitated patients like Karen Quinlan held the same privacy right as did competent patients. The difference lay only in that incapacitated patients needed the assistance of a proxy to discover and declare the decision the patient would make if competent to do so. The court imagined a transient moment of lucidity for Ms. Quinlan in order to convey the nature of the decision that a proxy would be asked to make.

In the 1977 *Saikewicz* decision, where substituted judgment reached its full flower (*Superintendent of Belchertown State School v. Saikewicz*, 1977), the transient moment of lucidity became a complete rather than just a partial fiction. Joseph Saikewicz had always been profoundly retarded and could not understand his circumstances. Whereas in *Quinlan*, the court saw the proxy's task as that of reconstructing a prior decisionally capable self and determining its wishes about a current problem, the *Saikewicz* court was forced to imagine the existence of an unprecedented decisionally capable self suffering under unnatural constraints of irremediable ignorance. This was the only way it could determine what a temporarily aware and therefore entirely imaginary Joseph Saikewicz would face and what he would choose. If it did not perform this contortion, the court apparently thought it would be forced to treat never-capable persons differently from formerly capable persons in a way that would be fundamentally unfair. Perhaps it thought that according to the best interests standard, never-capable persons would always have to be treated.

Because personal values come strongly into play in end-of-life decisionmaking, the courts recognized that reliance on the best interests standard in cases like Karen Quinlan's might not be sufficient to take account of patients' values. There are obvious problems with using the substituted judgment standard instead, however, especially with patients like Joseph Saikewicz. Almost before the ink was dry on the *Quinlan* decision, courts and commentators began attempting to reformulate, rehabilitate, or replace it. Some of these efforts are discussed below. Still, substituted judgment can be a useful, if crude, decisionmaking tool, and many courts continue to apply it, requiring proxies to make "the decision the patient would make if competent." Indeed, the influential Court of Appeals for the District of Columbia recently strongly affirmed substituted judgment as the appropriate decision-making standard in end-of-life decisionmaking (*In re A.C.*, 1990).

Who Decides?

The families of adult decisionally incapable patients were the first to seek decisional authority in treatment refusal cases. Parents, adult children, siblings and other relatives, and long-time friends have all, in various circumstances, been given authority to make substituted judgments for decisionally incapable patients. Court-appointed guardians have also been appointed to make substituted judgments, when family and friends are unavailable or have been thought to have a conflict of interest making them inappropriate proxies.

It is important to recognize that *no* relative of a decisionally incapable adult patient has any legal decisionmaking authority for the patient unless the patient names that person as a proxy in a directive, or the court appoints that person as the patient's permanent or temporary guardian, or a state statute specifically conveys such authority. This seems puzzling at first, because not only do physicians and other caregivers rely extensively on family members for information and decisionmaking, but many courts recently have emphasized that life-and-death decisions are properly private and should be made whenever possible by agreement between physicians and family, rather than being judicially reviewed in every instance. That sounds like relatives are being given legal authority – and it also implies that patients who might prefer to have a friend or a lover as proxy will not be able to enforce their wishes if their families disapprove. However, the crucial matter, the basis for decision, is yet to be addressed. Understanding the basis for decision will clarify how caregivers should view the decision-making role of family members and others.

On What Basis?

A true substituted judgment is defined as what the patient would have wanted. Family and close friends are chosen as substitute decisionmakers because of what they know about the patient. Their personal experience with the patient gives them access to information, direct and indirect, about the patient's preferences, values, character, habits, beliefs, desires, fears, hopes, and plans. It is precisely this information that must be assembled into a prediction on the patient's behalf.

Relying on close, "interested" parties to determine accurately what the patient wants has its risks. Interested parties my not be objective, confusing their own interests with those of the patient. In contrast, court-appointed guardians acting as surrogate decisionmakers are substantially less likely to confuse patients' needs with their own. These guardians, of course, must go out and gather information about the patient – information that family and friends already have. Court appointment of guardians also ensures that patients who are alone, without relatives or other "natural" advocates, can still have the benefit of substituted judgment.[4]

Recently, courts and commentators have begun to realize with new clarity that reliance on judicial review of treatment decisions can be cumbersome, expensive, and time-consuming. Judicial review is also more likely to be abstract and "juiceless", and to result in conservative decisions (Burt, 1988; Wolf, 1990). Encouraging private decisional consensus where possible, perhaps with the help of a consulting ethics committee, is coming to be seen as more flexible, realistic, and potentially faithful to the patient's interests.

Whether the decisional forum is public or private, the authority enjoyed by family members according to substituted judgment is only the authority to provide to caregivers good-faith input on the patient's putative choice – to provide *evidence*. That this authority is unappealable by default in many cases does not necessarily mean the family has the right to decide; it means only that the family is presumptively the best means of discovering the patient's choice. Therefore, if there is reason to doubt that the family is best for this purpose, the caregiver (or a court if necessary) must rely not on the family but on the best proxy, who could be a friend, neighbor, or lover.

Many adults may be better represented by friends than by family members rendered distant geographically, temporally, or generationally. The difficulty is that in the absence of a written directive, it may not be easy for a caregiver to discern that a family member is not the best proxy, or that the family's choice reflects their own needs as much as it does the patient's interests. Some commentators (Dresser, 1986; Rhoden, 1988) have suggested that this is not a bad thing – that rigid separation of patients' interests from the interests of their moral communities is artificial, potentially impossible, and not particularly realistic or productive. Thus it is important that patients who wish to define their own moral communities and to distinguish their own wishes from the needs of their families write directives that can do so.

When an advance directive exists, the role of family and friends changes. No longer primary sources of evidence, family and friends become clarifiers and supplementers of the directive unless named as proxies. Family and friends do have a role and an interest in the honoring of any directive; where possible, they should be involved in the directive's formulation, or at least alerted to its existence while the author is still decisionally capable and can discuss it. However, families do not have the power to overrule or invalidate a directive because they disagree with it or are upset by it, and they should not be granted that power, unless it be by patients themselves. Only genuine, persuasive evidence from families that the directive should not be honored, for example because it is fraudulent or because the patient was mentally unbalanced, should be grounds for seeking consultation from an ethics committee or court.

The New Best Interests

The counterfactual contortions demanded by the substituted judgment standard in cases like *Saikewicz* have raised the question of whether substituted judgment really has a place in many cases (Annas, 1988; Dresser, 1986; Rhoden, 1988). Joseph Saikewicz's pain, fear, and resistance to blood transfusions and other aspects of his treatment just did not add up to a choice about treatment. Neither do patients with little or no accessible history present enough on which to base a genuine and distinctive choice. The introduction of substituted judgment permanently moved discussion beyond the patient's-choice-or-doctor's-choice dichotomy; but when information about patients and their preferences does not add up to enough to support a substituted judgment, it must be used in some other way.

Reexamining what the court did in the *Saikweicz* case led other courts, critics, and theorists to think more deeply about the best interests standard (Annas, 1979; Buchanan, 1979; Buchanan and Brock, 1986; Capron, 1984; Gutheil and Appelbaum, 1983; Hunter, 1985; President's Commission, 1983; Wolf *et al.*, 1987). The results of these efforts have been expounded extensively in the literature, and might be summed up in the following way: Patients make health care decisions in what they view as their own best interests. Their determination of their best interests comes from combining their own (nonmedical) beliefs and values; the physician's assessment of their best (medical) interests; and their preferences, feelings, and experiences. Thus, an advance directive or a true substituted judgment reflects the patient's best interests as the patient sees them. When a surrogate decisionmaker tries to determine what the patient would have wanted, the decisionmaker is determining the patient's best interests in this sense.

Joseph Saikewicz's beliefs and values were nonexistent or unknown. Medical opinion suggested that treatment could afford some chance of a short remission of his disease. Yet he responded to treatment with uncomprehending fear and pain that was harmful in itself and made treatment difficult and stressful. The court's reasoning about what he would have wanted could have been put this way: Because of his adverse response to treatment and his relatively small chance of a brief survival with the discomforts of treatment, it was in his best interests not to treat him.

This way of assembling the factors relevant to health care decisions on behalf of decisionally incapable patients has a satisfying consistency, as it places all information about the patient's preferences and probable choice on a continuum. A clear oral statement of the patient's wishes constitutes evidence equivalent to an advance directive. At the other end of the spectrum, an alone, unknown, comatose patient's future may be decided "objectively", solely according to medical judgment. In between, a "modified objective" standard can consider both "objective" medical information and "subjective" information about the patient's beliefs, values, and preferences, weighing each according to their persuasiveness. In 1976, the New Jersey Supreme Court refused to consider Karen Quinlan's conversations with friends about life-sustaining treatment in its decision about her because it rightly viewed them as casual, vague, and therefore not very helpful to its determination. But in a later decision introducing a "modified objective" standard of decision, the same court stated that it should have considered her statements, giving them only the weight they deserved, rather than disregarding them entirely because they were not decisive (*Matter of Conroy*, 1985).

Most courts now examine and weigh all such statements, and most find them persuasive. A few courts – for example, those in New York State and in Missouri – set very high evidentiary standards and have ordered treatment in cases where apparently reliable evidence, including advance directives and decisions by named proxies, supported the removal of treatment (*Cruzan v. Harmon*, 1988; *Evans v. Bellvue Hospital*, 1987). Distressing as these decisions are to patients and their advocates, they are still in a distinct minority. Moreover, reasonable decisions can still be made under such a "clear and convincing evidence" standard (Gianelli, 1990a; *In re A.K.*, 1989; *In re Guardianship of Browning*, 1990), and courts and legislatures are free to select less rigid evidentiary standards or to empower families as decisionmakers (Areen, 1987; *Cruzan v. Director*, 1990).

Acceptable Choice and the Quality of Life

Although it makes logical sense to employ this "new" best interests standard rather than substituted judgment in deciding on behalf of incompetent patients without advance directives, there is little reason to think that using different names will produce very different decisions, so long as the process is carefully undertaken under either standard. Whether both standards are equally likely to result in unacceptable quality of life judgments is a more difficult question to answer. Judicially reviewed decisions do, however, incorporate a brake against the temptation to devalue decisionally incapable patients: There are some choices that neither medicine nor society currently accepts as being in a patient's best interest, even if the patient is permanently incapacitated. Patients may autonomously make these choices, of course; but if they have neither done so nor left persuasive evidence that they would, it may be appropriate for surrogate decisionmakers to feel constrained not to make those decisions on their behalf. The range of choices acceptable under the new best interests standard will thus be somewhat narrowed, bounded by professional and societal consensus.[5]

Without a directive, many courts might hesitate to permit a proxy decisionmaker to refuse standard treatments that would undoubtedly prevent the death of patients not terminally ill – for example, antibiotics to cure pneumonia in a brain-injured but not comatose young adult. Artificial nutrition and hydration have been withdrawn from severely demented patients in some cases, where there is at least some evidence that the patient would have so chosen. Rebecca Dresser maintains that such decisions in the absence of directives rely excessively but covertly on the family's needs and interests and on quality of life judgments. She believes that although such factors do have some place in decisions, their role can only be appropriately limited if they are clearly acknowledged and balanced against whatever interests in continued life and/or potential recovery the incapacitated patient currently enjoys (Dresser, 1986). In a recent article, Nancy Rhoden takes a different approach, arguing persuasively for a presumption in favor of family choice when there is no directive (Rhoden, 1988).

Food and Fluids for Vegetative Patients: The Limits of Consensus

The withdrawal or withholding of artificial nutrition and hydration from patients in persistent vegetative states represents the single most troublesome and disputed choice to be faced in the absence of an advance directive. It pushes the boundaries of moral comfort for the community for two reasons: Patients in persistent vegetative states are arguably not "terminally ill" (many are projected to have nearly normal lifespans) and food and fluids, even delivered through sophisticated medical technology and therefore classifiable as "treatment", seem to have a symbolic, relational importance for caregivers and families that may make their nonprovision appear inhumane.

A few states have attempted to preclude patients from refusing nutrition and hydration by advance directive, or from refusing any treatment when in persistent vegetative states, for the foregoing reasons. Most courts, on the other hand, have been willing to withdraw nasogastric or gastrostomy tubes from patients in persistent vegetative states whose families are able to present credible evidence in support of their claim that the patient would have wanted withdrawal. Nonetheless, some states may continue to require that evidence of the patient's wishes be "clear and convincing" in order to overcome the state's interest in preserving the lives of patients when they are not terminally ill (*Cruzan v. Director*, 1990).

Ironically, continuing existence in a persistent vegetative state seems to be the archetypal situation that patients most wish to avoid ("I never want to be another Karen Ann Quinlan"). If more and more patients write directives and express wishes refusing artificially administered food and fluids and other interventions should they suffer from persistent vegetative state, perhaps the current reluctance to withdraw support from patients in persistent vegetative states will be overcome, making decisions easier for victims of accident or sudden illness, like Nancy Cruzan (*Cruzan v. Director*, 1990) and Paul Brophy (*Brophy v. New England Sinai Hospital*, 1986), who had no opportunity to write directives refusing artificial feeding. Indeed, a respected legal commentator has recently argued eloquently that withdrawal of nutrition and hydration from patients in persistent vegetative states is appropriate and cannot be construed as euthanasia (Cantor, 1989, 1990).

Clinicians should understand that "best interests" can have an expanded and comprehensive meaning that is able to account for the patient's individual character and choices to the maximum reasonable extent. If this new best interests standard is used for making decisions in the absence of a directive, clinicians, family, and friends may find the process of deciding for patients to be a little clearer – though not necessarily any easier.

"Mother's Day Syndrome" and Other Family Problems

How does one go about finding, and giving weight to, evidence about the patient's character and choices? Clinicians face many obstacles to the smooth resolution of treatment decisions. Perhaps the most mundane of these problems is lack of information about a patient. If sufficient information is not to be had, the temptation is to over-value the few pieces of information available, whatever their nature or source. The solution is simply to remember to weigh all information appropriately, especially when there is little to go on. The less information the clinician has about the patient, the more important prognosis and general medical information become.

Equally common, and more troubling, is having too much information that is conflicting and contradictory. What should the clinician do, for example, when a patient, who may or may not have written an advance directive, is demented and of questionable capacity, but is expressing choices? What if the choices flip-flop, or the patient's decision-making ability appears to wax and wane? Whether there is a directive or not, how is the clinician to pin the patient's "real" choices down?

And what about the patient whose family is in conflict, or the patient whose only child flies in from around the world after a 20-year absence from the family, and says "Father would have wanted everything!"? How should information from family members be regarded? May information from children thought to be exhibiting "Mother's Day Syndrome" – that is, children who seem to be afraid that any treatment withdrawal would label them uncaring and ungrateful survivors – be discounted as motivated by guilt? Or must the family be obeyed in all cases?

As stated earlier, any time an advance directive is in the picture, all other evidence of the patient's wishes must be viewed in its light. If any evidence the clinician has calls the directive's validity seriously into question (e.g., forgery of a signature, witness testimony that the patient was decisionally incapable at the time the directive was signed), only then may other information override the directive. Family disagreement calls for extremely sensitive management of the situation by the clinician, but it simply cannot justify disregarding a patient's advance directive. When there is doubt, the clinician should seek the assistance of an ethics committee or a court to make the best possible decision, if there is no other way to resolve the conflict. Private consensus may be used to reach a decision in the absence of a directive, or to interpret a directive without some outside consultation. The patient's autonomy requires that overriding the wishes clearly expressed in a directive should not be done lightly.

The patient with a directive should discuss it with family and friends when it is written. At the very least, family and friends should have notice of it, so that they may prepare to respect the patient's wishes even if they disagree with them. Perhaps an advocate for the patient will emerge, or be named by the patient, and be able to engage friends and family in fruitful discussion of the patient's wishes. To the extent that physicians and other caregivers can facilitate any of these things, they must do so. Ultimately, however, caregivers need to remember that although they have responsibilities toward their patients' families, their responsibilities to their patients are overriding when there is a conflict. If the directive can be honored, it must be honored, or turned over to one who will honor it. When there is a dispute in the family, the clinician who would otherwise honor a directive is not required to seek court approval before doing so simply because the family disagrees. Notice to the family of an intention to honor the directive is usually sufficient to permit the family to seek a court order if it wishes to do so.

Remember that, though family members are natural advocates for the patient, they have no automatic legal status as decisionmakers. Only the parents of minors and court-appointed guardians for minors and legally incompetent adults have that status. Unless a court or a special statute or an advance directive has said otherwise, the family of an incapacitated adult has only an evidentiary role, like the physician's, in determining the patient's wishes. The family possesses, and must assemble and examine, information about the patient in order to help determine what decisions will be in the patient's best interests. If the family's interests conflict with the patient's, their information is not reliable. If the patient has written a directive, their information is less persuasive. If the patient's most natural advocate is not a family member but a friend or a lover, that person's evidence should be most persuasive, especially when he or she has been named by the patient.

When there is no directive, or when there is a directive whose terms do not address the decision that is being faced, conflict in the family becomes more difficult to untangle. Caregivers must approach the decisions as a court would, by assembling and weighing all of the evidence to arrive at a decision that appears to be consistent with this patient's best interests. Discussing this decision and the evidence and reasoning underlying it with family and friends is a necessary first step. This includes the very difficult task of raising with family members any concerns that their stances are affected by their own grief and loss as well as by their regard for the patient's wishes.

Unless there are state laws in place giving to family members the authority to authorize termination of treatment for incapacitated adult patients in the absence of a directive,[6] there is, generally speaking, no legal requirement for the physician to seek a court's approval of a responsibly made decision about which the family disagrees (Areen, 1989). However, caregivers usually have far better access to legal resources, through their institutions, than families do. Caregivers should make sure that there is ample opportunity for discussion of the dilemma with the family, and the family should have the opportunity (perhaps even assistance) to seek a court resolution if it wishes, since the court is always available as the ultimate arbiter of who should properly choose for the patient. In making its determination, a court will assemble and critically examine the same sort of evidence as that already relied upon by the physician. Knowing this should help to reduce the physician's worries about involving the courts.

Courts in a growing number of states have declared their preference that decisions like this be made privately (Areen, 1987, 1988). Nonetheless, when disagreement persists, it may be necessary and is certainly appropriate to go to court for a final resoultion. Ethics committees offer excellent forums for examination of these disagreements as well (Hunter, 1985; King, 1988). Though committees must not make decisions, they should facilitate open and comprehensive discussion and can help resolve conflict and confusion without court involvement.

One problem faced by clinicians and family who must make choices for patients when there is no advance directive lies in determining how much evidence is enough. When this question is posed to the courts, they address it in terms of the evidentiary standards employed in civil suits. The burden of proof has thus fallen upon those seeking to show that the patient without a directive would have wanted treatment stopped, in the face of institutions and clinicians seeking to continue it. The ordinary civil standard of proof is "by a preponderance of the evidence", that is, more likely than not. Courts in several states – for example, New York and Missouri (*Cruzan v. Director*, 1990; *Cruzan v. Harmon*, 1988; *Evans v. Bellvue Hospital*, 1987; *In re A.K.*, 1989) have imposed a higher standard, that of "clear and convincing evidence"–which is more than a preponderance, but less than the criminal "beyond a reasonable doubt."

Caregivers have reasons to be concerned about the evidentiary standard applied in their states when disagreements about treatment in the absence of a directive reach the courts or when institutional policy favors treatment, because the effect of stringent standards of proof may be to presume that treatment is desirable, or desired, unless the patient's objections are "clear and convincing." Even if those objections fail to satisfy such a standard, however, the patient's best interests will not always require treatment, so that the existence of such standards still does not make clear what will happen when there is no directive. Patients and physicians in a jurisdiction whose courts apply the clear and convincing evidentiary standard will presumably be more successful in withholding and withdrawing treatment on the basis of an advance directive than without one, especially when the patient is not terminally ill or likely to die soon, or when the treatment in question includes artificial nutrition and hydration (See *Cruzan v. Director*, 1990). Of course, whenever there is no advance directive, physicians in all jurisdictions have the obligation to assemble evidence of the patient's preferences and to apply their best medical judgment in determining where the patient's best interests lie.

The Process of Decision

In sum, when directives are not available or not helpful, clinicians and others who would decide for the patient should determine the patient's best interest *as the patient would see it*. This means making use of as much evidence as is reasonably available of the patient's beliefs, values, preferences, and experiences,[7] as well as medical information and medical judgment. The credibility, relevance, and importance of all evidence must be assessed, and a decision must be reached on the basis of all of the evidence available. Conflicts within the family about decisions for the patient must be viewed in the light of the physician's duty to act in the patient's best interests. Where a state court or legislature has imposed a clear and convincing standard, the evidence available may not always meet this standard if there is no written directive, and sometimes judicial review may be advisable. Nonetheless, for the clinician, there is no essential difference between fulfilling the duty to the patient who has not written an advance directive and honoring a patient's advance directive. When a patient has conscientiously executed an advance directive, the physician's duty is simply that much easier to fulfill. Patients who have strong treatment preferences and patients who know or have reason to think that their families would make decisions for them that differ from those they would make for themselves will be much better assured of the decisions they want if they write directives – and if they discuss their directive beforehand with their families, their named proxies, and their physicians.

Interpreting Revocation

"And if I ever say I *do* want treatment, don't listen to me!" More and more frequently, the authors of advance directives are making declarations like this to their physicians, family members, and friends. People who seek to control their own future treatment decisions are becoming more sophisticated about the issues at stake, and more aware of threats to that control. The possibility of revocation is one such threat; so are caregivers' concerns about honoring the directives of patients who are chronically diminished in their mental capacity but not completely unresponsive. Many people who are alive today can expect to live for long periods with mild or severe irreversible cognitive impairment. They may not be able to interact with their surroundings to a meaningful extent, and they may not be able to make decisions for themselves (Callahan, 1987).

According to state living will statutes, all persons capable of giving a sign that is interpreted by someone as a revocation are considered to have revoked their directives. This wide-open revocation clause reflects a legislative preference for preserving life in the face of the irreversibility of directives – a discomfort that is often felt by caregivers, patients' families, and policymakers (Francis, 1989). Yet many authors of directives, concerned that well-meaning interference with their competent choices may result from the application of these clauses, are seeking ways to avoid "involuntary revocation." They have been trying to make their directives into arrangements that will stay binding on the physician no matter what they say later. Although completely precluding a change of mind is both wrong and impossible, perhaps some partial protection against involuntary revocation could be a good thing for some patients.

Consider the patient with chronic lung disease whose knowledge of her disease and familiarity with the experience of ventilator dependence in similarly affected relatives leads her to write a directive refusing, under any circumstances, to be placed on a ventilator.[8] She has discussed her decision thoroughly with her physicians and family; it is well-conceived, well-supported, and firm. During her first serious respiratory crisis, when she is frightened, in pain, and becoming obtunded, she is asked whether she would accept ventilator support and she says yes.

It is not clear whether this patient has the capacity to make autonomous decisions, though she is apparently on her way to becoming incapacitated. As we know, advance directives become effective only when the patient becomes decisionally incapable, so in this example, there is some question whether the directive has legal effect yet. But even if it does not, it clearly constitutes good evidence of the patient's views up to this point. Thus, whether this patient is decisionally capable or not, we must ask – just as we do in the classical "Ulysess contract", where Ulysses, tied to the mast of his ship and under the influence of the Sirens' songs, may or may not be decisionally capable – whether the patient's current wishes or her previous wishes should be honored.

We have already seen that to make sense of patients' rights to make autonomous decisions about their own health care, the standards used to measure the capacity for autonomous choice must be *minimal* standards (Danis *et al.*, 1988; Faden *et al.*, 1986). To encourage patients to exhibit high-level moral reasoning, have a coherent life plan and well-articulated values, and make forward-looking decisions that accord with a proper appreciation of all relevant facts and circumstances is to set standards that are vitally important as *guidelines* and *aspirations*. (See Chapter 2.) However, if these were *requirements*, so few people could meet them that health care decisionmaking would essentially be removed from the patient's control. Society permits apparently capable adults to make many important life decisions while under stresses and constraints of many kinds. There is no general requirement that decisionmaking be serene and pristine. Because there is no reason to treat health care decisions as fundamentally different from other decisions, to remove control of decisionmaking from patients by setting too high standards is unworkable and unfair.

It may nonetheless be thought prudent to require that the health care decisions accomplished by means of advance directives, because of their future-looking quality with its attendant increase in ignorance and uncertainty, must be "more autonomous" than other health choices. This may also unfairly invalidate some directives. However, advance directives that were not arrived at "more autonomously" are often less versatile, less easy for caregivers to understand and apply to the immense variety of clinical situations that may arise. If we wish to encourage patients to reflect a very high degree of decisional autonomy in their advance directives, even though they may not be required to, the problem of honoring revocations becomes even greater. Revocations of directives can exhibit high levels of autonomy, but are often less autonomous than directives and may even not be autonomous at all.

As a general rule, the more recent of two autonomous decisions should be honored (Buchanan and Brock, 1986). For advance directives, this means simply that a directive does not even become effective until the patient is decisionally incapable, since a patient with decisional capacity will be able to make an autonomous contemporaneous decision. Likewise, whenever an individual amends, updates, or even reaffirms a directive, a new autonomous decision is taking precedence over an old one. There is no hierarchy of autonomy among autonomous decisions (Faden *et al.*, 1986). The decisionally capable patient can decide on an impulse to tear up a document executed with the greatest of gravity, and a reaffirmation of a directive may require very little thought but still be autonomously made.

Ulysses had his crew tie him to the mast of his ship so that he could hear the Sirens' song. He told his men to ignore him when he asked to be released, as he knew he would do when he heard them sing. Was Ulysses capable of autonomous choice when he begged his crew to release him to the Sirens' allure? If he was, the reasoning above would require his release. If he was not, should not his prior directive prevent his release? Perhaps – except that here is a living, breathing, talking subject pleading with his crew, and that is a hard thing to ignore (Dresser, 1984; Winston *et al.*, 1982). Similarly, in drafting living will statutes, legislators and policymakers felt they could not ignore any patient's attempt to revoke a directive, because here the living person would be pleading not just to be released but to remain alive. Hence all statutory directives have revocation clauses that permit anyone to revoke a directive anytime, and in any way, regardless of decisional capacity.

But *should* a nonautonomous choice that comes later always trump a directive? Consider the case of the woman who finally agrees to go on a respirator. If we put her on the respirator and she regains full clarity of mind and requests that it be discontinued, and we do so, we have merely subjected her to a period of discomfort that might have been avoided. We run several risks by this course of action, however. If this patient is successfully weaned from the respirator, her change of mind may make us less willing to honor her directive the next time it comes up. We may feel the need to reexplore with this patient all of her expressed choices and preferences, to see whether they have changed as a result of this one change of mind. If she then reaffirms all of her other desires for refusing treatments, we may not quite believe her unless she writes and solemnizes a new directive.

A bigger risk of this course of action is that the patient may not regain her full decision-making capacity. Whether she becomes permanently respirator-dependent or is weaned from the respirator, she may not regain her previous level of mental ability. Instead she may fall anywhere on a continuum from complete unresponsiveness to mild dementia, fluctuating in her abilities or fixed at one level. Wherever she falls on the continuum of capacity, we will not be able to consult her for effective decisionmaking guidance. What has become of her directive? Can we use it as evidence of her wishes? But it was revoked. Or was only one of its provisions revoked? How do we know she would not also revoke other provisions now if she could? Should we make a practice of asking patients of questionable capacity whether they want the very treatments they have refused in their directives? Even if we do not, should we question whether any information about such a patient's past life and wishes has any value or relevance now?

The question of whether a revoked or partially revoked directive has value in future decisions about the care of the directive's author seems to have no better answer than that a careful evaluation of all of the circumstances is absolutely essential. The nature of the revocation is crucial, for a lot more can be learned from a decisive and spontaneous revocation than from an equivocal sound or gesture evoked from a seriously obtunded patient (Francis, 1989). A genuine and reliable complete or partial revocation should make a directive substantially less meaningful.

Revocation also calls into question other evidence of values and preferences, whether from the patient or from the patient's family, that is consistent with the directive and therefore inconsistent with its revocation – thereby potentially making decisionmaking after revocation of a directive even more problematic than it is when no directive was ever written. A possible solution is to construe all revocations as narrowly as appears possible under the circumstances. For example, a patient who revokes a refusal of ventilator support cannot necessarily be assumed to desire CPR. Decisions that appear to fall outside the scope of the revocation should be examined in light of all of the evidence ordinarily available about the patient's wishes, *including* consideration of the revocation itself. Decisions that appear to be substantially affected by the revocation are more appropriately decided by the "new best interests" standard – a reasonable consideration of medical judgment in light of the patient's values – than by simply doing everything in every case.

The decisional process after apparent revocation will be tricky, demanding, and controversial. Caregivers should not duck the challenge involved in decisions after revocation by switching to a life-at-all-costs policy, *except where* it is clear that this is what the patient intended to do by revocation; and it is unlikely that all revocations have this intended meaning.

Moreover, we cannot know for certain, in the case of the patient who revokes and does not regain decisional capacity, whether the revocation would stand if we could ask that patient again, magically and temporarily restored to capacity (as the court imagined Karen Quinlan when the substituted judgment standard was born). It is easy to imagine our ventilator patient saying, "Well, yes, I *did* revoke my directive; but I was confused and panicky then, and now, after that experience, I am clearer than ever about what I want." Imagining such reasoning for a patient who cannot now decide is consistent both with a declaration and with its revocation, and seems called for when the evidence appears overwhelming that the patient's revocation was "uncharacteristic." Yet such considerations appear to make it nearly impossible for a decisionmaker to stop oscillating between two poles: Relying on the values expressed in a directive or giving greater credibility to the revocation and its implications.

Decisionmakers who honor revocations will be stuck in that difficult oscillation. It seems unavoidable, and all that can be said is that they must honorably try to extricate themselves and their patients from it.

Revocation and the Future Factor

For the patient who pleads not to be listened to, there may be another solution: Establishing carefully limited circumstances under which the apparent revocation of an advance directive *should not be honored* for some patients. This possibility returns us to the problem of the "future factor", in a new guise, to be sure, but it is the same problem. Can caregivers rely on a patient's autonomous prior choice when some interpretations of the no-longer-autonomous patient's current interests would conflict with that choice?

Throughout this book it has been emphasized that the degree of autonomy patients are required to demonstrate, in making medical decisions generally and in writing advance directives in particular, is *not* higher than the basic minimal autonomy we all require of others in society when it comes to any significant self-regarding decisions in their lives – decisions, for example, about marriage, career, making investments, buying a home. It is just as vital for physicians to permit patients who are well-informed and acting freely to make decisions emotionally or impulsively or idiosyncratically, if that is their desire, as it is for physicians to encourage and support their patients in making scrupulously reasoned decisions that express their long-held values.

Physicians can and should do both these things without contradiction. The statement "You have a right to do this, but you are wrong to do so" embodies the physician's relationship to the patient who disagrees with medical advice – even when the patient's choice risks death.

Nonetheless, in order to be of genuine use to clinicians in making the choices patients want, advance directives should demonstrate a higher degree of reflection and foresight than patients' contemporaneous medical decisions must display. Thus, though *greater* decisional autonomy is not *required* for writers of advance directives, it will usually be there in a good directive.[9] Patients who are highly concerned that their wishes be understood and honored are well advised to take great care in conveying those wishes, and will naturally do so. They are setting for themselves a voluntary standard of high autonomy, in order to ensure their directive's effectiveness.

When these patients say "If I seem to revoke, don't listen", they are implicity claiming that the higher standard of autonomy reflected in their directives should outweigh the less autonomous revocations they are attempting to disown. Perhaps they are concerned that if they become demented as a result of Alzheimer's disease or other conditions in which the ability to communicate is less impaired than cognitive ability, they might *say* things that could be construed as revoking a directive – things that they do not now believe they could have the capacity to *mean*. These patients are claiming the right to value different actions, and changes in their moral identities, differently – claiming that they themselves should finally control the definition of their true selves, and rejecting an unknown, uncharacteristic, and diminished self.

The essence of this claim is no different from the claim that advance directives are valid even though, when they are applied, the patient's circumstances are changed. As discussed in Chapter 3, respect for the autonomy of decisionally capable patients with concern for their futures dictates that directives be honored, even when those patients have lost the current capacity to reaffirm the values on which their directives are based, precisely because those values are so important that the failure to honor them is a failure to respect the judgment and humanity of the decisionally capable patient. Patients who recognize the risk that their directives may not be followed have real concerns that their dignity will be violated and the meaning of their lives will be diminished if their choices are not followed, even though they also recognize that they may not fully perceive those violations at the time. It is undeniably troubling for caregivers to contemplate honoring a patient's directive when the now-incompetent patient could perhaps remain alive and without significant pain for some years, and perhaps there are instances where many caregivers would argue that the patient, in his or her directive, made a wrong decision. The real question is whether that moral uneasiness should outweigh the loss of trust, and the failure of respect for autonomy, that would result from a general reluctance to view directives as meaningful once the patient's decisional capacity is lost.

The claim that patients' choices about their own values and their own definitions of their true selves should control decisions about their treatment once their capacities have been irreversibly diminished appears in its most problematic form when the rejected self, though diminished and lacking mental capacity, has some capacity to respond to the environment and appears to want treatment the former, rejecting self has refused. If the patients who choose a higher standard of autonomy in writing their directives make explicit their desire to disavow purported revocations made when they lack decisional capacity, physicians and others asked to follow directives exemplifying these claims might be better prepared to implement them in the face of revocation. After all, it is common, and commonly regarded as admirable, for individuals to set for themselves higher than minimal standards in many areas – in moral behavior, in artistic, athletic, or academic achievement, in business or professional goals. Individuals who set high standards for themselves generally expect that other people will understand their reasons for setting high standards and will cooperate with their obedience to them. Thus, for example, a patient who has chosen a rigorous physical and mental rehabilitation program to maximize recovery from a stroke should be able to expect his or her physician's support in sticking to that regimen even though it is more ambitious than the physician usually prescribes. The general notion of sympathy with patients' self-imposed self-images and goals is a familiar and comfortable one.

However, applying that notion to directives and their revocation has somewhat different consequences. A patient who wishes to preclude nonautonomous revocations of a directive should state explicity, in writing and discussing the directive with caregivers, family, and friends, that the preparation of the directive reflects a high standard of autonomy, including careful reasoning, reflection, and foresight, and that any change in or revocation of the directive must exhibit a similarly high degree of autonomy in order to be valid. The directive should explain the reason for this unusual requirement – the author's high degree of concern for preserving these very important decisions and preferences against the risk that crises, illness, and diminished capacity could result in apparent changes of mind. The directive should state the patient's awareness that such a requirement is unusual in light of the revocation provisions in most directives, and give assurances of the patient's full understanding and accceptance of the consequences of this requirement.

Given such assurances, a clinician should feel able to implement a directive in the face of a revocation that does not appear comparably autonomous. In practical terms, a directive with these provisions enables the clinician not to *invite* revocation from the patient of questionable capacity – that is, not to ask whether the patient wants treatments previously refused. Instead, when the physician doubts the patient's decisional capacity, the patient might be told "We are doing X, and not doing Y, in accordance with your instructions" – thus giving the patient the opportunity to object but requiring the patient to be somewhat active in doing so. Patients who then object might be questioned as to whether they understand that their objection is a revocation of the directive they drafted especially to preclude revocation. This discussion should reveal to the physician whether the patient currently has the decisional capacity to revoke that this special provision of the directive requires. And of course, if the patient assures the physician that he or she is making a highly autonomous choice in revoking the directive, the revocation should be followed; it should *not* be possible to preclude *all* revocations categorically.

This kind of inquiry is fully in accord with the general process that physicians should follow anytime the patient has written a directive and a decision that is within the directive's province needs to be made. No directive takes effect until the patient has lost decisional capacity; but if the patient is functional and responsive to any degree, it may not be until the point of decision that the occasion arises to examine the patient's capacity.[10] Beginning this inquiry with a discussion of the existing directive can facilitate autonomous decisionmaking in patients of questionable capacity by reminding them of their own earlier thinking and placing their decision in a context of continuity with the past. This can readily be done in ways that do not pressure the patient's decision, either to conform to the directive or to repudiate it.

When the patient has documented and discussed a desire to minimize the likelihood of nonautonomous revocation, the clinician's role in this discussion is admittedly more difficult. It is certainly appropriate for clinicians to inform patients that they feel they cannot ignore apparent revocations, even though patients at the height of their capacity may really want that. The clinician who agrees to honor an "antirevocation" provision may face some very difficult decisions; patients cannot expect physicians to ignore every revocation, and the clinician will have to make individual judgments about the decisional capacity of patients seeking revocation.

Of course, even the most clearly and persuasively reasoned antirevocation provision, obeyed in good faith by a scrupulous physician and approved by a hospital ethics committee, might not survive legal challenge by a family member or other interested party. Public policy has good reasons for favoring ready revocation of advance directives. Nonetheless, highly motivated individuals who explicitly and specifically disagree with that policy as applied to themselves should have the opportunity to have their reasonable wishes honored by a willing physician.[11] If the advice herein is carefully followed, legal challenges are unlikely to be successful; but the prudent physician should be realistic enough to prepare to face legal challenge in such cases, and the reasonable patient must recognize and be prepared to live with the powerful moral and emotional barriers to acceptance of antirevocation clauses.

Conclusion

The patient's right to make his or her own medical decisions is one-half of the working basis for the physician-patient relationship, regardless of the patient's current capacity to make choices. The other half of the basis of the relationship is the physician's duty to use professional skill and judgment in the patient's best interests. Taken together, these two central principles comprise the general standard of medical decisionmaking: the patient's best interests as the patient sees them. The physician's expert judgment is directed toward formulating an opinion as to the patient's best medical interests and informing and advising the patient about the best course of action in the physician's opinion. The patient then has a moral responsibility to consider the physician's advice, but will also consider personal nonmedical values, preferences, experiences, and beliefs as important decision-making factors.

When the patient lacks current decision-making capacity, the standard of decision remains unchanged and the factors (from both physician and patient) that enter into the decision remain unchanged. There are, however, different decisional processes that can be used. One is the process of implementing an advance directive – whether an instruction directive or a proxy directive. If there is no directive, a substitute decisionmaker – one not named by the patient in a document – is identified, formally or informally, to examine and decide on the basis of those same factors.

When not made available in a directive, these factors will be found in the patient's past expressions, current apparent preferences, and medical condition. The decisionmaker may be a family member, friend, physician, court, or court-appointed guardian. Assistance and advice may come from other caregivers or even from a hospital ethics committee. Although advance directives are the best evidence of a patient's wishes, the same kind of evidence of patients' wishes is vital in every case.

If there is no directive, many decisions will accord with what the physician advises, largely for lack of other evidence of the patient's wishes. When there is a directive, however, and the physician hesitates for any reason to rely completely upon it, the standard of decision to be used still points to the directive. As a principal source of information about the patient, directives always have some role to play in determining what the patient would have wanted.

Notes

[1] The term "living will" was coined in 1969 by Louis Kutner (Kutner, 1969).

[2] It is important to recognize that the U.S. Supreme Court, when it permitted states to require clear and convincing evidence of a decisionally incapable patient's wish to refuse artificial nutrition and hydration (*Cruzan v. Director*, 1990), did *not* thereby rule that persons without written directives had chosen treatment. The *Cruzan* Court left largely unspecified the means by which patients could meet their evidentiary burdens, left the states free to choose a less demanding standard of proof (as many already have), and made clear that the reason for imposing a standard that might result in failure to act in accordance with some evidence of the patient's wishes is not a presumption about what those wishes are, but rather a desire to protect the best interests of decisionally incapable patients. Moreover, the facts faced by the Court only concerned refusal of artifical nutrition and hydration on behalf of a patient in a persistent vegetative state. Thus, the Court's willingness to permit states to look carefully at those particular refusals does not necessarily imply a similar willingness in the face of different treatment decisions regarding patients in different circumstances.

[3] It is beyond the scope of this book to address comprehensively the theory or policy whereby medical treatment decisions in default of advance directives are and should be made. There is a vast and growing literature on this subject; some important and comprehensive discussions may be found in Buchanan and Brock (1986); Burt (1988); Cohen (1991); Dresser (1986); Meisel (1989); President's Commission (1983); Rhoden (1988); Ruark *et al.* (1988); Steinbrook and Lo (1988); Weir and Gostin (1990); and Wolf *et al.* (1987).

[4] See the debate about these issues in Annas (1979), Baron (1978, 1979), Buchanan (1979), and Relman (1978).

[5] This reasoning largely parallels that of the Supreme Court in *Cruzan v. Director* (1990), though it would permit more nontreatment decisions than would the State of Missouri. According to this new best interests standard, the withdrawal of artifical nutrition and hydration has been accepted in a number of cases (*Brophy v. New England Sinai Hospital*, 1986; *Delio v. Westchester County Medical Center*, 1987; *In re Jobes*, 1987; *In re Peter*, 1987). Withholding treatment from a demented victim of a serious but treatable condition is a much more controversial proposition, even though competent patients, like Dax Cowart, Elizabeth Bouvia (*Bouvia v. Superior Court (Glenchur)*, 1986), William Bartling (*Bartling v. Superior Court*, 1984), or Beverly Requena (*In re Requena*, 1986), may autonomously refuse care.

Decisionmaking without advance directives will in many cases be difficult at best, because the issues are so complex, our convictions are so diverse, and legal guidance for many of the situations caregivers face is still quite imperfect. An example of an increasingly common dilemma is the elderly nursing home resident without an advance directive who has severe Alzheimer's disease and other chronic debilitating conditions, who is somewhat responsive to her environment and somewhat ill and unhappy, and who suddenly becomes acutely septic or develops a treatable pneumonia. Somebody – one or all of the members of the health care team, or one or all of the family members, who may be involved and caring or deeply divided – suggests not treating the patient with antibiotics, so that she will peacefully die (Brown and Thompson, 1979). Somebody else disagrees.

Disagreement in cases like this can at least ensure that all relevant information about the patient's current experience, prognosis, and past preferences and values is considered. The willingness of family, friends, and caregivers to discuss disagreements openly greatly increases the likelihood of reaching a decision that all parties can accept as in the patient's best interests as she would view them. See, e.g., Tomlinson and Brody (1988). But there are no firm rules here, and none of the circumstances that make some cases "easy"; no one clearly holds the decisional authority, and there is no terminal illness, no respirator in place, no do-not resuscitate order to discuss. It is still likely that at least some such disagreements will end in anger, bitterness, and the courtroom.

[6] Authorizing someone to make the decision requires a determination, or at least a presumption, that the person chosen will make the decision on the basis of the best evidence. Special statutes usually require some degree of consensus among family members in order to protect against self-interested decisions by relatives, and courts will scrutinize the motives of would-be decisionmakers for the same reason. In the absence of a legal proxy, then, disagreement between physicians and family requires careful scrutiny of the evidence and reasoning behind the opposing contentions, but the decision itself "belongs" to no one in particular. Although the family's approval under these circumstances is not required, hospital lawyers routinely advise obtaining approval from the family or from the court as a prudential matter.

Special statutes are, however, becoming more common. The Uniform Rights of the Terminally Ill Act (1990) now includes a provision permitting withdrawal of treatment from terminally ill persons without advance directives upon consent of specified relatives, who are given in order of priority in an extensive list. This provision is likely to influence state law.

[7] One means of recording patients' preferences that does not amount to writing a directive is the 'values history', which appears to be gaining popularity in long-term care settings (Lambert *et al.*, 1990).

[8] I am indebted to Erich Loewy, whose presentation of a similar case at the Society for Health and Human Values Annual Meeting, Arlington, Virginia, November 1987, helped to illuminate this problem for me.

[9] See Chapter 3 for further discussion of this important point.

[10] This works both ways: Because the patient's capacity may vary, a new inquiry may be needed at the time of decision even if the patient is already thought to be incompetent.

[11] There is clearly a risk here that this "antirevocation" maneuver will simply focus all of the most difficult questions on this clause rather than on the entire directive – without the benefit of the assurances and safeguards provided to the clinician by standard revocation clauses. The problem is undeniable. Nonetheless, there is also an undeniable need to address patients' strong desires on this very question. This is one way to do so. It is legally unproven; yet the moral underpinnings of advance directives suggest that it merits exploration.

Chapter Six

The Forecast For Advance Directives:
Indispensable or Superfluous?

> Because death is so profoundly personal, public
> reflection on it is unusual....[H]owever, such reflection
> must become more common if we are to deal
> responsibly with the modern circumstances of death
> (*Cruzan v. Director*, 1990, p. 4936 [(J. Stevens,
> dissenting)]).

Advance directives are popular these days. Patient advocacy groups, medical
ethics "think tanks", attorneys, and many health care institutions are
promoting them to patients and providers as useful and even indispensable
documents. Advocacy groups send subscribers wallet-size laminated "living
will" cards containing toll-free numbers for a central registry that can supply
callers with the full text of the patient's directive in emergencies. "Medic
Alert" bracelets, ordinarily used to alert emergency personnel to a patient's
health problems, have been designed to alert caregivers to the patient's
refusal of hospitalization and treatment (see *In re Finsterbach*, 1990). Federal
legislation has been passed requiring health care facilities to promote advance
directives in order to receive Medicare and Medicaid dollars (Patient Self-
Determination Act, 1990). At the same time, however, institutions, caregivers,
and sometimes patients' families fight hard to continue care for decisionally
incapable patients and to promote policies that preserve life and discourage
the cessation of treatment before death. This stark opposition could be a sign
of healthy diversity of values in a pluralistic culture; it could represent the
adversary viewpoints necessary, as in a court of law, for distilling the proper
perspective; or it could demonstrate collective ambivalence and confusion
over what advance directives are all about.

Advance Directives and Moral Communities

Widespread promotion of advance directives has its dangers, perhaps the greatest of which is that directives will be perceived as documents that lay down the law and close the conversation (Johnson, 1987). This book has sought to demonstrate that, on the contrary, advance directives *continue* the conversation between physician and patient. The sharing of responsibility in the doctor-patient relationship precludes patients from simply demanding compliance with directives, and frees clinicians from simply being either "compliant" or "noncompliant" with patients' demands, permitting them instead to be genuinely responsive to patients' wishes.

The idea that the physician-patient relationship should embody a continuing conversation and a sharing of the decision-making process (Katz, 1984; Szasz and Hollender, 1956) is hardly a new one, and it has its critics, both among those who believe that such mutuality can too easily threaten the autonomy of patients (Baron, 1987) and those who believe that patients are unable to participate equally in such a relationship (Ingelfinger, 1980). Authors of advance directives have a particular stake in characterizing the physician-patient relationship in this way, however: Directives are help-seeking documents by their very nature. Directives ask for the cooperation of caregivers, family, and friends in honoring the wishes they express. Though some directives ask only that others refrain from acting, while some clearly require actions, all directives nonetheless ask others to take a posture of assistance. In this way they create what Raymond Duff (1988) has called "moral communities." Patients who cannot leave the hospital against medical advice, or assert their own rights for themselves, must rely upon these created moral communities of decision to honor their wishes. We can, if we wish, use only the terminology of rights when talking about advance directives, but that language alone does not seem to capture the felt responsibilities of caregivers, nor to account adequately for all patients' needs for support and care at the end of life.

If we think of advance directives as creating moral communities, it seems almost inevitable that our view of the entirety of the decisionmaking process within the physician-patient relationship must become richer and deeper. Like the housekeeper who polishes the silver only to find that, in order to do the silver justice, the table must also be polished, the dining-room windows washed, and the new candlesticks set out, physicians who accept membership in the created moral communities of patients who write advance directives will soon see the need to begin their conversations with patients early in the relationship, and to engage their patients as fully as feasible in the decisionmaking process, in order to be prepared to do justice to the decisions that may come later and the directives that may follow.

When clinicians recognize that it is permissible for patients to write advance directives, and therefore it is right to try to implement them, they must then confront a natural human reluctance to raise difficult questions with patients. But that is just half the problem. If directives are to continue the conversation, how can a clinician who meets a decisionally incapacitated patient and his or her directive at the same time know whether that conversation was ever begun?

There is an easy answer: All who encounter a directive must presume it is the product of an autonomous decisionmaking process. Even the briefest and barest of directives, if it has a signature, a witness, some statement indicating the writer's seriousness of purpose and understanding of the consequences of honoring it, provides enough to support that presumption and therefore requires the clinician to try in good faith to apply it. If it cannot be applied to the decision at hand, that is because the language in the directive cannot be made to fit the facts and circumstances – *not* because the directive as a whole is somehow untrustworthy because the clinician faced with implementing it could not talk with the patient. Many directives may not be easy to apply to specific facts; but if the effort is made, and the directive is not discarded outright, it still stands as evidence that this patient had some concerns about end-of-life decisions, about oppressive treatment, about "dying well." Recognition of these concerns will help direct the clinician's further inquiry about the patient and the patient's wishes.

Moreover, as advance directives become more popular, more widely employed, and more familiar, more clinicians will talk with patients about their directives, and "corroborating evidence" of the patient's wishes will be easier to find in the medical record, in the directive itself, in the appointment of a proxy, the report of family and friends, and statements from other caregivers who observed or took part in discussions while the patient still had decisional capacity. Clinicians will come to expect such evidence, and to provide it routinely for the benefit of other clinicians who may encounter the patient and the directive. As doctors and patients communicate better and share the process of medical decisionmaking, end-of-life decisions should become easier to make.

This vision is highly optimistic, and perhaps only partially warranted. It is also possible that directives might never step fully into the system of medical records, physicians' orders, and institutional policies that control health care decisionmaking for most patients, remaining always just one of a number of competing and overlapping decisional priorities that need to be waded through by clinicians, or even becoming obsolete.

Are Directives Cost Containers?

How could this happen? Well, it could happen as a result of a misunderstanding of what directives are really all about. The argument of this book is that directives are about patients' choices, a way of preserving the patient's choices about certain important matters under certain adverse circumstances. But the very great majority of directives address themselves exclusively to refusing treatment. If it could be said that directives were really about refusing treatment, even about "the right to die", then it could be argued that directives will become obsolete as soon as we face enough system-wide cost containment pressure. After all, there is no need to refuse treatment that is not available or not offered.

Indeed, many factors other than patients' choices are beginning to influence the general views of both physicians and society about prolonged intensive end of life treatment. Cost containment pressures from government payers, from insurers, and from capitation model health care delivery systems; the need to increase the supply of donated organs; concern for the just allocation of scarce resources (such as intensive care beds); and extensive public discussion of individual treatment termination controversies are among the factors that appear to be moving us, however slowly, toward a social consensus about the moral impropriety of continuing treatment as far as it has heretofore been continued. There is no agreement about when is too far or how much is too much; but in the future, substantial agreement may be possible about the appropriateness of stopping at some point short of obvious futility.

If advance directives were simply a way of ensuring that patients are not "overtreated", they would become superfluous in a climate that discouraged overtreatment even in the absence of directives. Some clinicians might prefer this, finding it artificial to view advance directives in a way that purports to separate the patient's right of choice from clinical and policy judgments that less care is better. Day-to-day hospital practice presents a range of questions about treatment in which the matter of advance directives occasionally bobs up like a cork in the sea. It may appear, to clinicians and others whose first concern is giving good care in the hospital setting, that the easier and more logical approach to managing care in a highly complex setting is to develop and coordinate guidelines, policies, and procedures sanctioning less care for some patients in some illness categories. Thus, much attention is given to guidelines for termination of treatment for dying patients; Do-Not-Resuscitate policies and practices; the establishment of hospital ethics committees; and discussions of when nontreatment should be considered and for which patients, with the aim of bringing hospital practice into harmony with the recognition that doing less can be better (Cranford and Doudera, 1984; Engelhardt and Rie, 1986; New York State Task Force, 1986; President's Commission, 1983; Steinbrook and Lo, 1988; Teel, 1975; Tomlinson and Brody, 1988; Weinberg, 1988; Wolf *et al.*, 1987). The impact of existing policy, malpractice concerns, the involvement of nonphysician caregivers, even payment issues and "turf" disputes, all must be dealt with in order to accomplish that aim – and all help to dwarf advance directives as an issue. When the central question is how best to terminate treatment for a selected category of patients, advance directives are minor: nice things to have, but neither necessary nor sufficient, nor even the best way to terminate treatment.[1]

If, however, advance directives are viewed not as one means of giving less care but as a primary means of accomplishing the primary goal of mutual decisionmaking to serve the patient's perception of his or her own best interests, advance directives are not minor but crucial. Bringing hospital practice into harmony with patients' choices is conceptually different from a selective retreat from the medical-technological imperative in the name of better care – even though many outcomes will be much the same. If the patient's choice is central, caregiving relationships, policies, and practices will be geared to eliciting patients' choices. If there are to be limits placed on those choices by other important priorities and interests – such as cost containment, resource scarcity, and medical necessity – the conflict must be openly acknowledged and directly faced.

It is sometimes assumed that ethical caregiving and "death with dignity" always mean doing less for and to patients. Advance directives are associated with treatment refusal and the end of life; thus, there is a strong identification between the freedom of choice and the freedom to refuse treatment. Yet less care is not always what patients who wish to direct their care either want or need. As caregivers know, "death with dignity" implies as much emphasis upon the humane and supportive qualities of the patient's care as upon the termination of the lifesaving components of that care (Schiffer, 1987).

Advance directives are the primary means of ensuring that as many treatment decisions as possible are made by the patient rather than by someone else, or by a trusted proxy rather than a stranger. Yet because they emerged historically in response to a medical-technological imperative that appeared to attempt to evade death, directives are easy to misconstrue as only means of refusing treatment.

The reasons given by state legislatures for enacting living will laws, as expressed in the preambles and general purpose clauses of those laws, often demonstrate this mixture of meanings. North Carolina's statutory purpose clause is a good example:

> The General Assembly recognizes as a matter of public policy that an individual's rights include the right to a peaceful and natural death and that a patient or his representative has the fundamental right to control the decisions relating to the rendering of his own medical care, including the decision to have extraordinary means withheld or withdrawn in instances of a terminal condition (North Carolina Natural Death Act, 1983, § 90-320(a)).

This one sentence acknowledges three "rights": the right to a certain kind of death, the right to control one's treatment, and the right to refuse treatment, at least in the case of terminal illness.

Despite its popularity as a term (cf. Cohen, 1991; *Cruzan v. Director*, 1990; Meisel, 1989), the "right to die" has always seemed an odd sort of right to have, since it amounts to a right to do something about which, in the long run, no choice exists. Defining some deaths but not others as "natural" is also semantically troubling: it would seem that either all deaths are natural because everyone's death is naturally inevitable, or no death could be natural in a hospital or when the patient is connected to monitors, IVs, or any other "unnatural" accoutrements of medical technology. The right to a *peaceful* death is perhaps easier to understand, but when it stands alone we cannot tell whether it means that patients can require others to do things to make their deaths peaceful or merely require that others refrain from disturbing the peace of their deaths.

The other two rights recognized by the North Carolina legislature are less ambiguous. Refusal of treatment is a fairly straightforward negative right, the right to be left alone. The right to control one's treatment is much like the right to informed consent: Patients have the positive right to receive information and choose among therapies, or the negative right not to be touched unless the positive right to choose has been honored.

"Request" Directives

Is there some component of positive right associated with advance directives — the right to elect certain treatments or to have a certain kind of dying experience? Let us examine "request" directives, where patients ask for what has been irreverently but vividly labeled the "full-court press." This request, though rarely encountered in written directives, is far from unheard of. Some Orthodox Jews and followers of Islam even have difficulty accepting "brain death" as death. Many other patients, whether their motivations stem from belief in the sanctity of life or from fear of being disvalued by others when gravely ill, may choose to instruct their physicians to "do everything possible" (Zugler, 1989).

If directives are really more about patients' own choices than about refusing rather than receiving treatment, then it seems it should follow that "affirmative" directives, where extensive treatment is sought, should be honored just as readily as the more common directives refusing treatment. Nonetheless, we ought to question whether they should be viewed in exactly the same light as refusal directives, especially if we believe that society must move toward withholding and withdrawing care for patients in some cases.

This problem is often answered by observing that physicians cannot be compelled to do anything that is not in accordance with their medical judgment, and therefore, affirmative "request" directives and refusal directives may legitimately be treated differently. Refusal directives must be honored because patients may refuse any treatment, medical judgment notwithstanding, but some request directives cannot be honored without forcing physicians to *act* in derogation of their medical judgment, and such directives need not be honored (Brett and McCullough, 1986; Schneiderman *et al.*, 1990; Tomlinson and Brody, 1988).

This way of distinguishing between request directives and refusal directives defines them as embodying positive and negative rights, respectively. To say that physicians (or anyone) cannot be compelled to act against their will is to say that they do not have positive duties, duties to act affirmatively to uphold a patient's positive right to treatment. Refusals are different because the duty they impose upon caregivers is only to refrain from acting. Traditionally, in legal and moral reasoning, negative rights are much easier to identify and enforce than positive rights, and are seen as preferable in a society oriented to independence and autonomy. Positive rights – for example, the claimed right to health care itself – are considered hard to define and potentially burdensome.

This distinction, though superficially valid, is ultimately unsatisfying as a justification for honoring refusal directives but not request directives, because it implies that the physician's role in treatment refusal is a negative, hands-off posture. Every advance directive, regardless of its provisions, makes a limited positive claim on every attending physician who encounters it. First, the physician must read the directive and determine whether it can be applied to provide a decision under the circumstances. Second, if (and of course only if) the directive can be applied, the attending physician must implement it or pass it on to one who will. Failure to act on a directive that can be implement is not by itself blameworthy; but it is unprofessional, and morally wrong, to ignore a directive or to refuse to implement it without making reasonable efforts to find a physician who will. This is true for instruction directives, which require the physician to determine whether they can be implemented under the circumstances, and for proxy directives, which require the physician simply to recognize the surrogate decisionmaker and then either accept the surrogate's decision or pass it on. A directive is the vehicle for delineating the physician-patient relationship after the patient has lost the capacity to do so directly. There is either treatment by mutual agreement, or termination of the relationship without abandonment, by passing the care to a willing other.

Withholding treatment, withdrawing treatment, and providing treatment are therefore all positive acts in a meaningful moral sense. The relationship between physician and patient is mutual and complex and thus, even while the physician is not free to act without the patient's consent, the physician's action is not one of bare agency for the patient. The physician is responsible for assessing the directive in good faith and then, if it can be implemented, doing so or passing it on. The patient's choice drives the physician-patient relationship, but *everything* the physician does in accordance with that choice – including nothing at all – is an exercise of the physician's moral agency as well. Directives require clinicians to take responsibility for them; passing a directive on to one who will implement it is a responsible action and should be felt as such. By the same token, implementing a directive is not mere compliance; it, too, is a responsible act.

When an entire medical staff refuses to withdraw respiratory support from a comatose patient, or when the hospital has a policy against treatment withdrawal, law will term the continuation of unwanted treatment legal battery, and the patient can successfully sue for discontinuation of treatment and for damages from continued treatment. The Ohio decision *Leach v. Shapiro* (1984) is the first to explicitly acknowledge the patient's right to bring such a lawsuit,[2] though the characterization of unwanted treatment as battery has existed for centuries. According to this battery viewpoint, continuation of treatment, the failure to stop, is not distinguished from starting in the first place.

The physician also has the right to withdraw from any relationship so long as the patient is not abandoned. Of course, the physician who seeks to withdraw from a relationship in which the patient seeks the withdrawal of treatment also wants to leave the patient with the mechanisms of life support in place; yet physicians who refuse to withdraw treatment commit battery just as much as those who institute treatment without authorization. However, the courts generally permit a physician who objects to withdrawing treatment to pass the task on to a willing substitute, since by doing so the physician ensures that treatment is not continued even though someone else withdraws the treatment.[3] But what if there is no willing substitute? More and more often lately, treatment refusal cases have quickly become notorious, and physicians and institutions may be reluctant to become involved in notorious cases. If no physician within the institution will act, and there is no place willing to accept transfer of the patient, may the physician or the institution be required to withdraw treatment?

The answer in the law so far is a hesitant yes. When the patient's rights and interests in withdrawing from treatment are weighed against the physician's and institution's interests in acting according to their own values, the patient's rights are paramount (Annas, 1987; *In re Jobes*, 1987; *In re Requena*, 1986). But there are a number of open questions remaining; for example, what if the patient had timely notice of the physician's or the institution's policies against withdrawing treatment (Miles *et al.*, 1989)? And what if the patient's needs include the provision of palliative care and pain relief and other desired treatments, in addition to withdrawal or withholding of treatment? Must these needs too be met by some unwilling physician?[4]

Suppose a patient writes an advance directive wanting "everything" done in case of permanent coma, and the attending physician firmly believes that doing everything is wrong. We seem to be requiring a great deal of withdrawal action from physicians who *would* do everything; why should we not similarly require physicians to leave life support in place, which does not seem to be as much to ask?

This is the same question raised in treatment refusal cases that examine the state's interest in maintaining the integrity of the medical profession. As we saw in Chapter 2, the courts have found that the decision to refuse treatment is one that professional values can support. But are there some decisions to continue treatment that are beyond the pale of professional values (Schneiderman *et al.*, 1990)? If the answer is no, it appears to make it impossible for physicians to end relationships with patients, and we know that physicians are always free to end relationships so long as they do not abandon patients. Yet if there is nowhere else for the patient to turn, the law of abandonment might suggest that the physician cannot refuse to treat. This issue is arising with ever greater frequency with regard to the patient's ability to pay. Certainly a patient who can afford continued treatment is highly likely to find some physician who will give it; but with the changing health care financing climate, insurers and other payers are becoming more reluctant to view all end-of-life care as "necessary."

When the issue of payment for care enters the picture, the distinction between refusal and request directive is reasserted in a different way. Although the patient's right to the physician's respectful consideration of his or her directive is the same for both types of directive, many request directives also incorporate positive claims on resources that exceed those made by refusal directives and may also exceed the resources available. Thus, the central question to be asked about request directives is not whether caregivers should honor them, but whether there are other interests present that can override the patient's request for continued treatment. If the patient's choice cannot always rule the decisionmaking process, whose can outweigh it? The physician's? The payor's? Society's? When a physician refuses to perform a procedure, is that refusal valid when based on medical judgment? On professional values? On personal values? May society ask the physician to limit treatment based on social or fiscal policy? May social policy prevent a willing patient and a willing physician from undertaking some care?

Medical Judgment and Advance Directives

Can medical judgment outweigh the patient's decision? It is difficult to define medical judgment, to determine whether it can or should be free from the influence of professional and personal values. Every decision about whether to begin the sixth resuscitation in 24 hours on a failing patient, whether to transplant a third or fourth or fifth liver into a child, whether to risk last-ditch surgery on an unstable patient or to treat another bout of *Pneumocystis* pneumonia in an AIDS patient – all these choices have components of personal values and risk assessment such that the *patient's* desire to make those last efforts, just as much as the *patient's* desire to forgo them, should be decisive. But physicians' values are implicated in these choices as well. Will we then require physicians to do what they believe to be harmful to the patient, medically futile, and wasteful?

No, we need not. Again we must examine the nature of the request that all advance directives make. "Do everything" cannot be read to require the medical profession to give care that is not medically indicated (Brett and McCullough, 1986; Schneiderman *et al.*, 1990; Tomlinson and Brody, 1988, 1990), unless society finds specific reason to disagree with the profession's assessment. This is likewise the case for directives refusing treatment. After all, physicians often think that withdrawing treatment is medically inadvisable. However, recognizing the possibility of a clash of values, society has explicitly recognized the patient's right to withdraw "against medical advice."

Physicians faced with a patient's directive to "do everything" must be aware that their own personal values figure into their medical judgments, and that it is precisely here where patients' differing values must be respected as far as possible. The physician who helps a patient draft such a directive, or who has the opportunity to talk with the patient about it, must take all such opportunities to understand the values underlying the patient's choice. Differences in views of the quality of life, the importance of suffering, the meaning of "futile" and the like all must be resolved in the patient's favor, whether the directive refuses treatment or requests it.

However, a directive that attempts to bind the physician to a specific list of treatments without permitting the exercise of medical judgment (e.g., "I want a liver transplant" expressed by a medically unsuitable candidate) cannot be made binding upon any one physician unless the physician specifically accepts these terms – that is, unless the physician is willing to go along with the patient's attempt to make this directive no longer a directive but a contract. The patient who refuses to give consent for a DNR order need not be resuscitated if in the physician's judgment the resuscitation will not succeed (Tomlinson and Brody, 1988, 1990). Yet the patient who will survive after resuscitation, even briefly, maintains the right to choose that extension of life though the physician may disagree with that value choice (Tomlinson and Brody, 1988, 1990; Zugler, 1989).

The Impact of Scarcity and Cost

There has as yet been little discussion of whether continuation of treatment is socially desirable. Discussions of financing and rationing have only recently begun to turn explicitly toward this question (Callahan, 1987, 1990; Churchill, 1987; Engelhardt and Rie, 1986). What happens to the role of advance directives when social policy favors limiting patients' access to scarce resources and costly treatments (Emanuel, 1987)? When the backdrop against which patients declare their choices changes, will our views of acceptable choices change as well?

We have already agreed about some things. Society can pass brain-death statutes that are opposed by some religious groups. It can ration organ distribution so that a rich Johnny-come-lately cannot bump others off the transplant list. However, societal power to do such things should be carefully circumscribed, its rationale should be explicit, its necessity should be demonstrated convincingly, and its restrictions should be the least onerous possible.

One of the most provocative issues raised by the new cost-consciousness is the tension between individual rights and interests and the collective good. We have been particularly schizophrenic about this tension when it comes to health care (Callahan, 1987, 1990; Churchill, 1987; Mariner, 1988). Indeed, it seems ironic that patients' rights proponents devote so much argument to overcoming caregivers' strong beneficent impetus to do as much as possible to preserve the lives of patients who do not view their own benefit as their caregivers do, while at the same time we are beginning to realize that at the social policy level, cost considerations are becoming powerful reasons to offer less care (Callahan, 1987, 1990; Engelhardt and Rie, 1986). We are floundering in the attempt to determine whether the very old, severely handicapped infants, or transplant candidates should have access to all the resources they want at public expense, while we still aggressively debate the wisdom of treatment refusal with individual patients.

Caregivers often fail to recognize the extent to which considerations of cost are inextricably woven into their own health care decisions about their patients. The simplest and most obvious sign of this intimate relationship is the ethical proposition that physicians may choose whom they will serve. A critical implication of this traditional professional prerogative is not merely the right to choose only insured patients or to refuse Medicaid patients, but also to *limit one's patient load* to a number that makes it possible to serve well the patients one already has.

All good patient care has cost factors built in, in the form of time. Some minimum length of visit is necessary for good caregiving, as is a maximum number of patients seen per day. Very similar considerations govern institutional decisions about staffing of physicians and other health care personnel, the provision of ancillary services, and the filling of beds. A recent malpractice case that identified intensive care unit overbedding as the cause of harmful neglect of an accident victim is merely the first step toward open discussion of the competing needs of patients. Such discussion necessarily entails a comparison of the likelihood and magnitude of benefit to each patient from each intervention – essentially a cost-effectiveness comparison (Engelhardt and Rie, 1986).

Yet acknowledging the integral role of cost in all health care decisions does not answer the question of whether advance directives should have cost containment functions. Some patients refuse treatment in order to spare their families from the financial ruin that can attend catastrophic illness. This can be a valid and autonomous choice, however tragic such a choice may be.

However, many state "living will" statutes contain clauses that prohibit health insurers from making the execution of an advance directive a condition of insurance coverage. Most such statutes also contain clauses declaring that the death of a patient who refuses treatment by means of an advance directive shall not be considered suicide for any purpose – including denial of life insurance awards, which do not pay benefits for suicides. Thus, two very different sorts of attempts by insurers to save money through advance directives are forestalled by such clauses. On the other hand, persons who have written advance directives refusing treatment have for some time been maintaining that insurers should be free to offer lower rates to them by virtue of their advance directives,[5] just as many insurers now offer discounts to insureds who do not smoke, are not overweight, have exercise regimens, and take other preventive health measures.

The recognition that failing to implement an advance directive often increases the costs of care has begun to suggest to patients and families a new legal means of ensuring that caregivers follow directives or pass them on to others who will. Traditionally, patients who are treated successfully despite their refusals of care have not been particularly successful in their lawsuits for unauthorized treatment – not because they had no claim – they do (See Chapter 2) – but because they could claim no damages, the costs of the treatment being more than offset by the successful results. But now that life-prolonging care can easily run into thousands of dollars per day, some courts have shown themselves willing to hear argument that a patient who does not wish treatment should not have to pay the bill for it.

When a hospital or nursing home delays unreasonably in honoring an advance directive or terminating supports for a patient declared dead, the patient's estate may be excused from payment of the portion of the expenses unreasonably incurred (Cohen, 1987b; *Grace Plaza v. Elbaum*, 1990; Meyer, 1990; Weir and Gostin, 1990). What constitutes a reasonable delay is not settled, but should be determined by the amount of time necessary to take reasonable and timely action to ascertain the validity of the advance directive and the diagnosis. Hospitals will need to institute policies and procedures to handle these cases with dispatch; they will also wish to give patients and their families notice of these policies and opportunities to discuss cases fully and freely so that the need for resort to the courts is minimized.

Insurance "discounts" for advance directives would also benefit patients when disagreements about termination arise. It is in the insurer's interest to advocate for the patient when the patient's decision to terminate treatment is resisted by caregivers or institutions. If treatment is given despite the patient's objections, the insurer is less likely to reap the cost savings anticipated by the policy discount. With the insurer on the patient's side, and with the risk of getting stuck with a big treatment bill growing, hospitals will soon see the need to take their responsibilities to patients as seriously when it comes to nontreatment as treatment.[6]

The acknowledgment that advance directives can be used as cost containment devices, by patients or by their insurers, does not legitimate cost containment as a societal interest capable of generally overriding autonomous choice as expressed in advance directives. If cost considerations should be found to outweigh patients' directives in some circumstances, that calculus must be explicit and its necessity made apparent. There is no question but that we must develop a system of health care provision that is just and reasonable, and that the cost of care must play an important part in any such system. However, viewing advance directives as nothing but cost-cutting devices does not further that goal.

The American system of health care delivery has as yet failed to confront squarely most of the important questions that arise with regard to the provision of end-of-life care that is costly or in short supply (Callahan, 1987, 1990). If the only issue were the ability to pay, it would be possible to distinguish readily between request and refusal directives. When request directives make positive claims upon resources, it is possible (though certainly not obligatory) to argue that those claims may be denied if they cannot be paid for. In contrast, the negative right asserted by a refusal directive may not be ignored, even though still requiring the expenditures associated with care for the dying.

Paying for care is not, however, the only issue. The scarcity of resources, the priorities of the health planning, and the need to control costs could be advanced in justification of the argument that some care may be withheld from persons who want it, can pay for it, and could even derive at least marginal benefit from it. This argument is complex, controversial, and well beyond the scope of the discussion in this book (Englehardt and Rie, 1986; Havighurst and King, 1986). Its success would imply that patients' request directives could be overridden for the fiscal good of society or for the sake of other patients' claims to resources (whereas refusal directives, as we have seen, override state and medical interests asserted against them). This book takes no position on whether such an argument should succeed, but only seeks to emphasize that any decision to set limits on patients' ability to receive requested treatment must be made and discussed only as a matter of policy imperatives rather than one of interpreting directives, so that the difficult questions underlying this critical issue may be directly addressed.

Making Advance Directives Make Sense

The only view of advance directives that is coherent and useful to health care providers recognizes that all types of directives – instruction directives and proxy directives, refusal directives and request directives – are equal in several respects. All directives provide patients with a way of continuing control over their own health care decisions, and in that respect, the physician's duty is to attend to the directive and understand how it purports to guide decisions on the patient's behalf. All directives also provide physicians with the opportunity to refrain from implementing the directive, so long as they pass it on to one who will do so. In this way, the patient's right to make medical choices is balanced with the physician's freedom to choose whom to serve.

The decision not to follow a directive – that is, one that can in good faith be understood and applied – cannot be lightly made. Respect for patients and their rights and interests requires that such a decision be based upon careful moral deliberation. Only well-grounded and serious objections should suffice, and then only after as much discussion as seems necessary with patient, friends, family, colleagues, ethics committee, etc. Even physicians who have strong objections to the patient's choice *must* see to it that another physician agrees to honor that choice before they can withdraw. Even the most controversial directives – for example, directives refusing artificial nutrition and hydration – must be treated in this manner. Neither the type of directive nor the current social climate about end-of-life treatment affects these duties: Directives concern patients' choices, not the choices of physicians (Brett and McCullough, 1986; Schneiderman *et al.*, 1990) or of institutions (Miles *et al.*, 1989) or even of society (Callahan, 1987, 1990; Emanuel, 1987; Weinberg, 1988).

The important matter is determining what the directive says about the choice at hand. Perhaps most of the time, discerning what the patient wants will be easy. Either the decision faced will be specifically addressed in the directive or a designated decisionmaker or other reliable friend or family member will be able to state the patient's preference with confidence. But many times, a decision that reflects the patient's wishes can only be arrived at by extrapolating from a general picture of the patient's beliefs, values, and preferences that is provided by the directive itself and conversation with the patient's family and friends. For the clinician whose relationship with the patient does not begin until after the patient has lost decisional capacity, this process may be very difficult.

It is obviously preferable for physicians to discuss any directives as fully as possible with patients while they still retain the capacity to do so, and to encourage as much documentation of the patient's views as possible to help guide physicians who encounter the patient later. When that does not happen − and it will not happen as often as it should − it is the physician's responsibility to determine as clearly as possible the patient's views, without being overly influenced by his or her own personal and professional values or by popular morality.

This moral scrupulousness is demanding; but it is demanded by well-established and long-standing moral and legal convictions about patients and their choices. If this process does not bear fruit, only then may physicians look for guidance to other means of deciding for patients, using family values, "reasonable person" standards, and/or medical judgment to determine the patient's best interests.

The patient's duty, in writing a directive, is to strive to give others the best guidance possible. The consequence of failing to fulfill this duty is simply that physicians will find themselves unable in good faith to follow a directive because they cannot tell what following it entails. Thus, a too narrowly drawn directive, or vague statements of preference given to a designated proxy, may unavoidably be affected by the physician's perception of what other people might do or what policy suggests they ought to do.

We are being pulled in two directions at once in health care delivery. The tensions between individual rights and public policy interests are exacerbating daily, as pressure mounts to save lives with multiple liver transplants, organ retrievals from anencephalic babies, fetal tissue transplants, and temporary artificial hearts, while surgeons bemoan the shortage of organ donors and Medicare and Medicaid patients suffer from their inability to afford the purchase of drugs and preventive care. We have more to overcome than just our desire to save the lives of those who do not wish to be saved; we must also face directly the possibility that we may need to refuse to save some who wish to be saved.

In doing so, however, we must avoid a very great temptation: to assume that the desire for the good death and the attempt to reduce unnecessary treatment and conserve costs are the same. When patients are given information and make choices, whether on the spot or by means of advance directives, those choices may indeed be the most cost-effective, but in most cases cost effectiveness is not the patient's principal concern.

Even granting that what patients are offered to choose from is itself determined by both the medical profession's standards of good care and far-off public policy decisions about what resources will be made available, it is still *the patient's choice* that finally determines medical care. If – or, more likely, when – we must refuse some of what is chosen, in so doing we must not bypass the choice. The first step is to ascertain what the patient wants, or wanted, or would have wanted. Having acknowledged the patient's choice, we must honor it, or pass it on, unless we have made a policy choice that overrides it. Only in this way will it be possible for caregivers to preserve their own sense of relationship with patients in the face of policy pressures that seem determined to undermine the intimacy of health care for our own good.

Advance directives ultimately demonstrate the true nature of autonomy. Much criticism has been leveled at the primacy of autonomy in medical ethics; many have argued that physicians who leave their patients to their own unaided exercise of autonomy in fact abandon them. This volume has attempted to navigate the narrow channel that all good clinicians must travel daily: supporting and promoting the patient's exercise of autonomy without straying into either abandonment or paternalism.

Advance directives acknowledge that autonomy requires both responsibility, in thinking through choices and putting them in writing so they may be understood and honored, and community, in talking with others about choices and relying upon others to understand and honor them.[7] Advance directives also put the clinician's responsibility, the patient's responsibility, and the task of the patient's moral community in perspective. They embody decisions of the most deeply private and personal kind, about experiences in which people are most truly alone; at the same time they acknowledge dependence on the help of others in the service of those singular choices. The moral community serves the individual; the individual discharges responsibility to the community by considering, declaring, and sharing the choices the community acts to honor. The balance to be effected is fine, in all senses of the word: delicate, costly, even noble.

> The initial issues in advance directives concern our respect for the freedom of those who have the right to decide. But the further issues engage certain responsibilities to ourselves and to others, responsibilities that call on us to advise and be advised, to counsel and to be counseled, as we work out our notions about the ends befitting human lives. Until recently these questions have been obscured by the imperatives of a plot structure imposed by medical technology. Now they are in danger of being obscured by the imperatives of a moral philosophy insistent on the exclusive relevance of respect for freedom. But if there is such a thing as dying well – that is, dying in such a way that the narrative of our life is completed in a fitting way – then freedom

can be well or poorly used. It is toward a discernment of that difference that we now need to move. Aristotle mused on an idea of Solon's that no one should be called happy until death. He asked whether we can call a life well-lived until we have seen and understood the manner of its ending. Advance directives enhance our ability to choose well regarding the end of life. Beyond respect for freedom, the coherence of lives well-lived over time and in community is at stake in our deliberation about advance directives (Churchill, 1989, p. 179).

This is a book not only for patients but also for clinicians, whose role in making sense of advance directives is different from that of patients. Recognizing that their role is to serve patients in the responsible making of critical choices about their medical treatment, clinicians too perhaps should think about what the good life and the good death are, about how many ways of making choices there can be, how many different choices can embody living well and dying well, and how we each can serve each other in our own ways of coming to decisions of great moment and in compassionately honoring those decisions during the time that remains for every patient.

Notes

[1] For example, in the Hastings Center's comprehensive *Guidelines* (Wolf *et al.*, 1987), advance directives account for just 8 of 139 pages of suggestions for policy and procedures.

[2] Several cases since *Leach* have addressed the same issue. None has yet set precedent on the question, but more cases are pending (Cohen, 1987). Most recently, a New York trial judge responded to an appellate court's order in support of treatment withdrawal for a nursing home patient (*Elbaum v. Grace Plaza*, 1989) by ruling that the patient's family did not have to pay the $100,000 nursing home bill (*Grace Plaza v. Elbaum*, 1990; Meyer, 1990).

[3] Disputes will arise about the time lags incurred in finding a willing substitute–see discussion of cases in Cohen (1987) – but such disputes do not affect the essential point that the physician can avoid the charge of battery by properly withdrawing from the relationship, however "proper" is defined by courts.

[4] There is no sense minimizing the difficulty of these cases. When Elizabeth Bouvia first went to court to assert her right to refuse food, she was viewed by the court as attempting to starve herself while demanding extensive supportive care and pain relief from the hospital, and she lost (*Bouvia v. County of Riverside*, 1983). Later, however, she couched her need for pain relief and her disinclination to eat in less confrontational terms and succeeded in protecting her rights (*Bouvia v. Superior Court (Glenchur)*, 1986). One of the reasons for the persistence of the artificial distinction between action and inaction is that it permits us to avoid discussing euthanasia. Certainly there are many similarities between arguments in favor of euthanasia and those supporting treatment refusal and "death with dignity" (see, *e.g.*, *Cruzan v. Director*, 1990, Scalia, J., concurring; Engelhardt, 1986; Rachels, 1986). And much attention has been showered lately on the Netherlands' complex legal loophole that makes possible a policy of official inattention to certain carefully documented instances of voluntary euthanasia (Harper, 1987; Scholten, 1986; Singer and Siegler, 1990). This volume takes no position on euthanasia except

to point out (1) that there is great need for openness, procedure, and safeguards if any such policy is to be instituted, and (2) that the medical profession's involvement in voluntary euthanasia must be examined with the same sense of honesty and responsibility that has attended the best debate about the profession's role in withholding and withdrawal of treatment. This is not to say that the profession's conclusion should be the same on both questions.

[5] Nothing about advance directives is free from problems. It has been suggested to me by Larry Churchill that such insurance incentives, even though they are not conditions of coverage, could compromise the validity of the antirevocation clauses discussed in Chapter 5.

[6] Although clinicians may not be fully aware of the complexity of these decisions until one begins to go sour, insurers already play an important role in many treatment withdrawal decisions, simply because they must decide whether or not to pay for the continuation of treatment. Payment decisions are made by insurers on the basis of expert opinion about the propriety of treatment, and if the propriety of treatment is disputed, the insurer's experts may carry much weight – especially when they support the family's attempts to have treatment discontinued. In a dispute involving the hospital and the physician and their malpractice insurers as well as the patient's family and the patient's health insurer, the patient's insurer can be a major source of financial support for the patient's position, since expert opinion is expensive.

[7] The parsimonious view of autonomy that fails to acknowledge this richness may at last be in retreat. See Childress (1990).

Bibliography

Books and Articles

Amundsen, D.W.: 1978, 'The Physician's Obligation to Prolong Life: A Medical Duty Without Classical Roots', *Hastings Center Report* 8(4), 23-30.

Annas, G.: 1988, *Judging Medicine*, Humana Press, New Jersey.

Annas, G.: 1990, 'Nancy Cruzan and the Right to Die', *New England Journal of Medicine* 323, 670-673.

Annas, G.: 1979, 'Reconciling Quinlan and Saikewicz: Decision Making for the Terminally Ill Incompetent', *American Journal of Law and Medicine* 4, 367-396.

Annas, G. 1984, 'The Case of Elizabeth Bouvia', *Hastings Center Report* 14, 20-21.

Annas, G.: 1987, 'Transferring the Ethical Hot Potato', *Hastings Center Report* 17 (1), 20-21.

Annas, G.: 1986, 'Women as Fetal Containers', *Hastings Center Report* 16(6), 13-14.

Annas, G., and Glantz, L.H.: 1986, 'The Right of Elderly Patients to Refuse Life-Sustaining Treatment', *Milbank Quarterly* 64 (Supp. 2), 95-162.

Annas, G., *et al.*: 1990, 'Bioethicists' Statement on the U.S. Supreme Court's *Cruzan* Decision', *New England Journal of Medicine* 323, 686-687.

Appelbaum, P.S., *et al.*: 1987, *Informed Consent: Legal Theory and Clinical Practice*, Oxford University Press, New York.

Areen, J.: 1988, 'Legal Intrusions on Physician Independence', in N. King, L. Churchill, and A. Cross (eds.), *The Physician as Captain of the Ship: A Critical Reappraisal*, D. Reidel, Dordrecht, pp. 54-57.

Areen, J.: 1987, 'The Legal Status of Consent Obtained from Families of Adult Patients to Withhold or Withdraw Treatment', *Journal of the American Medical Association* 258, 229-235.

Areen, J., *et al.*: 1984, *Law, Science, and Medicine*, Foundation Press, NY, pp. 1112-1117.

Baron, C.: 1978, 'Assuring "Detached But Passionate Investigation and Decision": The Role of Guardians Ad Litem in Saikewicz-Type Cases', *American Journal of Law and Medicine* 4, 111-130.

Baron, C.: 1979, 'Medical Paternalism and the Rule of Law: A Reply to Dr. Relman', *American Journal of Law and Medicine* 4, 337-365.

Baron, C.: 1987, 'On Knowing One's Chains and Decking Them with Flowers: Limits on Patient Autonomy in "The Silent World of Doctor and Patient"', *Western New England Law Review* 9, 31-41.

Beauchamp, T., and Childress, J.: 1979, *Principles of Biomedical Ethics*, Oxford, New York.

Brett, A. and McCullough, L.: 1986, 'When Patients Request Specific Interventions: Defining the Limits of the Physician's Obligation', *New England Journal of Medicine* 315, 1347-1351.

Brown and Thompson: 1979, 'Nontreatment of Fever in Extended-Care Facilities', *New England Journal of Medicine* 300, 1246.

Buchanan, A.: 1979, 'Medical Paternalism or Legal Imperialism: Not the Only Alternatives for Handling Saikewicz-Type Cases', *American Journal of Law and Medicine* 5, 103-104.

Buchanan, A., and Brock, D.W.: 1986, 'Deciding for Others', *Milbank Quarterly* 64 (Supp 2), 17-94.

Burt, R.: 1979, *Taking Care of Strangers*, The Free Press, New York.

Burt, R.: 1988, 'Uncertainty and Medical Authority in the World of Jay Katz', *Law, Medicine and Health Care* 16, 190-195.

Callahan, D.: 1987, *Setting Limits: Medical Goals in an Aging Society*, Simon and Schuster, New York.

Callahan, D.: 1990, *What Kind of Life: The Limits of Medical Progress*, Simon & Schuster, NY.

Cantor, N.: 1989, 'The Permanently Unconscious Patient, Non-Feeding and Euthanasia,' *American Journal of Law and Medicine* 15, 381-437.

Cantor, N.: 1990, 'My Annotated Living Will', *Law, Medicine, and Health Care* 18, 114-122.

Capron, A.M.: 1984, 'Ironies and Tensions in Feeding the Dying', *Hastings Center Report* 14(5), 32-35.

Cassell, E.: 1985, *Talking With Patients*, Vol. I, MIT Press, Boston, pp. 53-55.

Childress, J.: 1990, 'The Place of Autonomy in Bioethics', *Hastings Center Report* 20 (no.1), 12-16.

Churchill, J.: 1989, 'Advance Directives: Beyond Respect for Freedom', in J.C. Hackler, R. Moseley, and D. Vawter (eds.), *Advance Directives in Medicine*, Praeger, NY, pp. 171-179.

Churchill, L.R.: 1987, *Rationing Health Care in America: Perceptions and Principles of Justice*, Notre Dame Press, Notre Dame, Indiana.

Cohen, E.: 1987, *Appointing a Proxy for Health-Care Decisions: Analysis and Chart of State Laws*, monograph available from the Society for the Right to Die, 250 West 57th Street, New York, NY 10017.

Cohen, E.: 1987, 'Civil Liability for Providing Unwanted Life Support', *BioLaw* 2(6), 499-503.

Cohen, E.: 1991, 'Terminal Care Decision making', in Dellinger A.(ed), *Health Care Facilities Law*, Little, Brown, Boston, pp. 657-740.

Comment: 1967, 'Informed Consent in Medical Malpractice', *California Law Review* 55, 1396.

Concern for Dying: 1986, 'The Latest Advice for Living Will Protection: Concern's Three-Pronged Strategy to Make Sure All of Your Treatment Decisions are Honored', *Concern for Dying Newsletter* 12 (No. 4), p.1.

Concern for Dying: 1986, *The Living Will and Other Advance Directives*, Concern for Dying, 250 West 57th Street, New York, NY, 10107.

Concern for Dying: 1990, 'Living Will', document available from Concern for Dying, 250 West 57th St., New York, NY 10107.

Cranford, R.E., and Doudera, A.E.: 1984, 'The Emergence of Institutional Ethics Committees', *Law, Medicine, and Health Care* 12, 13-20.

Culver, C., and Gert, B.: 1982, *Philosophy in Medicine*, Oxford, New York.

Danis, M., *et al.*: 1988: 'Patient and Family Preferences for Medical Intensive Care', *Journal of the American Medical Association* 260, 797-802.

De Lugo, J.: 1868, *Disputationes Scholasticae et Morales VI*, De Justicia et Jure, Disputation X, sec. I, n. 30, (trans.) D. Cronin: 1958, *The Moral Law In Regard to the Ordinary and Extraordinary Means of Conserving Life*, ThD Dissertation, Rome, p.64.

Dresser, R.: 1984, 'Bound to Treatment: The Ulysses Contract', *Hastings Center Report* 14 (3), 13-16.

Dresser, R.: 1986, 'Life, Death, and Incompetent Patients: Conceptual Infirmities and Hidden Values in the Law', *Arizona Law Review* 28, 371-405.

Dresser, R., and Robertson, J: 1989, 'Quality of Life and Non-Treatment Decisions for Incompetent Patients: A Critique of the Orthodox Approach', *Law, Medicine, and Health Care* 17, 234-244.

Duff, R.: 1988, 'Unshared and Shared Decisionmaking: Reflections on Helplessness and Healing', in N. King, L. Churchill, and A. Cross (eds): *The Physician as Captain of the Ship: A Critical Reappraisal*, Kluwer Academic, Dordrecht, 191-221.

Dworkin, R.: 1986, 'Autonomy and the Demented Self', *Milbank Quarterly* 64 (supp. 2), 4-16.

Emanuel, E.: 1987, 'A Communal Vision of Care for Incompetent Patients', *Hastings Center Report* 17 (5), 15-20.

Emanuel, L., and Emanuel, E.: 1989, 'The Medical Directive: A New Comprehensive Advance Care Document', *Journal of the American Medical Association* 261, 3288-3293.

Engelhardt, H.T., Jr.: 1986, *The Foundations of Bioethics*, Oxford University Press, N. Y.

Engelhardt,, H.T., Jr., and Rie, M.: 1986, 'Intensive Care Units, Scarce Resources, and Conflicting Principles of Justice', *Journal of the American Medical Association* 255, 1159-1164.

Faden, R. and Beachamp, T.L., in collaboration with King, N.M.P.: 1986, *A History and Theory of Informed Consent*, Oxford University Press, New York.

Feinberg, J.: 1984, *Harm To Others*, Oxford University Press, New York.

Francis, L.: 1989, 'The Evanescence of Living Wills', *Real Property Probate & Trust Journal* 24, 141-164.

Gelfand: 1987,'Living Will Statutes: The First Decade', *Wisconsin Law Review* 1987, 737.

Gianelli, D.: 1990, 'Missouri's "Cruzan Bills" Address Treatment Withdrawal', *American Medical News* Jan. 26, p.1.

Gianelli, D.: 1990, 'Missouri Reverses Position, Wants Out of Cruzan Case', *American Medical News*, September 28, 1990, p.1.

Gianelli, D.: 1990, 'The Last Battle? New Witnesses Agree: Nancy Cruzan Would Want Tube-Feeding Stopped', *American Medical News*, November 16, p.1.

Gostin, L.: 1989, 'Family Privacy and Persistent Vegetative State: A Symposium on the *Linares* Case', *Law, Medicine and Health Care* 17, 295-346.

Gutheil, T.G. and Appelbaum, P.S.: 1983, 'Substituted Judgment: Best Interests in Disguise', *Hastings Center Report* 13(3), 8-11.

Harper, T.: 1987, 'Where Euthanasia Is a Way of Death', *Medical Economics*, Nov. 23, pp. 23-28.

Havighurst, C., and King, N.: 1986, 'Liver Transplantation in Massachusetts: Public Policymaking as Morality Play?, *Indiana Law Review* 19, 955-987.

Hippocrates, *The Art*, reprinted in S. Reiser *et al.* (eds.): 1977, *Ethics in Medicine: Historical Perspectives and Contemporary Concerns*, Massachusetts Institute of Technology Press, Cambridge, MA, p.6.

Hunter, K.: 1985, 'Limiting Treatment in a Social Vacuum', *Archives of Internal Medicine* 145, 716-719.

Ingelfinger, F.: 1980, 'Arrogance', *New England Journal of Medicine* 303, 1507-1511.

Johnson, S.H.: 1987, 'Sequential Domination, Autonomy, and Living Wills', *Western New England Law Review* 9, 113-137.

Juengst, E., and Weil, C.: 1989, 'Interpreting Proxy Directives: Clinical Decision-Making and the Durable Power of Attorney for Health Care', in C. Hackler, R. Moseley, and D. Vanter (eds.), *Advance Directives in Medicine*, Praeger, pp 21-37.

Kane, F.: 1985, 'Keeping Elizabeth Bouvia Alive for the Public Good', *Hastings Center Report* 15 (6), 5-8.

Katz, J.: 1972, *Experimentation With Human Beings*, Russell Sage Foundation, New York.

Katz, J.: 1984, *The Silent World of Doctor and Patient*, Free Press, New York.

Kayser-Jones, J. and Kapp, M.: 1989, 'Advocacy for the Mentally Impaired Elderly: A Case Study', *American Journal of Law and Medicine* 14, 353-376.

King, N.M.P.: 1988, 'Ethics Committees: Talking the Captain Through Troubled Waters', in N.M.P. King, L.R. Churchill, and A.W. Cross (eds.), *The Physician as Captain of the Ship*: *A Critical Reappraisal*, D. Reidel, Dordrecht, pp. 223-241.

Kutner, L.: 1969, 'Due Proccess of Euthanasia: The Living Will, A Proposal', *Indiana Law Journal* 44, 539-554.

Lambert, P., Gibson, J., and Nathanson, P.: 'The Values History: An Innovation in Surrogate Medical Decision-Making', *Law, Medicine, and Health Care* 18, 202-212.

Lederer, D. and Brock, D.: 1987, 'Case Study: Surgical Risks and Advance Directives', *Hastings Center Report* 17 (4), 18-19.

Legal Advisors Committee, Concern for Dying: 1983, 'The Right to Refuse Treatment: A Model Act', *American Journal of Public Health* 73, 918-921.

Lo, B.: 1990, 'Assessing Decision-Making Capacity', *Law, Medicine and Health Care* 18, 193-201.

Loewy, E.H.: 1987, 'Treatment Decisions in the Mentally Impaired', *New England Journal of Medicine* 317, 1465-1469.

Mariner, W.: 1988, 'Social Goals and Doctors' Roles', in N.M.P. King, L.R. Churchill, and A.W. Cross (eds.), *The Physician as Captain of the Ship*: *A Critical Reappraisal*, D. Reidel, Dordrecht, The Netherlands, pp. 177-187.

McCoid, A.H.: 1957, 'A Reappraisal of Liability for Unauthorized Medical Treatment', *Minnesota Law Review* 41, 381-434.

Meisel, A.: 1979, 'The "Exceptions" to the Informed Consent Doctrine: Striking a Balance Between Competing Values in Medical Decision-making', *Wisconsin Law Review* 1979, 413-488.

Meisel, A.: 1989, *The Right to Die*, John Wiley & Sons, New York.

Meyer, H.: 1990, 'Nursing Home Cannot Collect Fees In Right-To-Die Case', *American Medical News*, Feb. 16, p.8.

Miles, S., Singer, P., and Siegler, M.: 1989, 'Conflicts Between Patients' Wishes to Forego Treatment and the Policies of Health Care Facilities', *New England Journal of Medicine* 321, 48-50.

Note: 1970,'Restructuring Informed Consent: Legal Therapy for the Doctor-Patient Relationship', *Yale Law Review* 79, 1533.

Parfit, D.: 1984, *Reasons and Persons*, Oxford University Press.
Pernick, M.: 1982, 'The Patient's Role in Medical Decision-making: A Social History of Informed Consent in Medical Therapy', in *Making Health Care Decisions*, Vol. 3, *Studies on the Foundations of Informed Consent*, President's Commission for the Study of Ethical Problems in Medicine and Biomedical and Behavioral Research, U.S. Government Printing Office, Washington, DC, pp. 1-35.
Plant, M.: 1968, 'An Analysis of Informed Consent', *Fordham Law Review* 36, 639.
President's Commission for the Study of Ethical Problems in Medicine and Biomedical and Behavorial Research: 1982, *Making Health-Care Decisions*, U.S. Government Printing Office, Washington, DC.
President's Commission for the Study of Ethical Problems in Medicine and Biomedical and Behavorial Research: 1983, *Deciding to Forego Life-Sustaining Treatment*, U.S. Government Printing Office, Washington, DC.

Rachels, J.: 1986, *The End of Life*: *Euthanasia and Morality*, Oxford University Press, Oxford.
Ramsey, P.: 1978, 'The *Saikewicz* Precedent: What's Good For an Incompetent Patient?', *Hastings Center Report* 8(6), 36-42.
Relman, A.: 1978, 'The Saikewicz Decision: A Medical Viewpoint', *American Journal of Law and Medicine* 4, 233-237.
Rhoden, N.K.: 1987, 'The Judge in the Delivery Room: The Emergence of Court-Ordered Cesareans', *California Law Review* 74, 1951.
Rhoden, N.K.: 1988, 'Litigating Life and Death', *Harvard Law Review* 102, 375-446.
Rhoden, N.K.: 1990, 'The Limits of Legal Objectivity', *North Carolina Law Review* 68, 845-865.
Roth, L.H., Meisel, A., and Lidz, C.W.: 1977, 'Tests of Competency to Consent to Treatment', *American Journal of Psychiatry* 134, 279-284.
Ruark, J.E., *et al.*: 1988, 'Initiating and Withdrawing Life Support: Principles and Practice in Adult Medicine', *New England Journal of Medicine* 318, 25-30.

Schneiderman, L., Jecker, N., and Jonsen, A.: 1990, 'Medical Futility: Its Meaning and Ethical Implications,' *Annals of Internal Medicine* 112, 949-954.
Schiffer, C. F.: 1987, '"DNR" Doesn't Stand for "Do Not Respect"', *Medical Economics* Feb. 2, 29-32.
Scholten, H.-J.: 1986, 'Court Decision: Justification of Active Euthanasia', *Medicine and Law* 5, 169-172.
Schucking, E.: 1985, 'Death at a New York Hospital', *Law, Medicine, and Health Care* 13 (6), 261-268.
Scofield, G.: 1987, 'Cause for Celebration, and Cause for Concern', *Concern for Dying Newsletter* 13 (No. 3), pp. 1-2.
Singer, P., and Siegler, M.: 1990,'Euthanasia–A Critique', *New England Journal of Medicine* 322, 1881-1883.

Society for the Right to Die: 1981, 1981-1984, 1985, 1987, *Handbook of Living Will Laws*, Society for the Right to Die, 250 West 57th Street, NY, 10107.

Society for the Right to Die: 1985, *The Physician and the Hopelessly Ill Patient*, Society for the Right to Die, 250 West 57th Street, New York, NY, 10107.

Society for the Right to Die: 1990, 'Living Will Declaration', document available from Society for the Right to Die, 250 West 57th Street, New York, NY, 10107.

Society for the Right to Die: 1988, *Checklist Chart of Living Will Laws*, available from Society for the Right to Die, 250 West 57th Street, New York, NY, 10107.

Society for the Right to Die: 1989, 'Tube Feeding Law in the United States' (chart), 250 West 57th Street, New York, NY, 10107.

Soto, D.: 1582, *Theologia Morales*, Tractatus de Justicia et Jure, Book 5, q. 2, art. 1, D. Cronin (trans.): 1958, *The Moral Law In Regard to the Ordinary and Extraordinary Means of Conserving Life*, ThD Dissertation, Rome, p. 51.

Starr, P.: 1982, *The Social Transformation of American Medicine*, Basic Books, NY.

Steinbrook, R. and Lo, B.: 1988, 'Artificial Feeding–Solid Ground, Not a Slippery Slope', *New England Journal of Medicine* 318, 286-290.

Stevens, R.: 1971, *American Medicine and the Public Interest*, Yale University Press, New Haven, CT.

Szasz, T. and Hollender, M.: 1956, 'The Basic Models of the Doctor-Patient Relationship', *Archives of Internal Medicine* 97, 585-592.

Teel, K.: 1975, 'The Physician's Dilemma–A Doctor's View: What the Law Should Be', *Baylor Law Review* 27, 6-9.

Thomas, L.: 1975, *The Lives of a Cell: Notes of a Biology Watcher*, Bantam Books, New York, pp. 35-42.

Tomlinson, T. and Brody, H.: 1988, 'Ethics and Communication in Do-Not Rususcitate Orders', *New England Journal of Medicine* 318, 43-46.

Tomlinson, T., and Brophy, H.: 1990, 'Futility and the Ethics of Resuscitation', *Journal of the American Medical Association* 264, 1276-1280.

Tribe, L.: 1978, *American Constitutional Law*, Foundation Press, NY.

U.S. Congress, Office of Technology Assessment: 1987, *Life-Sustaining Technologies and the Elderly*, U.S. Government Printing Office, Washington, DC, p. 40.

Veatch, R. and Callahan, D.: 1984, 'Is Autonomy an Outmoded Value?', *Hastings Center Report* 14(5), 38.

Waltz, J.R. and Scheuneman, T.: 1970, 'Informed Consent to Therapy', *Northwestern University Law Review* 64, 628.

Wanzer, S., *et al.*: 1984, 'The Physician's Responsibility Toward Hopelessly Ill Patients', *New England Journal of Medicine* 310, 955-959.

Wanzer, S., *et al.*: 1989, 'The Physician's Responsibility Toward Hopelessly Ill Patients: A Second Look', *New England Journal of Medicine* 320, 844-849.

Weinberg, J.: 1988, 'Whose Right Is It Anyway? Individualism, Community, and the Right To Die: A Commentary on the New Jersey Experience', *Hastings Law Journal* 40, 119-167.

Weir, R., and Gostin, L.: 1990, 'Decisions to Abate Life-Sustaining Treatment for Nonautonomous Patients: Ethical Standards and Legal Liability for Physicians After *Cruzan*', *Journal of the American Medical Association* 264, 1846-1853.

Winston, M.E., *et al.*: 1982, 'Case Study: Can A Subject Consent to a "Ulysses Contract"?' *Hastings Center Report* 12(4), 26-28.

Wolf, S.M.: 1990, 'Nancy Beth Cruzan: In No Voice At All', *Hastings Center Report* 20 (1), 38-41.

Wolf, S.M., *et al.*: 1987, *Guidelines on the Termination of Life-Sustaining Treatment and the Care of the Dying*, The Hastings Center, Briarcliff Manor, New York.

World Medical Assembly: 1964, 'Declaration of Helsinki: Recommendations Guiding Medical Doctors in Biomedical Research Involving Human Subjects', *New England Journal of Medicine* 271, 473.

Zugler, A: 1989, 'High Hopes', *Journal of the American Medical Association* 262, 2988.

Cases and Statutes

Application of President and Directors of Georgetown College, Inc., 331 F.2d 100, *petition for rehearing en banc denied*, 331 F.2d 1010 (D.C. Cir. 1964), *cert. denied*, 377 U.S. 978 (1964).

Arizona Medical Treatment Decision Act, ARIZ. REV. STAT. ANN. §§36-3201-3210 (1986).

Barber v. Superior Court, 147 Cal. App. 3d 1006, 195 Cal. Rptr 486 (1983).

Bartling v. Superior Court, 163 Cal. App. 3d 186, 209 Cal. Rptr. 220 (Ct. App. 1984).

Berkey v. Anderson, 1 Cal App. 3d 790, 82 Cal. Rptr. 67 (1969).

Bouvia v. County of Riverside, No. 159780 (Cal. Super. Ct. Riverside County Dec. 16, 1983) (Hews, J.).

Bouvia v. Superior Court (Glenchur), 179 Cal. App. 3d 1127, 225 Cal. Rptr. 297 (Ct. App. 1986), *review denied* (Cal. June 5, 1986).

Brophy v. New England Sinai Hospital, Inc., 398 Mass. 417, 497 N.E.2d 626 (1986).

Brown v. Hughes, 94 Colo. 295, 30 P.2d 259 (1934).

California Natural Death Act, CAL. HEALTH & SAFETY CODE §§7185-7195 (West Supp. 1989).

Canterbury v. Spence, 464 F.2d 772 (D.C. Cir. 1972).

Carpenter v. Blake, 60 Barb. N.Y. 488 (1871).

Cobbs v. Grant, 104 Cal. Rptr. 505, 502 P.2d 1 (1972).

Colorado Medical Treatment Decision Act, COLO. REV. STAT. §§15-18-101-113 (Supp. 1989).

Connecticut Removal of Life Support Systems Act, CONN. GEN. STAT. §§19a-570-575 (Supp. 1989).

Cooper v. Roberts, 220 Pa. Super. 260, 286 A.2d 647 (1971).

Corbett v. D'Alessandro, 487 So. 2d 368 (Fla. Dist. Ct. App.), *review denied*, 492 So. 2d 1331 (Fla. 1986).

Cruzan v. Director, Missouri Dept. of Health, 111 L. Ed. 2d 224, 110 S. Ct. 2841, 58 U.S.L.W. 4916 (U.S., June 26, 1990).

Cruzan v. Harmon, 760 S.W. 2d 408 (Mo. 1988), aff'd *sub nom.* Cruzan v. Director, Missouri Dep't of Health, 58 U.S.L.W. 4916 (U.S., June 26, 1990).

Department of Health and Human Services: 1989, 'Protection of Human Subjects,' *Code of Federal Regulations* 45, §§46.101-46.409.

Delio v. Westchester County Medical Center, 129 A.D.2d 1, 516 N.Y.S.2d 677 (App. Div. 2d
    Dept. 1987).

Elbaum v. Grace Plaza of Great Neck, Inc., 148 A.2d 244, 544 N.Y.S.2d 840 (2nd Dept. 1989).
Evans v. Bellvue Hospital (Wirth), No. 16536 87, N.Y. Sup. Ct., N.Y. County (July 27, 1987);
    N.Y.L.J. July 28, 1987, at 11, column 1.

Food and Drug Administration: 1990, 'Protection of Human Subjects', *Code of Federal
    Regulations* 21, §§50.1-50.48, 56.101-56.124.
Fortner v. Koch, 272 Mich. 273, 261 N.W. 762 (1935).
Fosmire v. Nicoleau, 75 N.Y.2d 218, 551 N.E.2d 77 (1990).

Grace Plaza v. Elbaum, Index No. 19068/88, N.Y. Supreme Ct. (Nassau Co., Jan. 9, 1990).
Gray v. Grunnagle, 423 Pa. 144, 223 A.2d 663 (1966).
Gray v. Romeo, 709 F. Supp. 325 (D. RI 1988).

In re A.C., 533 A.2d 611 (D.C. Ct. App. 1987), *rev'd*, 573 A.2d 1235 1990).
In re A.C., 573 A.2d 1235 (D.C. Ct. App. 1990), *rev'g* 533 A.2d 611 (1987).
In re A.K., RJ1 No. 26796, N.Y. Sup. Ct., Warren County (Feb. 16, 1989).
In re Finsterbach (N.Y. Sup. Ct. Oneida County, June 12, 1990).
In re Greenspan, No. 67903 (Ill. Supreme Ct., July 9, 1990).
In re Guardianship of Browning, No. 74,174 (Fla. Supreme Ct, Sept. 13, 1990), *aff'g* 543 So.2d
    258 (Fla. Dist Ct. App.), *clarified*, No. 88-02887 (Dist. Ct. App. May 3, 1989).
'In re Jamaica Hospital,' *New York Law Journal*, May 17, 1985, p.15.
In re Jobes, 108 N.J. 394, 529 A.2d 434 (1987).
In re Melideo, 390 NYS2d 523 (NY Supreme Ct. 1976).
In re Osborne, 294 A.2d 372 (D.C. App 1972).
In re Peter, 188 N.J. 365, 529 A.2d 419 (1987).
In re Quinlan, 70 N.J. 10, 355 A.2d 647 (1976).
In re Requena, 213 N.J. Super. 475, 517 A.2d 886 (Super. Ct. Ch. Div.), *aff'd*, 213 N.J. Super.
    443, 517 A.2d 869 (Super. Ct. App. Div. 1986) (per curiam).
In re Rodas, No. 86PR139 (Colo. Dist. Ct. Mesa County Jan. 22, 1987) (Buss, J.).
In re Westchester County Med. Center (O'Connor), 72 N.Y.2d 517, 531 N.E.2d 607 (N.Y. Ct.
    App. 1988).
Indiana Living Wills and Life-Prolonging Procedures Act, IND. CODE ANN. §§16-8-11-1-22
    (Burns Supp. 1989).

Jacobson v. Massachusetts, 197 U.S. 11 (1905).

Leach v. Shapiro, 13 Ohio App. 3d 393, 469 N.E.2d 1047 (Ct. App. 1984).

Maine Uniform Rights of the Terminally Ill Act, ME. REV. STAT. ANN. tit. 18a, §§5-701-714.
Maryland Life-Sustaining Procedures Act, MD. HEALTH-GENERAL CODE ANN. §§5-601-614
    (Supp. 1988).
Matter of Conroy, 98 N.J. 321, 486 A.2d 1209 (1985).
McFall v. Shimp, 10 Pa. D.&.C. 3d 90 (Allegheny Ct. Comm. Pleas, 1978).
Mohr v. Williams, 95 Minn. 261, 104 N.W. 12 (1905).

Natanson v. Kline, 186 Kan. 393, 350 P.2d 1093, *opinion on denial of motion for rehearing*, 187 Kan. 186, 354 P.2d 670 (1960).
New Hampshire Terminal Care Document Act, N.H. REV. STAT. ANN. §§137-H:1-H:16 (Supp. 1988).
North Carolina Durable Power of Attorney Act, N.C. GEN. STAT. §32A-1-14 (1987).
North Carolina Right to Natural Death Act, N.C. GEN. STAT. ANN. §§90-320-322 (1985).

Oklahoma Hydration and Nutrition for Incompetent Patients Act, Okla. Stat. Ann. tit. 63, §§3080.1-.2 (Supp. 1991).
Oklahoma Natural Death Act, Okla. Stat. Ann. tit. 63, §§3101-3111 (Supp. 1991).

Patient Self-Determination Act, §§4206-4207, 4751, Omnibus Budget Reconciliation Act of 1990, P.L. 101-508 (101st Cong. 2nd Sess., Nov. 5, 1990).
Pratt v. Davis, 224 Ill. 300, 79 N.E. 562 (1906).

Randolph v. City of New York, 117 A.D.2d 44, 501 N.Y.S.2d 837 (1986).

Salgo v. Leland Stanford Jr. University Board of Trustees, 317 P.2d 170 (1957).
Satz v. Perlmutter, 362 So. 2d 160 (Fla. Ct. App. 1978), *aff'd with opinion*, 379 So. 2d 359 (Fla. Ct. App. 1980).
Schloendorff v. Society of New York Hospitals, 211 N.Y. 125, 105 N.E. 92 (1914).
Slater v. Baker and Stapleton, 95 Eng. Rep. 860 (K.B. 1767).
Strunk v. Strunk, 445 S.W.2d 145 (Ky. 1969).
Superintendent of Belchertown State School v. Saikewicz, 373 Mass. 728, 370 N.E.2d 417 (1977).

Tennessee Right to Natural Death Act, TENN. CODE ANN. §§32-11-101-110 (Supp. 1988).
Texas Natural Death Act, TEX. REV.CIV. STAT. ANN. art. 4590h (Vernon Supp. 1989).
Truman v. Thomas, 165 Cal. Rptr. 308, 611 P.2d 902 (1980).

Uniform Durable Power of Attorney Act, 8 Uniform Laws Annotated 74 (1982).
Uniform Rights of the Terminally Ill Act, §§1-18, 9B Uniform Laws Annotated 67-81 (Supp. 1990).
Utah Personal Choice and Living Will Act, UTAH CODE ANN. §§75-2-1101-1118 (Supp. 1988).

Appendix

Advance Directive Statutes, State-by-State Listing[1]

Alabama Natural Death Act [1981], Ala. Code §§22-8A-1 to-10 (1984).
Alaska Rights of Terminally Ill Act [1986], Alaska Stat. §§18.12.010 to -.100(1986).
Alaska Statutory Form Power of Attorney Act [1988], Alaska Stat. §§13.26.332 to 13.26.353
    (H.B. 491 signed June 6, 1988).
Arizona Medical Treatment Decision Act [1985], Ariz. Rev. Stat. §§36-3201 to -3210 (1986).
Arizona Powers of Attorney Act [1974], Ariz. Rev. Stat. Ann. §§14-5501 to -5502 (Supp. 1989).
Arkansas Rights of the Terminally Ill or Permanently Unconscious Act [1987], Ark. Code Ann.
    §§20-17-201 to -218 (Supp. 1987).

California Natural Death Act [1976], Cal. Health & Safety Code §§7185 to 7195 (West Supp.
    1989).
California Statutory Form Durable Power of Attorney for Health Care Act [1984, 1985, 1988],
    Cal. Civil Code §§2430 to 2444 (West Supp. 1990).
Colorado Medical Treatment Decision Act [1985, 1989], Colo. Rev. Stat. §§15-18-101 to -113
    (H.B. 1036 signed March 29, 1989).
Colorado Powers of Attorney Act [1983], Colo. Rev. Stat. §§ 15-14-501 to -502 (1987).
Connecticut Removal of Life Support Systems Act [1985], Conn. Gen. Stat. §§19a-570 to -575
    (Supp. 1989).

Delaware Death with Dignity Act [1982, 1983], Del. Code Ann. tit. 16, §§2501 to 2509 (1983).
District of Columbia Natural Death Act of 1981 [1982], D.C. Code Ann. §§6-2421 to -2430
    (Supp. 1988).
District of Columbia Health-Care Decisions Act [1988], D.C. Code Ann. §§21-2201 to -2212
    (1989).

Florida Life-Prolonging Procedure Act [1984, 1985, 1990], Fla. Stat. Ann. §§765.01 to -.15
    (H.B. 513 enacted without signature June 30, 1990).

---

[1] *Source: Society for the Right to Die Fact Sheet*, August 27, 1990.

Florida Durable Power of Attorney Act [1974, 1977, 1983, 1988, 1990], Fla. Stat. Ann. §709.08 (S.B. 748 signed July 2, 1990); Act [designating a health care surrogate], S.B. 798 (signed July 2, 1990).

Georgia Living Wills Act [1984, 1986, 1987, 1989], Ga. Code Ann. §§31-32-1 to -12 (1985 & Supp. 1989).
Georgia Durable Power of Attorney for Health Care Act [1990], Ga. Code §§31-36-1 to -36 (H.B. 999 signed April 11, 1990).

Hawaii Medical Treatment Decisions Act [1986], Hawaii Rev. Stat. §§327D-1 to -27 (Supp. 1988).
Hawaii Uniform Durable Power of Attorney Act [1989], Hawaii Rev. Stat. §§551D-1 to -7 (Supp. 1989), health care decisions authorized by Medical Treatment Decisions Act, Hawaii Rev. Stat. §237D-2 (Supp. 1988).

Idaho Natural Death Act [1977, 1986, 1988], Idaho Code §§39-4501 to -4509 (1985 & Supp. 1989).
Illinois Living Will Act [1984, 1988], Ill. Ann. Stat. ch. 110 1/2, §§701 to 710 (Smith-Hurd Supp. 1989).
Illinois Powers of Attorney for Health Care Act [1987, 1988], Ill. Ann. Stat. ch 110 1/2, §§804-1 to 11 (Smith-Hurd Supp. 1989).
Indiana Living Wills and Life-Prolonging Procedures Act [1985], Ind. Code Ann. §§16-8-11-1 to -22 (Burns Supp. 1989).
Iowa Life-sustaining Procedures Act [1985, 1987], Iowa Code Ann. §§144A.1 to-.11 (1989).
Iowa Power of Attorney Act [1975], Iowa Code §§633.705 to -.706 (Supp. 1989), health care decisions authorized by Iowa Life-sustaining Procedures Act, §144A.7(a)(1989).

Kansas Natural Death Act [1979], Kan. Stat. Ann. §§65-28,101 to -28,109 (1985).
Kansas Durable Power of Attorney for Health Care Act [1989], H.B. 2009 (signed April 7, 1989).
Kentucky Living Will Act [1990], 1990 Ky. Acts, ch. 122 (H.B. 113 signed March 23, 1990).
Kentucky Health Care Surrogate Act [1990], 1990 Ky. Acts, ch. 123 (S.B. 88 signed March 23, 1990).

Louisiana Life-Sustaining Procedures Act [1984, 1985], La. Rev. Stat. Ann. §§40:1299.58.1 to -.10 (West Supp. 1989).

Maine Uniform Rights of the Terminally Ill Act [1985, 1990], Me. Rev. Stat. Ann. tit. 18a, §§5-701 to -714 (Supp. 1990).
Maine Powers of Attorney Act [1986], Me. Rev. Stat. Ann. tit. 18-A, §5-501 (Supp. 1989).
Maryland Life-Sustaining Procedures Act [1985, 1986, 1987], Md. Health-General Code Ann. §§5-601 to -614 (Supp. 1988).
Maryland Durable Power of Attorney Act [1969, 1974], Md. Est. & Trust Code Ann. §§13-601 to -603 (1974), as interpreted by 73 *Opinions of the Attorney General* [Opinion No. 88-046 (October 17, 1988)].
Minnesota Adult Health Care Decisions Act [1989], Minn. Stat. §§145B.01 to -.17 (Supp. 1990).
Mississippi Withdrawal of Life-Saving Mechanisms Act [1984], Miss. Code Ann. §§41-41-101 to -121 (Supp. 1988).

Mississippi Durable Power of Attorney for Health Care Act [1990], S.B. 2599 (signed April 9, 1990).

Missouri Life Support Declarations Act [1985], Mo. Ann. Stat. §§459.010 to-.055 (Vernon Supp. 1989).

Montana Living Will Act [1985, 1989], Mont. Code Ann. §§50-9-101 to -104, -111, -201 to -206 (1987).

Nevada Witholding or Withdrawal of Life-Sustaining Procedures Act [1977, 1985, 1987], Nev. Rev. Stat. §§449.540 to -.690 (1986 & Supp. 1988).

Nevada Durable Power of Attorney for Health Care Act [1987], Nev. Rev. Stat. Ann. §§449.800 to -.860 (Supp. 1989).

New Hampshire Terminal Care Document Act [1985], N.H. Rev. Stat. Ann. §§137-H:1 to - H:16 (Supp. 1988).

New Jersey Act [1972], N.J. Stat. Ann. §46:2B-8 (Supp. 1989).

New Mexico Right to Die Act [1977, 1984], N.M. Stat. Ann. §§24-7-1 to -11 (1986).

New Mexico Act (providing for the appointment of a conservator or other protective orders) [1989], N.M. Stat. Ann. §§45-5-501 to -502 (H.B. 510 signed April 5, 1989).

New York Health Care Agents and Proxies Act, S.B. 6176-A (signed July 22, 1990).

North Carolina Right to Natural Death Act [1977, 1979, 1981, 1983], N.C. Gen. Stat. §§90-320 to -322 (1985).

North Carolina Power of Attorney Act [1983], N.C. Stat. §§32A-8 to -14(1987).

North Dakota Rights of the Terminally Ill Act [1989], N.D. Cent. Code §§23-06.4-01 to -14 (Supp. 1989).

Ohio Power of Attorney Act for Health Care [1989], Ohio Rev. Code Ann. §§1337.11 to -.17 (Anderson 1989).

Oklahoma Natural Death Act [1985, 1987, 1990], Okla. Stat. Ann. tit. 63, §§3101-3111 (Supp. 1991).

Oklahoma Hydration & Nutrition for Incompetent Patients Act [1987, 1990], Okla. Stat. Ann. tit. 63, §§3080.1 to -.2 (Supp. 1991).

Oregon Rights with Respect to Terminal Illness Act [1977, 1983], Or. Rev. Stat. §§97.050 to -.090 (1984).

Oregon Durable Power of Attorney for Health Care Act [1989], Ore. Rev. Stat. §§127.505 to -.585 (1989).

Pennsylvania Durable Powers of Attorney Act [1982], Pa. Stat. Ann. tit. 20, §§5604 to 5607 (Supp. 1989)

Rhode Island Health Care Power of Attorney Act [1986, 1989], R.I. Gen. Laws §§23-4.10-1 to -2 (1989).

South Carolina Death with Dignity Act [1986, 1988], S.C. Code Ann. §§44-77-10 to -160 (Law. Co-op Supp. 1988).

South Carolina Powers of Attorney Act [1986, 1990], S.C. Code Ann. §§62-5-501 to -502 (H.B. 4444 signed May 14, 1990).

South Dakota Durable Powers of Attorney Act [1977, 1979, 1990], S.D. Codified Laws Ann. §§59-7-2.1 to -4(H.B. 1233 signed February 24, 1990).

Tennessee Right to Natural Death Act [1985], Tenn. Code Ann. §§32-11-101 to -110 (Supp. 1988).

Tennessee Durable Power of Attorney for Health Care [1990], Tenn. Code Ann. tit. 34, ch. 6 (H.B. 2345 signed April 9, 1990).

Texas Natural Death Act [1977, 1979, 1983, 1985], Tex. Rev. Civ. Stat. Ann. art. 450h (Vernon Supp. 1989).

Texas Durable Power of Attorney for Health Care Act [1989], Tex. Rev. Civ. Stat. tit. 71, ch. 20, art. 4590h-1 (Vernon 1989).

Utah Personal Choice and Living Will Act [1985, 1988], Utah Code Ann. §§75-2-1101 to -1118 (Supp. 1988).

Vermont Terminal Care Document Act [1982], Vt. Stat. Ann. tit. 18, §§5251-5262 and tit. 13, §1801 (1987).

Vermont Durable Powers of Attorney for Health Care Act [1987], Vt. Stat. Ann. tit. 14, ch. 121, §§3451 to 3467 (Supp. 1988).

Virginia Natural Death Act [1983, 1988, 1989], Va. Code §§54.1-2981 to -2992 (1988).

Virginia Durable Power of Attorney Act [1954, 1968, 1987], Va. Code §§11-9.1 to 9.4 (19__), health care decisions authorized by Va. Code §37.1-1134.4 (1990) (surrogate decisionmaking statute).

Washington Natural Death Act [1979], Wash. Rev. Code Ann. §§70.122.010 to -.905 (Supp. 1989).

Washington Durable Power of Attorney-Health Care Decisions Act [1989], Wash. Rev. Code Ann. 11.94.010 (H.B. 1952 signed May 3, 1989).

West Virginia Natural Death Act [1984], W. Va. Code §§16-30-1 to -10 (1985).

West Virginia Medical Power of Attorney Act [1990], W. Va. Code §§16-30a-1 to -20 (H.B. 4197 signed March 15, 1990).

Wisconsin Natural Death Act [1984, 1986, 1988], Wisc. Stat. Ann. §§154.01 to -.15 (West 1989).

Wisconsin Power of Attorney for Health Care Act [1990], 1989 Wisc. Act 200 (H.B. 305 signed April 12, 1990).

Wyoming Act [1984, 1985, 1987], Wyo. Stat. §§33-22-101 to -109 (1988).

Index

Clinical Medical Ethics

KLUWER ACADEMIC PUBLISHERS – DORDRECHT / BOSTON / LONDON